Samuel A. Chambers
Money Has No Value

Samuel A. Chambers

Money Has No Value

—

DE GRUYTER

ISBN (Paperback) 978-3-11-076090-3
ISBN (Hardcover) 978-3-11-076072-9
e-ISBN (PDF) 978-3-11-076077-4
e-ISBN (EPUB) 978-3-11-079674-2

Library of Congress Control Number: 2023936598

Bibliographic information published by the Deutsche Nationalbibliothek
The Deutsche Nationalbibliothek lists this publication in the Deutsche Nationalbibliografie;
detailed bibliographic data are available on the internet at http://dnb.dnb.de.

© 2023 Walter de Gruyter GmbH, Berlin/Boston
Cover image: Michigan near Trumbull, photographer: Lester K. Spence
Printing and binding: CPI books GmbH, Leck

www.degruyter.com

To Rebecca

Advance praise

"The provocative, counterintuitive title challenges us to think as deeply as Sam Chambers has done in *Money Has No Value*. In doing so, we see how meticulous scholarship and relentless logic can take us to a new level of understanding beyond the confused debates that have dogged the theory of money for centuries."

– **Geoffrey Ingham, Professor Emeritus at Cambridge University,** **author of** ***The Nature of Money***

"Money, Chambers shows in this important book, is at heart always a social relation of credit. But what would it mean for a credit theory of money to take seriously the role of the state as one of the primary sites of capitalist production? Building on a powerful re-reading of early-twentieth century theories of credit, *Money Has No Value* offers a seminal intervention in foundational debates over the nature of money and carves out an original place for a novel conception of credit money. Chambers questions not just received orthodox wisdom but also deftly challenges recent revisionist understandings of money. Brilliant, elegant, and written with revisionist verve, *Money Has No Value* is an essential contribution for theorists, historians, and students of contemporary money alike."

– **Stefan Eich, Georgetown University,** **author of** ***The Currency of Politics***

"Chambers takes on an immense and dual task: recalibrate the immensely complicated scholarship on money in order to rethink the tangled web of assumptions we hold about it. That he does so with such originality, rigor, and clarity is even more impressive. The stakes for understanding money have never been higher, and this book – one of the most important of its kind – rises to the challenge."

– **Jacob Swanson, Georgetown University**

https://doi.org/10.1515/9783110760774-001

Acknowledgements

Though they gave me no explicit teachings on the topic that I can recall today, there can be no doubt that my parents taught me important lessons about money. From my father I learned that you could not realize money's "value" without spending it; there was thus no reason to hold on to it. From my mother I learned that you could not survive – literally could not eat – without money; this, it turns out, was a very good reason to hold on to it. When I compared and combined their approaches, I got a glimpse of the mysteries and paradoxes of money. Money is both nothing and everything at the same time. I thank my parents for making it possible for me to spend my life pursuing such mysteries and paradoxes.

Like so many before me, I wrote this book in an effort to climb out of the money rabbit-hole into which I had fallen. Along the way up, I benefitted enormously from the aid, support, and traveling companionship of my students. The intellectual spark for this book came from early undergraduate seminars on capitalism. When those classes turned to money I saw a flash: money grabbed these students in a way I had seen no topic do in quite some time. Their fascination with money became my own, as I tried to understand money well enough to teach it to them. To grasp money to those depths, I needed the significant help of a unique group of graduate students. We learned money together: through multiple seminars that I taught, through undergraduate classes we taught together, and in Perry Mehrling's online banking and finance course, which a group of us took together. I owe a series of debts (think of them as maturing bonds) to various cohorts of students over the past eight years. I am particularly grateful to the following: Cécile Cadet, Em Cytrynbaum, Rothin Datta, Conrad Jacober, Felicia Jing, David Johnson, Henry Scott, Ben Taylor, and Darko Vinketa.

Portions of this book – including excised portions, the exclusion of which proved essential to making this book a book – were first presented as papers and talks to a variety of audiences, whose criticism, feedback, and encouragement shaped the project in countless ways. It is a deep privilege to be able to share one's work in this manner and I take great pleasure in specifically acknowledging the following individual organizers and institutional hosts: Heikki Ikäheimo, University of New South Wales; Julen Etxabe, PDX theory workshop; Tamara Metz, Reed College; Jake Swanson, Cornell University; Stefan Eich, Georgetown University; Anthony Lanz and Deme Kasimis, University of Chicago; Philip Wohlstetter, Red May Seattle; Amin Samman and Martijn Konings, Finance and Society Network, City, University of London; Patrick Murray, Creighton University.

https://doi.org/10.1515/9783110760774-002

Certain passages from various chapters of the book first appeared in Chambers, Samuel, "The Money Array," *Finance and Society*, 9, no. 2 (2023): 1–20. Thanks to the lead editor, Amin Samman, for permission.

For feedback on various drafts of chapters along the way, I am pleased to acknowledge Rebecca Brown, Rothin Datta, Alan Finlayson, Henry Scott, Adam Sheingate, and Joshua Simon. A number of generous souls read the entire manuscript. Such an act creates debt that cannot be redeemed – but perhaps it can circulate. Deep thanks to Rebecca Brown, Geoff Ingham, Christopher Robinson, and John Seery. Ben Taylor copyedited the entire manuscript, engaging with both the language and ideas at an incomparable level of depth. Ben also remains the undefeated champion in starting arguments (both intellectual and grammatical) that I can never win. Here I express my extensive gratitude and leave it to Ben to decide the use-value.

With an insider's view that proved invaluable, Alex Andre helped me to understand how traders talk, think, and act. With grace and good humor, Tim Schere endured an almost endless series of simple and silly questions about money markets. Thanks to both of them for helping me enormously in the effort to link the theory of money with today's money-market practices.

A book is much more than words, and its creation requires much more than an author. It has been a genuine pleasure to work with the professionals at De Gruyter. Thanks to: Faye Leerink, for initial interest in the project; two anonymous reviewers, for giving me energy, insights, incisive criticisms, and wonderful suggestions; Gerhard Boomgaarden, for seeing the big picture, how this book fit into it, and for steadfast support; Mark Petrie for peerless copyediting; and Lucy Jarman, for working so ably and deftly *with* me to make it across the finish line. Everyone knows the cliche "never judge a book by its cover," but in this case I can only hope the work on the inside lives up to the art on the outside. That art was created by my colleague and friend Lester Spence, who shot the original photograph. I am both thankful and delighted that he kindly allowed me to use it for the cover.

Very few of the arguments in this book were not first tried out on Paul Mariz, and the final form of them all has been inflected by our unique collaboration. Whatever I understand about blockchain I owe to Paul; all my arguments about crypto might as well be co-authored. Paul did not necessarily *read* this book, but he can see its *shape* better than anyone – and he has helped me to see it too. For that, I am grateful.

As always, I owe it all to Rebecca.

Contents

Advance praise —— VII

Acknowledgements —— IX

Preface —— 1

Introduction —— 9
1   What is "Money"? —— 9
2   A Non-Disciplinary Study of Money Relations —— 11
3   Capitalism, Value, and Money —— 14
4   Credit (i. e., Debt) —— 17
5   Indexing the Money Array —— 21

Chapter One
How to Do the Theory of Money —— 30
1   A Note on Method —— 30
2   "What Is Money?" Redux —— 31
3   The Strange History of Theories of Money —— 34
4   Conceptual and Historical Accounts – and Capitalist Social Orders —— 36
5   Against Functionalism: The Ontology of Money —— 40

Chapter Two
The Matrix of Money Theories —— 45
1   Money Sources —— 45
2   Money Choices —— 47
3   The Matrix —— 59

Chapter Three
Money "Is" Credit —— 62
1   What Is Economic Exchange? —— 62
2   A True *Credit* Theory of Money —— 72
3   Beyond the Quantity Theorem —— 83

Chapter Four
Money Theories Today —— 87
1   Money and Credit Redux —— 88

2   The Myth of Community Debt —— **92**
3   Origin Stories: From Barter to *Wergeld* and Chartalism —— **98**

Chapter Five
From Money/Credit to Money-Credit —— 107
1   The Ontology of Credit —— **107**
2   Five Theses on Credit and Money —— **111**
3   Liquid Goat Money and Illiquid US Treasuries —— **120**
4   Money and State Money —— **130**

Chapter Six
Money Markets —— 137
1   Money Problems —— **137**
2   Money Creation, Part 1; or, What Is a Loan? —— **140**
3   The "Price" of Money —— **151**
4   The Logic of the Derivative —— **155**

Chapter Seven
Money Today —— 166
1   Is It Money? —— **166**
2   World Money —— **168**
3   Money Creation, Part 2 —— **173**
4   Bitcoin: Digital Metallism —— **179**
5   The Ontology of Bitcoin —— **184**
6   Crypto Markets —— **189**
7   Money and Capitalism —— **195**

Bibliography —— 196

Preface

Money Parables: From Coin to Edict to Crypto

For a very long time the story of money was straightforwardly told through coins. Digging up old coins as artifacts of previous civilizations seemed to reveal a thing called "money," understood as bits of metal of certain weights. In the typical tale, the metal was "rare" and thus thought to have some intrinsic value, and in turn the coins – *the money* – had value because they contained a specified weight of the metal. Because money itself possessed value, and because it was generic and standardized and would not spoil, we could exchange it for the wide variety of other things we needed or wanted – things that were of value precisely because they satisfied those needs or wants directly (in a way money could never do).

But money, as this story goes, was very much *like* those other things (commodities) in that both money and commodities were thought to have fundamental value. In this narrative, shoes have intrinsic value (a value in their use, use-value) because they keep your feet warm and dry, or they protect you from rocks and glass when you go for a walk; money has intrinsic value because it contains valuable metal. We want the shoes so we can wear them, but we want the money so we can buy the shoes (or anything else we might prefer). In this tale, money is a commodity (just like any other) with direct and positive value. The story could be rendered more complex by the issuance of credit (a promise to pay money at some point in the future), but one need not worry much about those complications because at root money itself was essentially coins, and therefore relatively simple to understand in its nature. The moral of this tale: money has value because money is, and should be, a commodity with its own intrinsic value; money should therefore be "sound money" in that it should contain the value it says it does.

I cannot overstate this next point: though that story has been told throughout history (and repeated especially forcefully since at least the eighteenth century), it has never been true. *Never.* Even in those historical periods when coins seemed to preponderate, *money* was never a weighted quantity of *metal* (with intrinsic commodity value). Rather, the coin was a *token* or *symbol*, a *claim ticket* within a relation of credit and debt. It mattered not whether the ticket itself had any value. The money token could just be a piece of paper; the money symbol could be mere lines on a clay tablet, marks on a paper ledger, or digits on a computer spreadsheet.

There were particular societies, of course, where the object used as token of money – say a gold or silver coin – was itself a good that had both some intrinsic

https://doi.org/10.1515/9783110760774-003

use-value and a market exchange-value. Gold can famously be used to fill dental cavities and has sometimes played small roles in industrial production, while most precious metals can serve as raw materials (production commodities) in the making of jewelry. Thus anyone wishing to buy gold or silver for those productive uses would have to accept the going market price. However, in those cases where a commodity served as the money token, its commodity value (as a metal) was always less than its money value (as a claim of denominated credit/debt). Within a properly functioning coinage system, money-gold always has a higher denomination (and thus seems to be "worth" *more*) than the market price of commodity-gold. For just this reason, the monetary system breaks down the moment that relation inverts, for if commodity-gold is worth more than money-gold, no one will continue to use gold coins as money; they will hoard them for their commodity exchange-value. This means that money can never be sound, because to be "sound" is no longer to be money. Hence we can refer to these coinage systems as having or using "commodity money" only in the very limited sense that their money tokens were composed of a commodity, but the nature of their money was not that of a commodity. *Money is not and has never been a commodity in this sense* – and money's nature would not change if those societies substituted paper money or any other symbolic representation for the coin tokens.

Money as a commodity proves to be the oldest, most dominant, and most frequently told story about money. It forms the backbone of the treatment of money by modern economics, and this book will engage in great depth with that narrative, along with a strong series of criticisms of it. But for now we set this story aside in order to move to the more recent and quite dramatic *turn*, by which a new narrative of money has quickly started to take hold.

Over the past fifteen years, people have been abandoning this old yarn (about bits of metal) in droves, and though it still survives intact in the skeletal structure of neoclassical economics, many have been surprised by the speed with which some writers and thinkers have moved on to a radically different account. In the ongoing aftermath of the great financial crisis (GFC) of 2008, there have been many new course corrections in the tale of money, but all largely orbit around one particular rejection of the old narrative. The new account of money dispenses with the commodity story in the starkest manner, by proclaiming the following: money is not bits of metal with intrinsic value, because money is *nothing more than fiction.*

One could generate countless examples, both popular and academic, that defend this thesis, so we can pick almost at random. Take Jacob Goldstein's 2020 book, *Money: The True Story of a Made-Up Thing.* The title says it all: money is fabricated, nothing more than a *story* we tell. But in case any readers miss the point, Goldstein titles his preface with the declaration, "Money is fiction." At its core, this new narrative re-grounds the value of money by substituting social value for commodity value: money has value only if and insofar as everyone believes it does. A 2021 *New York Times* article presents the new common sense by quoting an ostensible expert on money, Neil Buchanan, as follows: "Monetary systems depend on 'a leap of faith.' People accept it because others accept it, making money one big 'group delusion'" (Coy, 10 December 2021, quoting Buchanan 2013).

Here we have money as nothing more than a kind of shared faith – hence ephemeral and precarious. This new narrative resonates with so many readers because it rises to the surface amid the tumultuous wakes of both the GFC and the coronavirus pandemic; it captures the important sense that whatever money is or has been in the past, money today feels both mysterious and conspiratorial – manipulated by shadowy figures, important but intangible, beyond our control. It also resonates with broader ideas about a historical change in money, a shift from sound metallic money to so-called "fiat money" – a putative *type* of money that depends solely on the decree or edict of the government. As societies have abandoned faith in a variety of governmental institutions, they have in turn lost trust in money itself. At this same moment, they begin to tell a tale of money as itself nothing other than a made-up bedtime story. The moral of this second narrative: money has whatever value it is believed or decreed to have. Money is therefore no longer "sound" (or never was) because all money is mere fiat money.

This recent tale of money has roots in the past, and I freely admit that it better conveys certain elements of money's nature; it captures more of the history of money practices than the old story. Moreover, it is a basic fact of markets that the prices of both commodities and financial assets can be moved by the collective beliefs of market actors (e.g., meme stocks). Nevertheless, money is neither mass delusion nor simply shared faith, and no government or other issuing agency can establish value in money by fiat. Governments, of course, have played and continue to play an enormous role in monetary systems; as with so many elements of the life of a society, governments have enormous power to shape and impact money. Yet neither money's origin nor its end lies with the government, or any other central authority. Chapter 4 engages in depth with state theories of money and explores the complex relation between money and state powers. For now we only need to underscore that money is not made up – it is very much real – and this means that we cannot change money (and money practices) either by abolishing it or making it up anew.

At this juncture we come face to face with bitcoin and the larger project of cryptocurrencies, whose original and very much explicit goal was precisely to create a new form of money. While crypto seems like (and in some sense is) a brand *new* story of money, we must first understand it as a momentous *wrinkle* in the post-2008 narrative. The invention of crypto would arguably have never occurred were it not for the undoing of the old tale (money is bits of metal, with real value) and its replacement by the new (money is fiction, with value decreed by the government). Our second money story serves as a condition of possibility for crypto's rise: only in a context in which large swathes of people believe that money's value is nothing other than an index of what people think money is worth, might we witness the results we have seen over the past few years with crypto – people paying increasingly large sums of real money (bank credits denominated in dollars, euros, etc.) in order to take ownership of a sequence of numbers on a distributed ledger (a blockchain). In November 2021 the price of a bitcoin reached a high of $68,000; if ever there were a time when "group delusion" was the best explanation for the putative "value of money," it was at that moment. As Matt Levine pithily puts it: "Much of crypto economics consists of some version of 'if you assume this thing is valuable, then it is valuable'" (Levine, 14 February 2022).

But crypto is much more than merely a component of the new money narrative. Rather, crypto constitutes an ingenious and dangerous new development precisely because it powerfully *combines* the old story with the new. On the one hand, crypto is openly and expressly *made up*, because, quite literally, someone (or some algorithm) just writes lines of computer code and crypto tokens magically come into existence. On the other hand, crypto purports to be of intrinsic value in a much more essential manner. Tracing its origins to the 2008 white paper that announced both Bitcoin (the computing protocol) and bitcoins (the digital tokens), crypto evangelists (especially early on) insisted that crypto was valuable for the same reasons as commodity money: because its supply was definitively limited, and because it had some intrinsic use-value (with crypto this use-value is vaguely ascribed to the value of the blockchain as a technology).

Crypto therefore leverages the new narrative (money is fiction, it can be invented) while calling on the reassurances of the old narrative (money has intrinsic value, it can be isolated as a singular entity beyond the control of bankers and politicians). Starting with the white paper, the hope for crypto was always for it to be "digital cash," where the word "cash" (just like "currency"[1] in "cryptocurrency") functions as a synonym for "coins" in the original tale of money as bits of metal. Bitcoin is also bits, in the bare sense that it is nothing other than computer code that occupies bits of computer memory. But unlike bits of metal, which had value because the metal had real-world use, the bits of computer code have value only because we assume they do. And if enough people make such an assumption, then they will pay real money (credits denominated in national currencies from actual bank accounts) to buy a token (a string of alphanumeric characters),

---

1 For more on the slippery term "currency," see Chapter 3, Footnote 19.

which can then later be sold again for more real money. In other words, the promise of cryptocurrency is to function like gold and silver function in the original myth of money as valuable bits of metal.

Of course, if actual metallic coins were never money in the way the original money narrative propounds (i. e., as objects of intrinsic value), then cryptocurrency can never be money either. Never. Chapter 7 makes that argument in full, but here we need to do something much simpler: to trace the short but intense development of cryptocurrency in relation to both its promise and its practice vis-à-vis money. Recent events in crypto and the crypto markets tell their own important story about money. In a word, the development of crypto – from proof-of-work tokens like bitcoin to stablecoins like tether – can serve as a powerful parable of money.

Let us start with an outline of this tale, and then fill in the needed detail:
1) In 2008, the Satoshi white paper announces bitcoin as the first cryptocurrency, designed specifically as a digital version of *cash*, understood as standalone, non-bank money that does not depend on any trusted third party (Nakamoto 2008: 1).
2) In its early history, bitcoin and other cryptocurrencies fail, repeatedly, to function as money.
3) In 2012, J. R. Willett publishes "The Second Bitcoin Whitepaper," which explicitly specifies the need for a trusted entity, the existence of which will solve crypto's major problems of "instability and insecurity" (dacoinminster 2012). Willett's mastercoin becomes the protocol on which tether, the first stablecoin, is based.
4) In 2019, tether surpasses bitcoin in daily trading volume.
5) By early 2022 the Tether institution has just under $80B in tether tokens issued, and ranks third (behind bitcoin and ethereum) for total outstanding value of issued tokens. In daily trading volume tether is two to four times the size of bitcoin.[2]

We can reformulate the above timeline to produce our own pithy tale: crypto set out to revolutionize money, to literally create a new form of money never seen in history, and instead, within a few short years it managed only to *reinvent one of the oldest forms of money – bank money*. As I elaborate in Chapter 7, bitcoin is not, and has never been, money. Tether, in contrast, is in fact money. But here's the rub: tether is not crypto (its tokens are not decentralized because they are issued as ex-

---

2 Specifically, as of spring 2022 tether fluctuated around an average of $75B daily trading volume (+/– $20B), compared to $35B daily (+/– $10B) for bitcoin.

plicit liabilities of the Tether institution), and as money tether is not new at all; it's quite old.

The key to the entire story of crypto (up to now) lies in understanding, first, the fundamental facts of the rise of stablecoins, and second, the basic structure of the three dominant stablecoins (the coins issued by the Tether, Circle, and Binance institutions[3]). We can take tether as our case study: the Tether institution (Tether Limited, Inc.) is a shadow bank, and the tether token is bank money. Each tether token, worth $1, functions just like a $1 deposit in a bank account: the $1 is a denomination of debt owed by the institution to the holder of the token/deposit account. To spend tether is just like writing a check: the recipient is agreeing to accept debt on the Tether institution in exchange for whatever they are selling.

Tether is bank money, and the rise of stablecoins is nothing less than the crypto universe's reinvention of bank money (outside the regulatory environment). Crypto has become exactly the thing it set out to avoid; stablecoins are the reinvention of standard banking, all while pretending to be radically new. Crypto was founded on the mythical promise of trustless money. But in its initial incarnations (bitcoin, ethereum, etc.), it failed entirely at being money – though importantly, it did achieve some success as a speculative asset. And so, in an effort to develop a crypto version of money – under the guise of "stablecoins" – we found ourselves with just more shadow banks, albeit ones dressed in slightly different clothing, and operating almost completely unregulated.

* * *

What is the moral to this final story? Perhaps it is premature to draw any definitive lessons while crypto remains both in its infancy and still subject to dramatic change. Although, if the future of crypto looks anything like the present, then we can safely conclude that crypto will not "revolutionize money" (as so many crypto startups promise on their websites). Nonetheless, the development of crypto

---

3 Here I treat only the putatively successful stablecoins while underlining that the successes all prove isomorphic with shadow banks. Other types of stablecoins have been proposed, or even implemented, but never sustained. They include: 1) so-called "commodity-backed" coins meant to have one-to-one backing by gold or oil, with Digix as a failed version, well known within crypto communities; 2) algorithmic stablecoins where one coin is meant to algorithmically hold steady the value of another, most famously luna and terra, which collapsed spectacularly in 2022 and were for a brief moment well known far and wide; 3) decentralized finance coins, which function much like brokerage margin accounts, and probably provide the closest example to a viable form of crypto money (see Chapter 7) but, nevertheless, play an absolutely tiny role in the overall story (to date) of crypto.

from 2008 to 2022 (the movement from the promise of digital gold to the dominance of stablecoins) does teach us something significant about money – namely, the overriding importance of *bank money.*

Bank money can be traced back at least 1,000 years, to the thirteenth-century Venetian money markets (Mueller 2019). This book will not engage that history in depth. Instead, many of its early chapters schematize the history of theories of money. As the book traces these histories, it simultaneously builds out its own, richer theory of money. Within this framework we will see that the nature of money can never be rendered simple (money is not a base element or primary particle). Moreover, money always takes myriad forms: there is a variety of money, a hierarchy of different monies.

At the same time, it may serve as a useful guide along the way, a watchword of sorts, to keep in mind the central importance of bank money. In a significant sense, within today's societies, all money (we might even say, all "real money") is bank money. Put differently, if you want a simple *check* for determining whether something is money and, if so, what type of money it is (with what quality), you can always ask yourself: Who and where is the bank? To paraphrase a famous movie line: *show me the debtor.*

If you cannot come up with any answer at all – if there appears to be no bank, no debtor of any sort – it's very likely that whatever you are looking at is not money. And if the answer is "my friend Bob," then you know you are dealing with a *lower* quality of money than if the answer is "Deutsche Bank." In turn, if the answer is the US Federal Reserve or the European Central Bank, then you know you have a *higher* quality of money on your hands. Regardless of the details, before beginning the journey that this book charts toward a theory of money, know that you can be guided along the way by remaining on the lookout for bank money (our North Star), by always checking for the debtor. We can close here with a clear and concise contemporary example that highlights the significance of thinking about money as bank money.

When Russia invaded Ukraine in February 2022, both the United States and its European allies responded quickly with a tacit declaration of "economic war" on Russia (Tooze, 27 February 2022). This war took many forms, but its most important initial thrust was the unprecedented action of freezing Central Bank of Russia (CBR) assets held on other central banks. At the time, these frozen assets amounted to an estimated $630 billion, with over $400 billion in foreign exchange reserves, approximately $100 billion of which was held on the US Federal Reserve (Klein 2022). In the early days of the war, it was commonplace in the United States to see headlines like this: "$100 Billion. Russia's Treasure in the U.S. Should Be Turned Against Putin." The basic argument was that President Biden's administration (presumably in coordination with the Fed) should do more than "freeze" these assets; they should "seize" or "liquidate" them in order to put them to work against Russia or for Ukraine. The demand was simple: take Russia's money and use it to support the Ukrainian war effort (Tribe and Lewin 2022).

But what does that demand really mean? Russia's $100 billion appears in the form of a deposit account they hold on the US Federal Reserve. Therefore, prior to the start of the war, the Fed's balance sheet included a line on its liability column, as follows: "$100 billion deposit – CBR." The $100 billion in question is the Fed's *debt*; it is nothing more or less than what the Fed *owes* to the CBR. The sanctions against Russia manifest in the Fed refusing to honor that debt – that is, intentionally defaulting and therefore rejecting any Russian attempts to transfer that debt to someone else. Concretely, if Russia tries to spend their Fed deposits by buying rubles from another bank, the Fed will withhold payment and the transaction will fail. In other words, Russia's check will bounce.

Crucially, however, because Russia's deposits at the Fed take the form of debt for the Fed, *there is absolutely nothing to seize*, liquidate, distribute, or otherwise give to Ukraine. Before the war started, the Fed listed the $100 billion CBR deposit as a liability; after the invasion when sanctions are imposed, the Fed *draws a line* through that debt.[4] The Fed was not holding gold bars for Russia, so it cannot confiscate those bars and send them to Ukraine. Money, as we shall see, is never the site of positive value, but rather always a relation of credit/debt. In refusing to maintain that relation, which is precisely what the US declaration of economic war accomplished, one can effectively erase the debt, but this does not itself create positive money. Money is always the relation, so destroying the debt destroys the money.

---

4 Of course, the elimination of this liability favorably alters the Fed's balance sheet (by decreasing their liabilities without changing their assets), and if they so choose, they may then create a new liability – say, to the Ukrainians. But they could do this regardless of the status of the Russian liability. As we will see, the extinguishment of debt destroys money, and the creation of new debt creates it, but there is no need for the former to precede the latter.

Introduction

1 What is "Money"?

Money is not a thing – not an empirical object of any sort. If we insist on defining money as a singular concrete entity, we will consistently and repeatedly misidentify money, fail to grasp it as a worldly phenomenon, and ultimately produce only false theories of money. Rather, the concept "money" comprises a relation. Money is nothing less (or more) than this money relation. The tricky part consists in grasping the nature of that relation.

To carry out that task, this book starts with, and consistently calls for, a fundamental reversal of our everyday understandings of money. Most readers will naturally assume that "money" names *stuff*: things such as gold bars or silver coins; paper bank notes or digital bank deposits; perhaps other financial assets such as stocks, bonds, or derivatives; and maybe even digital "coins" or assets like bitcoin.[1]

This book will ask readers to reconsider that assumption and, in essence, to rename those instruments. Both a $20 bill and $20 in my bank deposit account are what we will call *money stuff*, but the money *thing* (the stuff) is not money *itself*. Rather, the money stuff must be grasped as merely a ticket, a token, or a claim. Those things that we like to call money always point beyond themselves, to two other parties: the agent in possession of the money stuff (the creditor), who in turn holds a claim on or against another party (the debtor).

The shift lies in seeing money not as the token, but as the *relation* between creditor and debtor. The token/ticket/claim *symbolizes* or *represents* the money relation; it is the only "thing" that can stand in for money, but it always remains just that – *a stand-in* for a more complex money relation. Furthermore, this representative token cannot be equated with or substituted for the full money relation.

To effect this reversal means not to see money as one thing (the money stuff) but rather to grasp money as the concatenation of three entities: creditor, token/symbol of credit/debt, and debtor. Properly understood, "money" must always include all three elements. In this book we will see that treatments of money often go astray because they either elide this last element (the debtor) or presume that as

---

1 "Stuff" and "things" are merely synonyms. The general approach to money as some sort of material entity (stuff or things) includes both the analog and the digital. The emphasis here lies not with a difference between the physically tangible and an ostensive intangibility of the digital (ledger numbers), but with the broad idea of money as a thing of positive value – regardless of whether this "thing" takes the form of a metallic coin or the balance in a PayPal account.

https://doi.org/10.1515/9783110760774-004

long as there is someone (creditor) in possession of money stuff (token), then we have an instance of "money." But without all three elements – including the debtor – we do not have money. In many such instances we have an *owner* and an *asset*, but we do not have *money* because we do not have a complete money relation.

Finally, we note a "fourth dimension" to money: the money concatenation (token, creditor, debtor) must necessarily be *denominated* in a "money of account." This phrase "money of account" indicates not any *particular* money thing (which is always concrete and material, even if it is only digits on a spreadsheet) but rather the utterly abstract denomination of money stuff *in its countability* – in dollars, euros, yuan, etc. Every money relation also includes this fourth dimension of *denomination*.[2]

Across the history of theories of money there has been an overwhelming temptation to study money through direct analysis of the money stuff. Such an approach tacitly yet powerfully assumes that *money is the money stuff.* This empirical seduction makes a kind of logical sense, especially when one considers the nature of historical (especially anthropological and archeological) evidence: as noted in the Preface, according to the early story of money, if we find coins and notes, we think we have found money.

But we can see from the above elucidation of the money relation that a proper explanation or account of money absolutely cannot be propounded strictly through

---

2 The concept "denomination" powerfully, but potentially confusingly, combines two meanings of the word. It includes both the older meaning of *name* or *naming* of the credit/debt (pounds, dollars, etc.) and also the mathematical association with units, which appears in money terms as *quantity* (5, 20, etc.). Different denominations can thus range across both *quantity* (smaller or larger denominations) and *type* or *kind* (rupees or pesos). *Denomination* includes both type and number – e. g., 31 euros or 16 pesos. This concept is related to but distinct from the notion of "money space" that I develop most fully in Chapter 5. To say that any token of credit/debt must be denominated in money of account indicates a kind of virtual or conceptual *space* for money (the space of dollars, euros, etc.). No credit/debt can be money without being *named* in this way. However, my own concept of money space is not abstractly conceptual but concretely phenomenological – money space is the worldly space in which credit/debt circulates – and is therefore distinct from denomination in money of account. (Thanks to Ben Taylor for critical clarification on this point.) In addition to space, we can also consider the conceptual and phenomenological question of time. The creditor/debtor relationship is necessarily *temporal* because for money to exist there must be debt, something owed and putatively to be paid back. To the extent that we can speak of the value of money, it always remains *future value*. John Maynard Keynes understood this point deeply and well: "Money is, above all, a subtle device for linking the present to the future" (Keynes 1936: 183). Stefan Eich lucidly expands on Keynes's point by describing money as a "battlefield of conflicting conceptions of the future" (Eich 2022: xiv). Eich's *The Currency of Politics* appeared in print just as this book was going to press; hence proper engagement with his important work must itself be deferred to the future.

an empirical investigation of the money token. The assumption of money as the money stuff proves false. Indeed, to focus narrowly on the money stuff would be to profoundly misunderstand money by ignoring the full complexity of money in its four-dimensionality. Worse, by focusing on a concrete thing, we run the risk of repeatedly mistaking some *other* thing – such as a commodity or a technology – for money.[3]

2 A Non-Disciplinary Study of Money Relations

The only viable theory of money must be a theory of *money relations*. Here, however, we encounter a second temptation: to reduce money relations to some other, putatively more primary or dominant, relations. Many well-known and popular accounts of money assert that "money is a social relation," but they take that phrase to indicate either that money's value is *established* by prior social relations, or literally that money is a thing whose existence *depends on* such social relations.

This book's insistence on the primacy of *money relations* operates quite differently. The point is not that money "depends on" social relations, but that money *is* a relation. There is no such thing as money itself; there are only money relations. Hence this book takes as a guiding methodological conjecture what it ultimately seeks to prove: the money relation can never be *derived* from any other form or type of relation.[4] This is to say that one cannot subsume money relations within

---

3 This section poses the question that the entire book tries to answer: "What is money?" Throughout the book it may be helpful to think of this question as *less* like (1) "what is oil?" and more like (2) "what is photosynthesis?" Grammatically, these seem similar, but the first asks about an *object*, while the second inquires into the nature of a *process*. The difference matters. One would assume a definitional response to (1) but expect a fuller elaboration and deeper explanation for (2). Put differently, if money is like oil, then we probably already recognize it as the stuff in our wallets and in our bank accounts. We think we already know the answer: a $20 bill is money. But if we make the heuristic assumption that money is like a complicated, dynamic process, then we will need to learn much more about it before we can understand its very being. This distinction also helps to clarify why my initial account of money in this chapter should not be taken for "my definition" of money (as if money were an object to be defined) but rather understood as the first of many layered efforts to conceptualize money. For more on this methodological point, see Chapter 1, Section 2.
4 In Chapter 1, I develop further an important point indicated here concerning the historical nature of this study of money. I reject any strictly logical (and therefore atemporal) approach to money, and this means that my "methodological conjectures" or "cautionary prescriptions" (see Footnote 7) must not be confused with the *assumptions* of formal logic. I am therefore not falling prey to the logical fallacy of "assuming the conclusion"; quite the contrary, I am avoiding precisely that error by refusing to assume that money can be understood fully either by its own "natural properties" or by its determination within a previously given social or political system. Operating

a theory of society or politics or culture without fundamentally misunderstanding money (and, perhaps attendantly, without misconstruing society or politics or culture). To the extent that money relations are irreducible to supposedly "prior" relations, we might say that the money relation itself proves fundamental. However, we must immediately clarify that this is a very odd fundament because the money relation is never pure. Money relations are always hybrid relations – simultaneously economic, social, cultural, and political.

This basic fact about money has significant implications for the *type* of theory one produces when trying to account for money. Most significantly for my purposes here at the outset, it dictates that one cannot produce a *disciplinary* theory of money: a *political* or *sociological* or strictly *economic* theory of money would always be a deficient theory of money because it would necessarily be limited in its understanding of the money relation. To clarify this point, we can consider the general limitations of three different *disciplinary* theories of money.

1) Sociology

    Money is fundamentally a social relation because it binds debtor to creditor, and creditor to debtor. Yet no prior social theory can properly account for money. The reduction of money to a constituted element within the social order (what I call the "sociological reduction") misconstrues the very nature of money because while money relations surely cannot stand outside of society, they themselves are constitutive of the social order.

2) Political Science

    Money is an intrinsically political relation because it is a relation of power – creditor and debtor are never equal within the money relation – and thus of hierarchy (and potentially of domination). The money relation always has the capacity to become a direct relation of force (should the unequal power of the money relation be translated into a relation of domination beyond the terms of credit and debt). All money relations are ultimately enforceable by nonmonetary forms of coercion and violence, which means there can be no "theory of money" that is not bound up with a "theory of politics." Money cannot be studied in isolation from politics. Nevertheless, money can also never be determined by or completely contained within a larger theory of politics precisely because the money relation is not just *any* sort of power relation. It has distinct origins and unique implications that are irreducible to the political, even while they are indissociable from the political.

---

as if money relations are unique will then make it possible to marshal arguments that ultimately illuminate this very phenomenon, but such arguments will be distinct, not deductions from a prior assumption of truth. Thanks to Joshua Simon for discussion on this question of logic.

3) Economics

Money is perhaps the quintessential economic relation because it binds individuals and groups to one another *across* the realms of production, distribution, exchange, and consumption. However, classical and neoclassical economics have repeatedly given inadequate, often bankrupt, accounts of money,[5] primarily because they both presume to start with putatively natural and transhistorical economic forces and then derive money from that basis. Money, however, cannot be explained by universal economic laws[6] but rather must always be understood within the context of a historically contingent social order.

In sum, money is always already social, political, and economic; hence no viable theory of money can bracket any of those dimensions. Readers coming to this book from any particular disciplinary context may all wish to register the same complaint, though in different forms: the scholar from each discipline will find too much in the book from the outside fields and not enough from their own discipline. Or they may feel that the conclusions the book draws are not directed *back* to their discipline, in the form of the work's "implications" for sociology, political science, economics, etc. My only defense, my only hope: that all disciplines prove equally disappointed. This would indicate my other, larger aim: not for interdisciplinarity but for non- or anti-disciplinarity. That is, I write here not as a political theorist foraging in the history of economic thought (and then framing those materials in terms recognizable to political scientists and philosophers) but rather as a student and scholar of the money relation itself. Throughout this book I aim primarily to illuminate the money relation as brightly as possible. Put differently, my goal is to develop the best theory of money, but to do that requires refusing, on the one hand, the guiding assumptions or methodological frames of any extant disciplines and, on the other, the criteria of "output" or "impact" by which each discipline judges works within its field. Instead, drawing from all of those fields (and

---

5 Starting in Chapter 1, I will set out some of the details of this "failure" of prior theories of money. Here I point mainly to two categories of theory: 1) economic theories that say nothing about money at all (or specifically assert that money can be excluded from economic models) and 2) theories of money as a material of intrinsic value. The former fail because they do not attempt to explain money; the latter fail because they are *false* historically (they fail to illuminate the concrete phenomenon of money in the world) and *misleading or distorting* conceptually (they lead to explanations and predictions that are themselves false).

6 There are none. Economic forces and relations are real, powerful, and irreducible, but social, legal, and property relations – contingent elements of a concrete social order – are the precondition for those forces and relations. We therefore cannot understand or explain economic forces without first understanding what type of economic forces we are dealing with, which means considering the social order in which we find such forces (Chambers 2022).

from others), I develop my own methods and frameworks as best suited to the subject at hand, and I orient my implications toward a much wider audience of readers across and beyond these fields.

3 Capitalism, Value, and Money

My first "cautionary prescription"[7] with regard to method: begin any study of money by situating it in history, and within society. A capitalist social order is one structured by and for money. Unlike previous social orders (e. g., feudal or tributary), the primary production of goods and services – including basic necessities – cannot even be begun without money. And the ultimate aim of such production processes is not the goods and services themselves but the money that can be gained through their sale. Money therefore proves essential not just to "the economy" but to the continued maintenance of the social order; life itself depends on money. It should therefore come as no surprise that in such societies the pursuits of life seem bound up with, if not overtaken by, the pursuit of money. In capitalist societies today, money appears to be the manifestation of value itself; money is the measure of value and the form in which value necessarily presents itself. The worth of a thing (sometimes even a person) is its price measured in money.

These simple facts about money tempt us to assume that money is value itself. It seems to us that to hold money (i. e., the money stuff) in our hand is to possess value, to grasp the essence of positive, intrinsic worth. Our daily social practices and institutions push us to conceive of money as value incarnate, to understand money as the substantive manifestation of value. But as we have already observed above, money is not what it seems.

Any effort to understand money must start here: money is not value itself; no form of the money stuff – *as money*, i. e., as part of the money relation – ever possesses any positive, intrinsic value. Within capitalist social orders the money stuff often seems to be the essential, positive location of value, the place where value crystallizes or condenses. However, to grasp money in its complex concatenation

---

7 I borrow this phrase from Michel Foucault, who used it carefully in his section on "method" in *The Will to Knowledge* (Foucault 1978). Such care was not always matched by Foucault's readers, who often took him to be laying down universal methodological principles or philosophical axioms. But Foucault's point was that the question of "how" to study objects in history could only be answered on the go, as it were, with an emergent set of guiding principles that helped orient those studies.

is to see an utterly contrary reality: the money stuff is never the site of positive value.[8]

This book develops this larger argument – that money does not incarnate value – from a number of different angles, but one way to initially orient ourselves around this new understanding of money is through a *metaphor*. To avoid any unnecessary confusion, I note that a good metaphor ought not function like a model or a concept, and mine is definitely not meant to be either. Quite the contrary, the "is" of the metaphor does not *equate* in formulaic fashion because the metaphor links two things that are absolutely not identical.[9] A metaphor produces *distanciation*; it defamiliarizes (Public Address 2021). Hence good metaphors convey meaning in a way that exceeds the literal (in a way that can even put philosophical concepts under pressure).[10] When I say "love is a rose," I try to indicate something important about love – not to suggest that one will find love by picking flowers.

Bearing the above in mind: *money is a pointer variable*. I draw the metaphor from the language of computer programming, which marks a fundamental difference between a "normal variable" (the standard kind) and a "pointer variable" (a special kind). A normal variable is just a location in computer memory that *stores a value*. Normal variables *have value*. In stark contrast, a pointer variable directly

---

[8] As I stress in this introduction, throughout this book I continually call on some very old, but at the same time quite lost, insights about money. For example, here are the first lines of the second chapter from an 1896 book called *The Science of Money*, which powerfully expresses the eponymous argument of my book:

> The laws of certain States ordain that either one of the several different coins weighing so many grains, or of pieces of paper of such a size, each called a pound, a dollar or franc, shall be "the unit of value." Important as they are, neither of these words, "unit," or "value," is defined in the law. Reasoning from its use in analogous cases, "unit" is a synonym for measure; but the meaning of "value" is not to be determined by analogy, for there is no analogous use of it in the statutes. When it is remembered that the ablest logicians of all countries, from Aristotle to Mill, have vainly endeavoured to give it form, it will begin to be seen how complex and obscure the nature of value must be, and therefore in what great uncertainty the statutes have involved all commercial relations, by using, without defining, this intricate term. Nor is its use a mere matter of speech, of interest alone to pedants or grammarians. *The existing law treats value as a thing, and measures our affairs and fortunes by means of assumed relations to this thing, which, we shall see as we go on, is not a thing at all.* (Del Mar 1896: 7–8, emphasis added)

Note that throughout this book all emphasis in quotations is original unless explicitly noted otherwise (as above).

[9] On this basis, Nietzsche argues for the superiority of metaphors over concepts: "Every concept arises from the equation of *unequal* things" (Nietzsche 1979: 83, emphasis added).

[10] Some argue that the failure of a philosophical metaphysics lies in its efforts "to pass off the metaphor for the concept" (Vinketa 2022: 66; see Kofman 1993: 15).

contains no value whatsoever. Instead, it literally *points to* another variable – that is, to a normal variable that contains value. But the pointer variable has no value; all it contains is an *address*, the physical memory address of the normal variable.[11]

So much the same can be said of money in the world as we have just said of the pointer variable in programming language. The raison d'être of the money stuff – of any coin, note, bill, check, or digital token – is not to contain, have, or incarnate value. *Money has no value.*[12] The value element of the money relation never lies *in* the money stuff, but rather can only be located *across* the entire *money array.* "Array" denotes an "ordered series," an "arrangement of quantities or symbols," or, in mathematics, "a matrix."[13] In referring to the "money array," we indicate not an array *of* money; rather, we designate money itself *as* the array. Money cannot be grasped as a *thing* or as any sort of simple relation; it can only be understood in the sense of an array. In choosing the term "array" to name this complicated, four-dimensional money relation, we also extend the programming metaphor. In programming, an array is at base nothing more than a table or spreadsheet, much like a basic money ledger. Importantly, however, a computer programming array is dynamic and multidimensional, and thus the references to value may constantly move and shift across the array.

The value dimension of money depends on the entire money apparatus: creditor, debtor, token, and denomination. If we isolate the money stuff, the token or claim itself, we do not find value in it, though we will observe that it wields a certain purchasing power in that agents may be willing to give valuable commodities in exchange for the claim of credit/debt.

---

11 For a detailed elaboration of the metaphor, built out in terms of the computer programming language C, please see the appendix to this chapter: "Money as a Pointer Variable."

12 As briefly mentioned in the Preface, and as will be discussed in much more detail in the following chapters, this thesis holds even when a commodity with value (use-value and exchange-value), such as gold, serves as the money token. Under such conditions, we must distinguish between commodity-gold and money-gold, and we must recognize that the value of the former only matters when it exceeds the denomination of the latter. See the detailed discussion of Schumpeter in Chapter 2.

13 A recent formulation by Ingham chimes with my use of "array." He writes: "Money is not a 'thing' that belongs to one or other of the institutions that it passes through and between. Rather, money consists in the *ensemble* of social relations ... [Money] is not created ex nihilo. The sovereign power to 'tap' the keyboard lies in the 'consolidated' *matrix* of credit-debt relations" (Ingham, forthcoming, emphasis added). For the definition of "array," see the *New Oxford American Dictionary.*

4 Credit (i. e., Debt)

This book builds from a rich vein of late nineteenth- and early twentieth-century writings on the history and theory of money. These works were often thought of as iconoclastic or strange at the time of their publication, and mostly they were quickly dismissed or forgotten. But for a brief period, they were numerous. Across their differences, we can read these works as arguing for a concept of money as a relation of credit (and therefore debt). This older body of literature shows that money has no value. Nonetheless, in their central focus on extant money practices, in their close scrutiny of given money stuff, these writings typically fail to grasp the wider money array. Hence, for my project, this body of work functions like a magnet, offering both a push and pull of attraction and repulsion.

This literature sharply illuminates a crucial fact that serves as a cornerstone of this book: any concrete example of the money material – a coin, a bill, a bank account, a digital token – will always be a marker of credit for the holder and a marker of debt for the issuer. "Credit" and "debt" are different names for the same thing; they distinguish not between different entities, but between different poles of a relationship.[14] The marker of credit/debt never itself *possesses value*, but only *measures* value denominated in a named money of account (euros, dollars, rupees). As detailed in the preceding section, we may think of the marker as the money *thing*, and we can even agree to call it by the name "money," yet we cannot forget that the thing is not actually money *itself.* Money always consists of the wider money relation, the credit/debt relation for which the thing simply serves as token. To spend or earn money then – to buy or sell – is simply to update and alter the array that records all credits and debts. To create money is merely

---

14 In making his own version of this clarification, Ingham puts the point nicely (in a passage I only came across after drafting my own formulation): "Credit and debt refer to the same thing seen from either side of the relation" (Ingham 2012: 122). Though I insist on this point throughout, I should clarify that not all writers on money maintain such consistency. Some authors intentionally allow the concept of "credit" to ossify; they thereby treat a "credit" as a site of positive value without a corresponding debt. In contrast, in my account what a creditor holds is *nothing other than a claim on a debtor.* For further illumination of this point, see my critical engagement with Stephanie Kelton in Chapter 6. In a related but distinct move, Tony Lawson reads various credit theories of money as arguing that "money is essentially debt, a liability *per se*" (Lawson 2022: 11). But this is incoherent: there can be no such thing as a liability per se. The concept of "liability" is fundamentally relational, and as such it cannot exist "in itself." My liability entangles me with a creditor, the agent I owe, and my debt is always their credit. Lawson stumbles into the nonsensical when he tries to discuss an intrinsic liability; this leads him to tie himself in knots trying to distinguish between "money" – which he claims, as debt, is "not visible" – and the "*markers* of money," such as coins, notes, and deposit accounts.

to issue debt that the holder then circulates as credit. These early works therefore frequently test the hypothesis (or, alternatively, advance the thesis) that *money is credit*.

Hence the importance and attraction of these works, which offer a succinct answer to our opening question. The most in-depth analysis of the money stuff will always give the same result: the token, claim, ticket, or voucher that is the money stuff can never be other or more than a symbol of credit (and thus of debt). This result must be taken as fundamental to any effort to understand money.

However, that very result cannot be fetishized or somehow taken as itself *establishing* a full-blown theory of money. Hence the repulsion, the need to move well beyond this literature. "Money is credit" proves inadequate as a theory of money because any narrow focus on the money stuff is insufficient. The money array must include not just the money stuff, the pointer, but also that to which it points (the creditor and debtor) and the denomination in money of account.

At an abstract level, we might describe money as the array itself, the overall accounting of the totality of credits and debts distributed throughout a multiplicity of denominations (multiple moneys of account). The nature of money is indelibly tied to this array. Yet we can never give an adequate account of money if we remain at too high a level of abstraction. We have to look at the contents of the array, which include specific moneys of account, concrete creditors and debtors, and a wide variety of money tokens.

One way to bring home this crucial point, which will arise again and again throughout the book, is to stress the deep ambivalence of the word "money." In using the term we find ourselves constantly substituting and conflating two different ideas: money as marker (*that* cheque for £47; *this* $20 bill) and money as the very money of account (GBP and USD). Moreover, cutting across and connecting these concrete and abstract levels, we find the definite existence of real creditors and debtors (individuals and institutions) who hold and exchange concrete money tokens, denominated in abstract moneys of account.

Tying these strands together leads to the conclusion that if we focus narrowly on the money stuff and ask the question "What is *that?*" then we are left with only one good answer, "It is credit," in the sense that it serves as a token of credit for its holder and a token of debt for the party upon which it makes a credit claim. The book develops and amplifies this argument that "money is credit" in a number of respects.

Simultaneously, however, the book also demonstrates that "What is money?" is absolutely not the same question as "What is the nature of the money stuff?" Whenever we limit our analysis to the money thing, we pose only the latter, narrower question. Yet this is an improper translation of "What is money?" and allowing it to guide the analysis severely limits any theory of money.

By insistently posing the broader question – what is money? – this book takes a subtle position on the "credit theory" of money. First, I strongly affirm the credit theory's core claim. The money stuff is an empirical entity, and if we inquire into its conceptual and practical nature, we will find that it is nothing other than a claim of credit/debt. The credit theory that arose at the turn of the twentieth century offers one of the richest resources for any effort to understand money today, and it provides an important background for the overall argument advanced here. In the debate between, on the one hand, metallists and commodity theorists, and, on the other, credit and claim theorists, the latter win – hands down. But to win a debate by proving one's opponent wrong is not equivalent to, nor does it logically entail, the validity or viability of your own theory. To construct a full-fledged theory of money requires much more than a critique of commodity theory, and the early twentieth-century credit theory cannot stand on its own.

Hence I depart from the credit theory in various ways. Primarily, *money*, in the broader sense of the money array, is not a thing; thus asserting that it *is* credit is never enough. On its own, "money is credit" cannot produce a fully robust theory of money, and therefore the argument today must look slightly different than that presented by the credit theorists a century ago. Whenever we encounter something purported to be the money stuff, we must ask ourselves: Does this entity function as a token or claim of credit/debt? Does it point to an identifiable creditor and debtor, and is it denominated in a (potential) money of account? In other words, can we locate the putative money stuff within a proper money array? If the answer is yes, then we will have shown how this money stuff functions as credit/debt, and in that sense it makes perfect sense to say money is credit (and thus debt). But the process of establishing something as money entails more than the designation of the money stuff. No matter how in depth the analysis, we cannot grasp money strictly by molecular analysis of the money stuff. If someone hands me a seashell, I cannot tell if it is "money" (that is, a token of credit that points to a debtor) simply by looking at the shell. Instead, we must always explicate the broader money relation, the concatenation of creditor, debtor, and denominated token of credit.

The basic idea of redescribing the money stuff as a claim of credit is nothing new: many of its core elements were detailed just over a century ago by A. Mitchell Innes.[15] After being forgotten for many decades, Innes's work – and, along with it,

---

[15] While his legal name was "Alfred Mitchell-Innes" his official publications bear attribution to "A. Mitchell Innes," sans hyphen (Wray and Bell 2004: 4). My concern lies not with his biography, so I simply refer to the published author as "Innes." Innes's work was effectively lost (never cited) for more than 75 years, before being rediscovered by L. Randall Wray, to whom anyone writing

a rudimentary credit theory of money – has today come into a sort of fashion. However, in this context, I want to underscore two points. First, Innes's writings were not sui generis. Joseph Schumpeter details a long lineage of "claim theories" of money, a line of descent in which Innes surely has a place, even if Schumpeter never read him (Schumpeter 1954). Second, despite the relative familiarity of Innes's name, a deep and sophisticated theory of money as credit simply has not yet been developed, and the radical implications of such a theory have not been fully explored. Quite to the contrary, at the very same moment that Innes's work has been uncovered (its insights celebrated), it has been simultaneously, even if unintentionally, reburied (its transformative implications blunted).[16] Just as the credit theory of money has been identified as a fundamental alternative to the dominant commodity theory, so has it simultaneously been misidentified as little more than a precursor to a state theory of money.

This book will frequently use the phrase, and defend the thesis, "money is credit," but it always does so in the context established just above: as an answer to the smaller question, "What is the nature of the money stuff?" While the short thesis "money is credit" powerfully disrupts a host of orthodox arguments for money as a positive site of value, we must remind ourselves that this phrase operates as shorthand; consequently, that claim must be taken in concert with a wider account of not only the nature of the money stuff but also the overall workings of the money array. To reiterate, "money array" names the quadripartite money relation. As an array, money pivots around the money token as a pointer (held by a creditor) that identifies a debt (held on a debtor) denominated in a specific money of account.[17]

Therefore the narrow claim for the money stuff as credit must consistently and repeatedly be set into the broader context of the money array. As long as our gaze remains confined to the money stuff, our account of money will remain limited to exploring the nature of that element in isolation. But such an explora-

---

about, or just trying to understand, money today owes an enormous debt for excavating and popularizing Innes's early articles.

16 Of the three most important and widely read authors who cite Innes prominently: one consistently subordinates his work to Georg Friedrich Knapp (Wray 2014); one thoroughly muddles the theory of money (Graeber 2011); and while the final one reads Innes incisively, he nevertheless depreciates a credit theory of money in favor of a sociological account of state-capitalist money (Ingham 2004a; Ingham 2004b).

17 Programming-languages tacitly presuppose either no denomination or a universal denomination of pure numerical number (established in the declaration of variables as integers or floating-point decimal numbers, etc.). In the concrete world, denominations are multiple and must be specified clearly. There is no such thing as a credit/debt of pure number (e. g., 22); it must be a credit/debt of specifiable denomination (e. g., \$22 or £22, etc.).

tion proves impossible: the token of credit/debt in itself is nothing.[18] To understand "money" we must trace the connections to which the money pointer points. This means that every time we see a putative instance of "money," we must look to the creditor and debtor, and often we must inquire further into the details of their balance sheets. As we will explore further later, not all money tokens are the same: first, because not all creditors and debtors are the same; second, relatedly, because not all moneys of account are the same.

The issues at stake here go well beyond the treatment of one author; they redound to the presentation of the entire history of theories of money. Recent work repeatedly parses that history into two categories: the orthodox theory that runs through classical political economy (mid-sixteenth to mid-nineteenth centuries), comes explicitly to the fore during the emergence of the neoclassical paradigm (late nineteenth century), and continues to be repeated in introductory economics textbooks to this day; and the heterodox alternative, a mixed bag of texts and arguments drawn from diverse quarters, all of which oppose or challenge the so-called orthodoxy. This narrative framing nicely supports contemporary accounts of money designed to offer their own distinct, present-day, theory. When given any length of overview of orthodoxy versus heterodoxy and then asked to choose between them, there really is no choice: the "orthodox" account proves false at almost every turn. But along the way these approaches get the history wrong, and do so in a way that has significant consequences for the theory of money. The plain truth is that, even working with simplified typologies, we can easily discern, at minimum, more than half a dozen *distinct alternatives* to the orthodox account.

5 Indexing the Money Array

This book is not another contribution to the "heterodox tradition." Quite the contrary: I reject the notion that we can properly conceptualize either the history of money or extant theories of money through the lens of the orthodox/heterodox binary. For just this reason the book begins, in Chapter 1, with a reconsideration of the history of theories of money. I title the chapter "How to Do the Theory of Money" to signal that history is not just a blank context, an empty container for "theory" as a work of abstraction. Rather, history is *made* and theory is a mode of *seeing*; both theory and history are things we *do*. Hence I start with methodological remarks that draw out the threads woven here concerning the type of questions we must ask in order to provide an adequate account of money. We cannot

---

18 Thanks to Paul Mariz for this essential notion.

take up the project of trying to grasp money without considering some much broader questions about how we understand history, theory, and their relation.

This first chapter establishes a working framework for both theorizing money and studying the history of prior theories. It also outlines the paradoxical history of theories of money before engaging in some detail with the dominant approach to money: functionalism. The functionalist approach to money – money is that which performs money functions – centers and dominates (even if tacitly) almost every introductory economics textbook. My critique of functionalism shows that despite putatively eschewing metaphysics, these simplified approaches tacitly presuppose their own (false) metaphysics of money. Ironically, they thereby serve to mark the importance of inquiring into the very being of money. Chapter 1 thereby lays important groundwork for later, theoretical chapters.

Before taking up those tasks, I first turn, in Chapter 2, to build my own broad typology of money theories. This matrix of money theories is not at all the telos of this book, but charting it early in the book allows me to situate my own theory in relation to that matrix, and therefore to illuminate its various contrasts with other theories – not only the orthodox account, but also a variety of unorthodox theories. By highlighting the differences between my account and these other "alternative" theories of money, I bring to light the power and distinctiveness of a theory that both *pushes* to its radical conclusion the thesis that the money token is credit, and *situates* that thesis within the broader context of the money array. As elaborated above, the money token is a pointer to a debtor, held by a creditor, and indexed in a money of account.

Chapter 3, "Money 'Is' Credit," takes up the so-called credit theory of money, considering it both in its historical context and in our own present. The quotation marks in the chapter's title underscore a point developed fully in this introduction, one that subtends the entire chapter: understood in the more limited sense as a theory of the nature of the money stuff, the extant credit theory provides a powerful starting point for reconceptualizing money today, but on its own, it cannot stand in for a proper *theory of money* because the money stuff must never be mistaken for the wider money relation. Thinkers such as Innes, R. G. Hawtrey, and Henry Macleod consistently prove that – at every turn, across swathes of history, and in theoretical terms – the money stuff is nothing other than credit. The late nineteenth- and early twentieth-century debates on money thus provide a definite critique of all versions of metallist or commodity theories of money, and this despite the fact that those latter theories never lost their dominant position within neoclassical economics (and hence in mainstream, everyday understandings of money).

This chapter develops a novel and, I submit, much more radical reading of Innes, designed to show that his conceptualization of money actually portends a new vision of "economic exchange," one completely at odds with the paradigm of neoclassical economics. Despite what all introductory textbooks still teach, at its core economic exchange is not the swapping of one commodity for another (two entities of the same kind) but the swapping of a commodity for a credit (two utterly different kinds of entities). Later in the book, this theory of economic exchange will provide a framework for a series of arguments that expand and develop my broader theory of the money array. At this juncture, the rereading of Innes and the development of a thicker understanding of the credit theory allows me to draw a much sharper contrast between credit theories and state theories of money.

Chapter 4, "Money Theories Today," both highlights and cashes out the importance of that contrast by engaging with the two dominant strands of "heterodox" money theory today, that of Geoffrey Ingham and his followers, on the one hand, and Randall Wray and his students, on the other. These writings, and the broader cohort of anti-orthodox works they call upon, all have the great merit of rejecting commodity theories of money (thereby undermining the teachings of modern introductory economics) and of learning from some of the key insights of the credit theory. Building from my radicalization of the credit theory in the previous chapter, I argue here that the broader sociological account of money that we see as a kind of foundation of these works (explicit in Wray's case, more tacit in Ingham's) proves limiting because it ultimately strives to treat money as a "thing" that is somehow endowed with value. To be clear, this approach does not naively take money as a "value-thing," in the sense of an empirical object with intrinsic value. Nevertheless, the state theory repeatedly falls back on the trope of money as an "institution" or a "tradition." In this narrative money has no value *but for* the sheer fact that society has "agreed" or collectively "believes" that it does.

The sources of this putative societal value of money may differ, but the edifice of the argument remains the same. We see its outline when journalists call on the post-2008 narrative of money that I described in the Preface, quoting experts to the effect that "money is a social institution ... It's like language. Its value depends on how many people agree to use it" (Coy, 10 December 2021).[19] These types of arguments manage to preserve the core of commodity theories of money while purporting to reject them, because ultimately they swap value *in* the money stuff for value *in* the money "institution."[20] We wind up in the same place: committed to the value

---

19 Here Coy, as journalist, quotes George Selgin of the Cato Institute, as expert on money. The quote comes from Coy's interview of Selgin.

20 Though I regret not having the space to address their work in detail, I would apply my broad challenge to the idea of money as an "institution" (posed in Chapter 4) to the significant work of Michel Aglietta and André Orléan, who, despite other significant differences, understand money in just these terms (Aglietta 2018: 67; Aglietta and Orléan 1998). When I describe the money "array," I

of money and therefore blinded to the actual, and quite complex, functioning of the money relation. In other words, to assert that money is accepted as payment *because* "everyone accepts it," one must ignore (rather naively) the long history of money relations in both capitalist and non-capitalist societies – a history replete with cases in which people routinely *cease to accept* tokens of credit as payment for goods, services, or previous debt. Calling money an "institution" tells us nothing about whether (and which) money relations in a particular society remain viable. More to the point, the question of whether money is accepted does not depend on some large and amorphous institution, but rather on the particular characteristics of the discrete money token, the concrete debtor on whom it makes a claim, and the specified money of account in which it is denominated.

Chapter 4 cuts at the root of these broad sociological accounts of money and challenges their vague reliance on "tradition" or "society" as a source for money's ostensible value. While it is doubtless true that money practices are bound up with all sorts of institutional systems and patterns – with norms, laws, and traditions themselves crucial to larger social and international orders – I demonstrate here the untenability of positing money as an institution that would somehow endow "money" with "value."

The title of Chapter 5, "From Money/Credit to Money-Credit," signals the most philosophical chapter of the book, wherein I consider seriously the question of the "nature" of the money stuff. Zooming in on the money token itself, I follow earlier credit theorists by asking after the very nature of the ticket, token, or claim. More-over, by leveraging my earlier work on the money array – that is, by framing the work here as a micro-level project carried out in a wider macro context – I propose to push that work much further than it has gone before. I do this by raising the genuinely ontological question of the *being* of the money stuff. What *is* the entity we refer to as "money" and that Keynes named "money proper"?

As already detailed in Chapter 3, any credit theory of money defends the claim that *all money is credit* – meaning that in each and every instance the nature of the money token is nothing other than a symbol of credit/debt. The late nineteenth- and early twentieth-century credit theorists all affirm this fundamental thesis. However, no one – then or now – has been willing to defend the corollary: *all credit is money* (i.e., there is only money-credit). Chapter 5 pushes a credit theory of money to its furthest ends by showing that a tenable theory of money must not only affirm the nature of the money stuff as credit but also demonstrate that any credit instrument can never be categorically distinguished from the money

---

am still using a metaphor to help capture the meaning and implication of money and money practices. Those scholars who describe money as an "institution" mean it much more literally.

stuff. Put simply, earlier writers argued: show me money stuff, and I'll reveal its nature as credit. Here I prove: show me a credit, and I'll reveal its nature as indistinguishable from money stuff. This means that one can never draw a fixed line between "money" and "credit."

In our everyday practices and discourses we can (and do) distinguish between promises to pay (credit) and actual payments (money). But this can only ever be a post hoc construction, not a categorial dichotomy. After all, in almost all cases "actual payment" is delivered in the form of further promises to pay (through the transfer of some other credit on a debtor). We can make empirical observations of money practices and measure the difference between credit that circulates and credit that fails to circulate, but this gives us only a descriptive or historical account of an emergent difference between money and credit – one that can always dissolve or even reverse. We can only *draw* the line between credit and money concretely, in history and in daily practice, while the line *itself* will constantly be blurring and shifting. At the ontological level, credit instruments and money tokens cannot be dissociated from one another; they are the same "stuff," what I call *money-credit*.

The conclusion of Chapter 5 brings the book to an important pivot point. Having explored the unique nature of the money stuff, located within the wider money array, the theory of money in an abstract sense proves complete to a greater or lesser degree. But to stop here – as most theoretical treatments of money do – would be to leave the understanding of money woefully underdeveloped. Indeed, my inclusion of the final two chapters itself poses a challenge to those works that would rest content with an abstract account of money.

Chapter 6 asserts that one cannot grasp money without exploring, even if only at a schematic level, the subject (and title) of this chapter, "Money Markets." Perhaps some readers may initially find the material addressed in this chapter prosaic. I spend a significant chunk of time first working through the elementary outlines of bank loans, then detailing some of the most basic components of today's money markets. But the finer points of those arguments are, in their own unique way, as conceptually complex as the footnotes on ontology from the preceding chapter. Today's money markets are simultaneously enormous, enormously complex, and enormously important – not just to economic forces and relations but to the entire constitution of contemporary capitalist social orders. Money markets form part of the bedrock of modern capitalist societies. If we cannot make sense of those markets, we cannot presume to understand money.

This chapter begins by developing a crucial complement to Chapter 3's revised theory of economic exchange as the swapping of commodities for money-credit: here we consider the idea of financial exchange as the swapping of money-credit for money-credit. Money markets are nothing more or less than markets in money-credits, functioning according to distinct precepts. To expound this notion I draw on Perry Mehrling's insightful illumination of the basic principle of banking as the swap of IOUs, and from there build to a working understanding of one of the most important money markets today, the "repo" market, valued at almost $7 trillion in transactions *daily*. At this point in the discussion, those readers who expected a boring, merely descriptive project will be surprised to discover that money markets operate according to a logic that can only be grasped properly through deep conceptualization and rigorous philosophizing.

The study of repo markets serves as the base for analyzing more complex financial instruments, especially derivatives. In this chapter I develop what I call the "logic of the derivative," an argument designed to show how non-money markets are treated like money markets (or better, how new money markets are created on the basis of commodities), with significant social, political, and economic effects. Importantly, I also address the thorny question of the "price" of money. The goal is to affirm both the central importance of markets in money, where traders surely see various prices for distinct money-credits, but also the fundamental thesis of the book that money has no value, and therefore has no price in the sense of a direct measure of that value. Overall this chapter serves as a bridge from the historical and theoretical work of the previous chapters to the more concrete political questions of the final chapter.

Chapter 7, "Money Today," addresses some of the biggest of today's money topics, using these examples to clarify the terms of the theory developed in the book, and mobilizing that theory to better highlight the shape of answers to such questions. The chapter briefly addresses today's "gold bugs," who think that money problems can be solved by returning to a place we never inhabited – to a sound (i.e., intrinsically valuable) money stuff. The point here is not just to show that this position is utterly wrong, both conceptually and historically, but to use the theory of money developed in this book to show precisely why and how it is wrong – and finally to indicate why so many would be attracted to such a nonsensical theory in the first place.

From there the chapter takes up the thorny question of "world money." I briefly show how, historically, it turns out that gold was never really *money* in the sense it has been taken to be. Then, perhaps even more counterintuitively, I explain why today it is not so simple as saying that "the dollar" is world money. The dollar is not money but merely the name for one of many moneys of account. And while world money today is typically denominated in dollars, and therefore always overlaps with US sovereign territory and the sphere of US influence, this does not make the direct issue of US debt the ultimate or only world money. In fact, world money today takes a different version of the same shape it took in the past – that of the derivative. Only a form of money that can move *across* both multiple denominations and geographic territories (across "money spaces") can aspire to world money, and only derivatives truly achieve this end.

Finally, here at the very end, I submit to the necessary compulsion that comes with concluding a book on money in 2022: to offer a more detailed discussion of bitcoin (and thus cryptocurrency in general). For readers who want the answers without reading the chapter: no, bitcoin is not money; no, bitcoin can never be money; yes, as others have suggested, bitcoin is a kind of *fake gold*, what I call a "faux commodity." But most significantly of all, I show that the fake-gold nature of bitcoin depends not merely on legions of bitcoin bros *pretending* that bitcoin is like gold (a too-simple particular thesis that operates according to the same logic as the too-simple general thesis that money is a mass delusion). Rather, bitcoin can function like a faux commodity only and precisely because it already functions *like* a derivative (though technically it is not one). In a word, bitcoins are like oil futures without spot prices. And this determination, I suggest in my own concluding lines, tells us something crucially important about capitalist social orders today.

* * *

Within the terms of this book's theory of money, we might accurately redescribe capitalism as an arrangement of society based upon the necessary availability of money-credits, which are drawn on to mobilize a system of production designed to generate more money-credits. Markets in money, built around and shaped by the principle not of economic exchange, but of financial exchange (the swapping of money-credits for money-credits), therefore prove central to capitalism. And the logic of financial exchange comes to play an increasingly dominant role not just within the sphere of the money markets but beyond it: through the logic of the derivative, markets in goods and services are routinely treated as if they were markets in money-credits. Money lies at the center of it all. But in order to make sense of any of it, we can never forget that money is not a substance, not a thing of value of any kind. Money is a pointer to concrete, denominated credit/debt relations, and as such, money has no value.

Money as a Pointer Variable

We can use programming language as a metaphor to grasp some of the fundamental conceptual truths about the nature of money. In particular, we can get a clearer sense of what the money token (the money stuff – coins, notes, spreadsheet entries) is and is not, and thereby clarify how money relates to *value*. Step one of this metaphor takes up the basic framework of the C programming language. For our very limited purposes, this gives us access to two types of variables.

A *normal variable* is nothing more than a location in computer memory that can store a value. For example "int x = 2;" is a line of C code that first *declares* a normal variable of the integer type and then *assigns* that normal variable the value 2.[21] When the program runs, the computer will allocate 4 bytes of memory for the variable x and then write the value 2 in that location in memory. We usually think of money like a normal variable: we assume that while money may have some symbolic or representational aspect, it nevertheless represents real value, located somewhere.

A *pointer variable* is unique: the only "value" it can contain is the physical memory address of a normal variable. The line "int *p;" declares an integer-type pointer variable (the "*" just means the variable is a pointer). And the line "p = &x;" assigns as the value of p the location in memory of x (the "&" just means memory location). The pointer variable points to the normal variable, and therefore it *points to value*. However, only the normal variable (x) could be said to contain value; all p contains is the address in physical memory of x. Money is like a pointer variable, not a normal variable.

Step two of the metaphor *modifies* the C programming language with two new rules:

I. **Every declaration of a normal variable requires a corresponding declaration of a pointer variable that points to that normal variable.**[22]

II. **All normal variables must be negative.**[23]

Rule (I) means that lines 2 and 3 of the code below *must follow*[24] line 1:

1) int v;
2) int *m;
3) m = &v;

---

21 For those completely new to the language of code, it could be helpful to think of lines of code like the statements of a god – that is, they are simply meant to bring into existence whatever they declare. This means you can read a line of code not as an argument/claim/assertion, but as the declaration of a new truth. The line of code that *says* "int x = 2;" *makes it the case* that an integer variable named x now exists, and that its value is 2.

22 This rule expresses that money is always "credit/debt," which means it is *credit and debt simultaneously.* Money must always have two "sides" to it because for it to be money, it must be a credit for one party and a debt for another.

23 This rule gives expression to money's "value form." Money itself has no value – is never the site of positive or intrinsic value – but money can have purchasing *power* because it functions as a value claim. Hence money can be one *form* that value takes within a capitalist system without itself having any value.

24 That is, literally: if a normal variable is declared without both the declaration of a pointer variable and the assignment of that pointer variable to the normal variable's location in memory, then the program will not compile.

We may then add a fourth and final line of code, declaring the value of v; v can take any value we want, but it must be negative. For example:

4)   v = −47;

The first two lines give us two working locations in computer memory: the one where the normal value (v) is written, and the one where the pointer variable (m) is written. After the first two lines, neither v nor m has any value at all assigned to it. Line 3 assigns to the pointer variable (m) *as its value* the location in memory of v. The "value" of m is nothing other than this memory address, a site for the possible value of v. And at this moment, v still has no value at all. Line 4 changes that fact by assigning v the value of −47.

These four lines of code are the entire "program" for this heuristic example, but they can illuminate a great deal about money and value.

A)   Whatever else we might say about value, we know that "47" is the *amount* of value in play. And yet, there is no positive value located anywhere in the code. The only normal variable, which is the type of variable to which we can *directly assign value*, in our program is v, and it has a negative value. *The normal variable (v) is a measure of debt.* We can think of the location where v is written into memory as lying within the liability column of a debtor: that debtor owes 47 units of value to someone else.
B)   *The pointer variable (m) is the measure of credit.* Importantly, because m is a pointer variable, it has no positive value assigned to it; m's "value" is the location in memory of v, the debt.
C)   *The credit cannot exist without the debt.*[25] If v is not declared in the program, m cannot be declared or assigned its value.
D)   The only manifestation of value in the program is negative value, debt, as expressed in the normal variable (v).
E)   The positive credit is the pointer variable (m), but m contains no intrinsic value whatsoever: it merely *references* value located elsewhere, and that value is negative (it is debt).

In other words, what we might otherwise wish to conceptualize as positive value is only ever credit, and credit can never be anything other than a claim on a debtor – a reference to value owed, which is negative value.

In programming languages a pointer variable is a "reference" to value located elsewhere. In this example, by requiring all normal variables to have negative value, I have underscored this truth: the value that money references is always debt. Only the *relation* between the pointer variable and the normal variable can *make value possible* in the program (in the system of money and value). Put differently, *the only positive value is the reference to a negative value.*

Without pointer variables there would be nothing like positive value at all. This is not despite, but rather because pointers themselves have no value. *The existence of value in the system depends on the essential role of a unique variable that has no value.* Moreover, the necessary and highest form of value in capitalism, money-value, is only ever a reference to negative value located elsewhere.

This metaphor conveys a truth about money: money has no value because the only *thing* one can possess is the money token, the pointer to value elsewhere, yet that money token points only to a denominated record of debt – not to positive, intrinsic value but to a record of negative value.

---

25 This fact within the metaphor tells us something of great significance about money: while we can rightly refer to money as "credit," we can never forget that credit is never anything more than a claim (held by the one who is owed) on a debtor (the one who owes).

Chapter One
How to Do the Theory of Money

1 A Note on Method

Any serious study of money must combine the historical and the theoretical, and sooner or later this simple fact forces the student of money to confront complex questions about the theory of history and the history of theory. In other words, the study of money inevitably raises thorny epistemological, ontological, and historiographical issues that many would reasonably wish to eschew, but which remain unavoidable so long as one refuses to settle for oversimplified accounts that would explain money based on its *functions*. Such accounts prove reductive and unhelpful, regardless of whether they take the shape of a crude empiricism that defines money by deducing its nature from the roles that it has played strictly *in history*, or if they manifest in an utterly abstract account that defines money based on its putative powers to solve logical or efficiency problems strictly *in theory*.

The first reduction we might call "functionalism": it illicitly transforms empirical facts (the money stuff currently performs these concrete functions) into general theory (money must exist *in order* to perform these functions; its very nature must be explained on the basis of these functions). As I show below, despite their ubiquity, functionalist theories of money always fail to identify the specificity of money. The second reduction we could name "theoreticism": it naively and wrongly assumes that the establishment of conceptual relations can itself serve to explain historical development.[1] Each of these reductions seeks to escape difficult questions about the relation between theory and history by narrowly explaining one in terms of the other. Yet neither pure historical description nor abstract logical positing will produce an adequate account of money. A history is not a theory, and no theory can truly *explain* history.

---

1 The term "development" has a long and problematic history in economic thought because it has often been understood in linear or even teleological terms, in the sense that all societies "ought to develop" toward some end point of advanced industrial/commercial/global capitalism. I use the phrase "historical development" only to indicate historical change (transformation of a social order) that can be grasped in relation to both the past and the future. Such change can include growth or disintegration, improvement or decline, and it can be radically discontinuous. Societies do not *evolve* (species evolve); they do not grow naturally; they are not headed toward the same end point (there is no end point); and none can be judged by comparing its position on a purported path of development relative to others or to a generic standard (there are no such standards).

https://doi.org/10.1515/9783110760774-005

In general terms we must start in the only place there is to occupy: a location *within history* (never outside it), but nonetheless *a location from which we can still theorize*. To *theorize* in this sense does not mean to postulate abstract and transhistorical elements and categories, but to try to see the world (*theoria*), to attempt to grasp conceptually (*begreifen*) the relations among elements as located within concrete (particular in time and place) social orders.[2] To put this point in the language of epistemology, we can say that knowledge is itself a product of history; to know is to know within history, not outside it. Such a claim in no way reduces to so-called relativism, since our location within the present does not confine us there; quite the contrary, that location affords us a view of the past, and provides us with the resources to try to understand the path from there to here. Furthermore, that same knowledge of history allows us to travel across time and place, to go first into the past and then back to the future (our present). Ontologically it means that we are not only creatures of history but also beings with the capacity both to know and to theorize history. The first point means that our being is always a *historical* being. The second point entails that our being is a *being*-historical. History is not just something we are "in" but something we "do" – hence the title of this chapter. In one sense it provides an overview of previous theories. However, I frame this issue as the question of "how to *do*" the theory of money: the point is not merely to document past efforts but to create a framework through which we can construct a new theory of money.

2 "What Is Money?" Redux

These brief methodological remarks on theory and history can help to clarify the specific nature of my theory of money, to say with more exactitude *how* I go about answering the question of the book, "What is money?" and how I distinguish my approach to the question from the many other authors who have tackled it. In

---

2 This form of *seeing* and *grasping* both exceeds and often rejects the terms of an empiricist epistemology, which commits itself to *observing* the world and fitting collected data into patterns (or testing hypotheses, or generating causal laws). Therefore when I say above that a history is not a theory, I include the work of empiricism within this very broad term "history." I distinguish theoretical work from an approach to money that would, first, generate a definition of money and then, second, operationalize that definition by testing gathered data for whether it fits the pre-constituted category. This epistemological approach would not get at what Ingham calls the "nature" of money (Ingham 2018: 845), or what we might call, using the language of ontology, the very "being" of money. In pointing toward the primacy of ontology, I follow a very long line of thinkers who have explored these philosophical issues in depth (Taylor 1985; Connolly 1987; Markell 2006).

some ways, I have already provided my answer: the Introduction presents directly the "money array." One could easily read the opening of that chapter to be directly *defining* money as the four-dimensional concatenation: creditor, token, debtor, and denominated money of account. Indeed, I do propose, in the most general sense, to use the term/concept "money" to refer to this clutch of ideas that I have captured with the name "money array."

However, because I reject the theoreticism described above, I also refuse to reduce my concept of the money array to an abstract "definition" that I (or anyone else) would simply stipulate in advance. In the chapters that follow, I intend to distinguish my account of the money array from an abstract or analytical "model" of money. I theorize money as the array of token/creditor/debtor/denomination not as an arbitrary or subjective postulation that I would then "apply" *to* the world. Rather, I conceptualize money *from* the world; the money array is an entity *of* the world. My account of money locates both money practices and theories of money within history, and from that starting point builds up a richer conception of money that can analyze, can make sense of, those very practices. Importantly, this leads to a theory of money that can distinguish money from other things, even if those things sometimes perform the same functions as money.

This approach – based on my understanding of the theory–history relation – also sharply differentiates my work from those authors who employ a wholly nominalist technique. That is to say, many writers propose to eschew the question "What is money?" – or better, to displace it onto the social orders they study. For them, money is whatever society says it is. As Viviana Zelizer puts the point: "Money is an abstraction that observers make from social interactions," and for this reason we can call *money* "all objects that have recognized, regularized exchange value in one social setting or another" (Zelizer 2000: 384; quoting Zelizer 1994: 21). Zelizer's nominalism naturally leads her to embrace a very long list of examples of money, starting (uncontroversially) with international currencies and ending (problematically) with "investment diamonds."

Throughout this book I will be at pains to draw a clear and tenable distinction between specific commodities (e.g., diamonds or gold) and money, just as I will consistently reject the more general idea that money is what society says it is. Money is not just a nominative that can be arbitrarily attached to certain objects or practices. While it surely matters what a particular society takes money to be, groups within society (perhaps even society as a whole) can certainly be *wrong* about what money is. I reject the nominalist approach precisely because any adequate theory of money must allow for this possibility. Diamonds are not money any more than frogs are fish. There can and often will be serious implications when that which is not money is treated as if it were, a fact lucidly illustrated by the spectacular implosion of the FTX crypto exchange in November 2022.[3]

In sum then, by taking a dialectical approach to theory and history, I reject both an abstract analytical formalism and a thin historical sociological nominalism. While we cannot use philosophical logic to "posit" the nature of money in some transhistorical sense, we also cannot reduce money to a mere name attached to myriad objects and practices in society. To put the point in the ontological language used in the previous section, while the being of money (what money *is*) is a *historical* being, it cannot be definitively determined or utterly contained by history – it remains a *being*-historical (Heidegger 1962).

This leads me to one final note on ontology. On the one hand, and to be clear, this book is not an ontological work. I believe any effort to *derive* a rich and robust theory of money by way of fundamental ontology would prove futile, and I have previously argued against the conflation of theorizing with ontologizing (Chambers 2014). On the other hand, this book necessarily raises ontological questions[4] because trying to theorize money while avoiding or eschewing ontology would be a fool's errand. For this reason I will occasionally recur to the language of ontology used in the previous pages. Money cannot be understood without rigorous conceptual, philosophical work, yet it also cannot be confined to a narrowly or strictly philosophical domain. In this context we turn to the *history* of *theories* of money, a topic that necessarily entangles history and theory in pursuit of the question of money.

---

3 See Chapter 7 for a detailed engagement with the nature of blockchain tokens and their differences from money. The collapse and eventual bankruptcy of FTX proved dramatic and complicated, and at the time of my writing the consequences remain far from fully sorted out. I cite the case here because the best early accounts of FTX's demise trace it directly to the failure of FTX's CEO, Sam Bankman-Fried, to distinguish between real money assets, on the one hand, and *magic beans* (i.e., the FTT token that FTX itself generated), on the other.

4 It does so in order to ensure that the project does not lose sight of the question "What *is* money?" To pose the question "what is" means to inquire into the being of an entity; "ontology" is nothing other than the study of (*logos*) or inquiry into being (*ontos*). Money cannot be grasped ostensively (by pointing to empirical examples) or even strictly historically (by mapping its historical appearances); rather, these activities presuppose our capacity to ask after the *ontos* of money – to figure out what it is. As I have made clear in this section, such an inquiry cannot be conducted outside or apart from history – *being is itself historical* – but as I will emphasize at various points in the book, the analysis will often require pausing at a particular moment and posing (or reposing) the ontological question "What is money?" – usually in the implicit form "What is the money stuff?" An empirical account of money that operates only at the level of epistemology will never be adequate to grasp the being of money. See Chapter 5 for much more on the ontology of money.

3 The Strange History of Theories of Money

The history of theories of money proves a tough tale to tell; hence it comes as no surprise that, to date, no one has told it well. I am not the writer to rectify this problem, and certainly not herein, but I can offer a well-drawn roadmap, and highlight certain locations on it that prove critical for the argument of this book.

First, and quite importantly, the development of theories of money does not map onto history; theories of money cannot be unfolded and explained chronologically because their history proves to be a *history of forgetting*. Insights into the nature of money emerge and sometimes even flourish at one point in time, only to disappear for decades or even centuries. At multiple moments in history, including recently, the "normal science" of money has coalesced around a few key elements taken as unquestioned facts or ineliminable guiding assumptions, yet the "facts" are false and the assumptions are frankly terrible. The fundamental elements of the dominant theory were disproved long ago, but in tracts that no one any longer reads or even remembers.[5]

Moreover, the history of money and the history of theories of money prove radically discontinuous because only at a certain historical moment did we gain (roughly) accurate historical and anthropological knowledge of the history of money and coinage. First, much of what was written about money prior to the very late nineteenth century made key assumptions about coinage (particularly concerning a standard of metallic value) that turned out to be incorrect. Second, the early history of money was not discovered until roughly this same period. Therefore anyone writing prior to the late nineteenth century simply did not know that money could be found in history 2,000 years earlier (in Mesopotamia in the period 3,000–2,500 BCE) than the history of coinage, nor that the early history of money was quite simply not a history of coins but of measures of credit/debt – listed in abstract units of account, and recorded on clay tablets. In a certain crude sense then, the history of theories of money really only begins near the end of the nineteenth century.

Serendipitously but significantly, this means that the relevant history of theories of money coincides with the (retroactive) establishment of the neoclassical paradigm of economics. As the story goes, three writers in the 1870s all "independ-

---

5 Complicating matters further, most of the significant historical debates over money are not academic/scientific/theoretical debates but practical/political/policy debates (Schumpeter 1954: 276). This poses to readers a real hermeneutic challenge: to distinguish an author's practical position on policy questions of the day from claims about the nature of money. For the purposes of this project, I bracket almost entirely this historiographical issue, focusing my reading on fundamental arguments concerning the nature of money.

ently discovered" the theory of marginal utility, thereby effecting the "marginalist revolution" and its decisive break with classical political economy (see Mirowski 1988). The latter had reached its pinnacle in writings that stretched from the late eighteenth century (Adam Smith's *Wealth of Nations*, 1776) to the early (David Ricardo's *Principles*, 1817) and mid-nineteenth century (Karl Marx's *Capital*, 1867[6]). Two of the foundational works for the so-called orthodox theory of money were written by two (out of three) "co-founders" of the neoclassical paradigm – namely, William Stanley Jevons and Carl Menger.

This historical coincidence (between the so-called origin of the neoclassical paradigm and the establishment of a somewhat more complete historical record regarding money) makes it deceptively easy (but also dangerous) to gloss the history of theories of money. First, one starts with the short and accessible books by Menger and Jevons, summarizing their main arguments. One may then be tempted (herein lies the first danger) to follow their lead by projecting their argument for money both back and forward in time – back to claim that all of the essential truths of this theory are found in the "greats" (mainly Smith[7] and Ricardo, but sometimes also Aristotle) and forward to claim the universal and enduring truth of the theory (as distilled in contemporary textbooks). These basic moves comprise a set piece that produces *the orthodox theory of money* as a timeless theory of the nature of money, containing a few clear and simple tenets. Of course, with the establishment of the orthodoxy, it naturally follows to group all the major alternatives or challenges to this single theory and name them *heterodox*. In a short series of steps, we have thus produced a binary debate, reducing the messy theory of histories of money to a choice between orthodoxy and heterodoxy.

Such a typology proves tempting, and one finds it reemerging even in some of the most sophisticated and rigorous overviews of money theory.[8] But the trade-off is not worth it. To pose the question "What is money?" is to ask a series of concrete historical questions, and also to raise a sequence of deeply conceptual or philo-

---

6 Most writers, non-Marxist and Marxist alike, simply include Marx directly within "classical political economy." But the best readers of Marx have always rightly insisted that Marx was not a member of the classical paradigm who merely criticized certain authors within it; rather, Marx conceived of his mature project as a fundamental critique of the whole paradigm. Nevertheless, in taking classical political economy as his object of critique, Marx thereby worked with (and against) its principles and precepts. Of course, Marx was not a neoclassical thinker, so in the *break* between the classical and neoclassical paradigms, Marx must still fall on the former side of the divide.

7 The attribution of this theory to Smith proves at best tenuous (see Cencini 1988), but that attribution nevertheless plays a key role in the narrative.

8 Ingham's massive and hugely important work on money represents by far the most prominent and sophisticated example. For much more on Ingham, see especially Chapter 2 and Chapter 4.

sophical issues. This latter point entails that no good theory of money can avoid complex metaphysical problems, eschew theoretical complexity, or evade philosophical dilemmas. That is to say, any viable theory of money must not only make sense of the practical history of money – as empirical object, as social practice, as technology – but also connect that history to a conceptual framework that interprets the nature (metaphysics) or being (ontology) of money. Reducing theories of money to two camps – orthodox or heterodox – untenably limits the variety of possible linkages between money practices and money concepts.[9] Careful examination of the history of writings on money clearly reveals a large number of ways (far more than two) to make these connections.

We need, then, a way to do justice to the complexity of the theory and the messiness of the history without ultimately getting lost in either. Mine undoubtedly remains a project of disentanglement, yet I aim to create categories that help to make sense of the various theories, while avoiding any urge to distill them to some supposed essence.

4 Conceptual and Historical Accounts – and Capitalist Social Orders

The dominant understanding of money pivots around a set of conceptual claims (sometimes described as "logical" claims) about money's "nature" – about the very *being* of money (hence ontology). Frequently these theoretical arguments are then mobilized to tell a tale of money's historical emergence. In many standard (textbook) accounts we find a theory of money that proves utterly abstract and ahistorical (it explains money without concrete reference to history), yet that account has enormous implications for how we understand money's history – be-

---

9 There are at least two distinct problems with the orthodox/heterodox framing. First, it oversimplifies, as I show in detail in Chapter 2. But second, and just as important, the critique of "orthodoxy" as articulated by self-identified "heterodox" theorists elides the extent to which, while quite wrong about money's nature, orthodox theory actually tells us something important about money's practical and ideological effects within a capitalist social order. Martijn Konings formulates this crucial point incisively:

> In its eagerness to reject the orthodox understanding of money as incorrect, heterodox theory has generally been blind to the work done by that conception, how it articulates and adds force to the regulative imaginaries and affective structuration of capitalist life. That is, to argue that we ought to take orthodox conceptions of money more seriously is to suggest not that we should celebrate their descriptive credentials but rather that we should take them seriously as an expression of a particular imaginary that has certain effects. (Konings 2018: 6)

cause *the deductive logic is meant to stand in for history.* I address this phenomenon concretely in the following section, via my critique of functionalist accounts, which presume we can know money's actual history through philosophical positing of its functions. These theories of money allow their authors to provide money's "history" without ever discussing actual history.[10]

The fact that my project necessarily and intentionally *combines* theoretical and historical work heightens the need to clarify and circumscribe the historical or conceptual nature of any specific claims I make along the way. First, my account will never ignore history, nor attempt to rewrite it through philosophical hypostatization. Further, the overwhelming historical evidence reveals that the history of money is a history of social relations of credit/debt within and between societies. Frequently the symbols or tokens of those relations of credit/debt *have become fetish objects* both for the members of those societies and also for theorists of economic activity, such that the claims to credit were understood to have intrinsic value themselves. Nonetheless, taking a wider view, the money objects themselves never "possess" value in any intrinsic way, but are always only perceived to have such value because they successfully function as claims on future value, as symbols or tokens of credit/debt. My theory of money takes account of both the historical record of money as credit/debt and the significant political, social, and economic practices in which money as credit/debt appears as a form of value in those social orders. Indeed, within capitalist societies money may appear as the ultimate form of value.

I understand a capitalist social order as a unique and peculiar organization of society. Capitalism is not an independent "economic system" that a society or nation-state would or could *choose*. Rather, a capitalist social order (a capitalist society) is one in which a capitalist mode of production predominates. "Mode of production" is neither an overly technical term, nor in my account (unlike in some Marxist discourse) is it an enchanted one; it has no special powers. It merely names the organization, structure, and dominant practices of production in a given social order. In a tributary mode of production, small-scale producers, who have direct access to the means of production, produce for themselves directly, while some state structure extracts part of that product through a system of taxation or direct domination. In a feudal mode of production, serfs produce for their own families and for that of their lords (to whom they are bonded by law and so-

---

10 The alternative is simply to presume such history in advance – as if it were given or known – and then use it as support for the conceptual argument.

cial custom), while the lords, in turn, have been granted title to the land (by the monarch) that the serf works.[11]

> In a capitalist social order, the capitalist use of the market – the use of the market for money-making – transforms the entire mode of production of society, such that production becomes production for profitable exchange. Under capitalism, most goods and services are produced not for direct consumption by either the producers or those they are closely linked to in society. Instead, even the most basic necessities (food, shelter, clothing) are produced as commodities for sale on the market, and such necessities can only be accessed through the market. (Chambers 2022: 59)

Perhaps most significantly, a capitalist mode of production is not a natural or inevitable development from the "nature" of *homo economicus*. Quite the contrary, a capitalist mode of production is historically contingent. Capitalism emerges for the first time only because of a matrix of prior conditions – namely, trade and money practices along with a set of social and legal property relations.[12] In any attempt to grasp the nature of money within a capitalist social order, history therefore matters fundamentally since the very economic forces within that order depend for their existence on these prior historical conditions.

At the same time, once a capitalist social order comes into being, and once capitalist structures come to predominate, such orders absolutely do unleash genuine and significant forces and relations into the world. Economic forces in a capitalist social order are different from those in a feudal social order, and they are not merely the product of law or political will. Those forces are no less real for being historically contingent. Therefore, in analyzing in close detail the nature of money and commodities within capitalist social orders, I will make a series of conceptual arguments about the nature of money and its relation to other elements in a social order. These will frequently be claims of entanglement and also

---

11 No mode of production is ever a pure type. Indeed, Jairus Banaji has shown that the closest we can find to an ideal-type model of a feudal mode of production is not western Europe prior to the emergence of capitalism but eastern Europe *after* the rise of capitalism (Banaji 2010: 82). In any case, my rough descriptions in the text above are meant to be schematic and heuristic.

12 The date and content of those earliest forms of capitalism are much debated. In my reading of this literature, Ellen Meiksins Wood and Banaji offer the most significant and convincing accounts. Wood focuses on the first appearance of the total reorganization of one sector of production within a specific country, according to the profit imperatives of the market; she argues that this happens first in English food production in the sixteenth century (Wood 2002). Banaji looks to wider practices within global trade that implemented capitalist relations – the use and organization of markets for making profit. This form of commercial capitalism can be dated back as early as the twelfth to fourteenth centuries, and certainly provided one condition of possibility for the later emergence of a distinctly capitalist society (Banaji 2020).

entailment, arguments that take their own deductive form – that is, *given* certain structural relations within society, other relations must follow. I want to stress that these are always *conceptual* and *theoretical* arguments about the nature of money (and commodities) within those social orders. Such arguments depend on history (and prior historical development), *but they are not themselves historical arguments.* They do not explain or predict the past or future historical development of these social orders. Thus, for example, when I describe relations between commodities and other commodities, and between commodities and money (and between buyers and sellers and producers and consumers), I am not describing historical change, not giving an account of events that happened diachronically in history. Any necessary relations – relations of entailment or determination – should be understood strictly in the sense of *conceptual relational requirements, not historical determinations.*

To reiterate, however, those conceptual arguments presuppose and rest on a specific set of prior historical developments: they have validity only for and within a capitalist social order. Transported to a different mode of production (e. g., feudal or tributary), none of these conceptual relations would necessarily hold because the categories themselves depend on a given historical and institutional configuration. This means that the starting point for conceptual analysis is itself historical, and it depends specifically on the existence of a social order structured by the production of commodities for exchange and profit. This is necessarily a monetary economy, so both money and commodities have already come into historical existence prior to our description of the conceptual relations between them.

Finally, this approach also circumscribes my own use of ontology in exploring money because it means that when I inquire into the *being* of money – by posing the question *"What is money?"* – I am specifically inquiring into the being of money today, the being of money under capitalism. History itself provides the necessary conditions for capitalist money because capitalism is a historical social order (not a universal form), and to grasp the being of money under capitalism may be to illuminate aspects of money's existence in prior historical periods. However, we must resist any inclination to transpose to prior historical periods the nature of money under capitalism.[13]

---

13 In an effort to describe his own understanding of the relation between history and ontology, Marx wrote:

In the anatomy of man there is a key to the anatomy of the ape. The indications of the higher types in the subordinate types of animal life *can only be understood, on the other hand, if the higher type itself is already well known.* ...However ... [we must not] obliterate all historical dif-

5 Against Functionalism: The Ontology of Money

As Schumpeter helpfully documents, between the 1870s and the middle of the twentieth century a certain common sense about the fundamentals of money began to congeal within economic writings, especially in the United States (Schumpeter 1954). This standard and standardizing approach to money eschews any rigorous conceptual work (dismissed as "metaphysics") and insists on a crudely functionalist account of money, as expressed in a phrase oft repeated during this period: "Money is that money does."[14] Francis A. Walker offers this proverb while laying out a line of reasoning that has animated accounts of money for 150 years: to understand what money *is*, simply look to the functions money performs (what it *does*). This logic, which underwrites textbook approaches to money today, asks "What is money?" and answers by listing "the functions of money" (Mankiw 2010: 80). Therefore money "is": medium of exchange, means of payment,

---

ferences and see in all forms of society the bourgeois forms [i.e., the contemporary forms]. (Marx 1996: 151, emphasis added)

The first sentence is quite famous, and it suggests that later forms of historical development can serve as aids to scientific understanding of earlier historical forms. But the second sentence, where I have added emphasis, is often forgotten. Marx says that the anatomy of man provides a key to the anatomy of the ape, but he immediately clarifies that the anatomy of the ape absolutely *does not* contain the key to the anatomy of man. Nothing in the ape's anatomy (nothing in the structure of a prior social order) can tell us in advance how history will develop, or what future social orders will emerge. Marx rejects teleology. Finally, while Marx thinks later developments can enrich our understanding of earlier forms, he explicitly cautions against a tendency to project present forms into the past. Apes are not human beings, and they may be different from us in ways that we, who benefit from an understanding of human anatomy, simply cannot grasp. We therefore ought to limit our most rigorous arguments to an account of the present. When I say in the text above that I "circumscribe my ontological approach," I follow Marx's suggestion here. (For much more on this text, and on the historical and ontological study of social orders, see Chambers 2014.)

14 The phrase comes from Francis A. Walker's 1879 book *Money and Its Relations to Trade and Industry* (Walker 1879: 1). However, the line is typically misquoted as "money is as money does," and attributed only to "Walker" (Fisher 2010 [1928]: 18; Kemmerer 1935: 8), or it is misquoted as "money is what money does" – either without attribution (Ingham 2018: 842) or with misattribution to Walker's 1878 book *Money* (Walker 1878; Ingham 2004a: 205). Ingham actually cites Schumpeter (1954) in both Walker references, but for the record, Schumpeter is the only author I can find who gets the wording of the Walker quote correct (Schumpeter 1954: 1052). However, while Schumpeter cites four different Walker books, he does not explicitly mention the 1879 source for the famous line (Schumpeter 1954: 861, 906, 1042, 1046).

store of value, and unit of account.[15] After defining these functions, the textbooks all move on to other matters, but it helps to go back to Walker's original presentation because he uses striking language to complete his logic: "Always and everywhere that which does the money-work is the money-thing" (Walker 1879: 2).

Notice the subtle transformation that occurs over the course of these deductive steps: Walker starts by posing the question what *money* is and ends by telling his readers what the *money thing* is. In other words, *the functionalist account of money rests on a fundamental conflation of money with the money thing.*

This functionalist account implies an untenable ontology. Walker's own contemporary Alexander Del Mar thoroughly skewers Walker's functionalist definition of money, describing the theory as "no more applicable to money than to steam engines, or cartwheels." Del Mar insists that Walker's account (like all the functionalist accounts that will follow) proves incapable of *"distinguishing money"* from things that are not money, but which might themselves carry out the enumerated functions. This leaves us with a "definition without any definitive idea behind it" (Del Mar 1896: 26, emphasis added). Functionalism provides the form of a definition – "money is the thing that performs money functions" – but the definition itself can only ever be empty or circular: empty, if it cannot answer the question of what makes money functions *the functions of money* rather than something else; circular, if it defines the functions of money by reference to its previous definition of money.[16] In straightforward terms, to theorize money as the thing that performs the four standard textbook functions is to say

---

15 To be more precise, most modern textbooks actually list only three functions; they elide "means of payment," implying that the category of "medium of exchange" includes the means of payment function (Mankiw 2010: 81). By erasing the temporal gap essential to the means of payment function, this move lends support to the myth that economic exchange can be modeled on the basis of barter. Dropping means of payment also completely erases a distinction crucial to many nineteenth- and early twentieth-century debates, wherein different authors attempted to build the theory of money from one function or the other, with significant consequences (Ingham 2018: 841–42). Hawtrey, for example, in his *Currency and Credit* (1919), focuses almost exclusively on means of payment, while Keynes explicitly rejects the Mengerian fixation on medium of exchange (Keynes 1930: 3).

16 It would be a mistake to think of functionalism as an old argument about money that has merely persisted in the textbooks. Rather, the most explicit efforts of neoclassical economists to theorize money today involve resuscitating a new functionalism. Here I point specifically to Tony Lawson's social positioning theory, which explicitly defends a functionalist account (Lawson 2016; Lawson 2022). I do not engage with Lawson's work in depth, mainly because I take Ingham's critique to be definitive, and Ingham shows starkly how Lawson "falls inadvertently into [functionalism's] trap" (Ingham 2018: 842).

very little at all *about money*;[17] many things that are not money can and do also perform those functions.[18]

More insidiously, a functionalist definition tempts us to adopt a broader functionalist mode of *historical* explanation. In other words, defining money as "that which performs money functions" encourages the view that money only emerges in history *because it performs those functions*. This account answers the properly historical question "Why did money become an element in ancient social orders?" with an abstractly logical (and entirely ahistorical) answer – namely, "because money performs money functions and thus filled a *need* for money that all societies always have." In short, functionalism lures us into believing barter-myth nonsense.[19]

This brings me to the tacit ontology of the functionalist definition. While writers in this tradition, especially early and mid-twentieth-century thinkers, wish to dismiss all deep conceptual work with the pejorative "metaphysics," Walker's own logic entails a strong set of ontological claims (even if Walker and his followers never offer an explicit defense of these tenets). Walker's reasoning leads to the conclusion that the money thing is money, and money is the money thing. The being of money dwells within the material object or technology that performs money's identified functions. We can always answer the question "What is money?" by pointing to specific objects or concrete practices. Moneyness is always bound up with, tethered to, and found in, money stuff.

Keynes was one of the first writers to recognize the inadequacy of this ontology. The opening passages of his *A Treatise on Money* (1930) issue a thoroughgoing rejection of such an approach. In response to the singular ontology by which money is money stuff, Keynes suggests a two-level analysis: 1) "money of account"[20] provides the "description or title of money" and "is the *primary concept* of a theory of money"; while, 2) "money derives its character from its relation to

---

17 Alvaro Cencini makes the point incisively: "It is not true that the functions played by money determine its nature; on the contrary, the nature of money determines the functions it can play" (Cencini 1988: 30).

18 Commodities can serve as store of value and medium of exchange, and with precisely written contracts, almost anything can serve as a means of payment (e.g., "I promise to deliver three interpretive dances by December 1, 2023"). Lest there be any confusion, these examples do not provide evidence that interpretive dances are money but rather serve as further evidence against the claim that money can be defined functionally.

19 For the definitive critique of functionalist historical explanation, see Nietzsche 1967; for the definitive explosion of the myth of barter, see Graeber 2011, whom I discuss in Chapter 3.

20 In the original 1930 publication, Keynes hyphenates the phrase as "money-of-account." Mercifully, the editors of Keynes's collected works removed the hyphens; I follow them here for both consistency and ease of reading (Keynes 1978).

the money of account" and "is the thing which answers the description" given by money of account (Keynes 1930: 3). In keeping with standard usage, Keynes still assigns the word "money" to "the thing," but the very nature of this money stuff depends on a relation to a prior concept of money (which for Keynes is money of account). One cannot understand what money is without grasping this two-level, or doubled, relation between the money stuff and the ontologically prior concept of money.[21]

On the one hand, Keynes provides a piercing and important insight: money is not the money stuff, and whatever we wish to say about the money thing must be placed into relation with a broader, more rigorously conceptual analysis of "money." This, I contend, must be seen as a singular contribution to the theory of money because Keynes supplies his readers with the resources they need to reject outright any functionalist theory of money, and to challenge any account that tries to derive a full theory of money from analysis of the money token. We will find the essence of money neither in a chemical analysis of a silver coin nor in a bare description of how and when that coin was held (as store of value) or changed hands (as means of payment, medium of exchange).

On the other hand, while Keynes was right to *distinguish* the money thing from the *primary concept* of money, he was wrong to attribute that concept to money of account. As briefly detailed in the Introduction, *money of account* names that crucial "fourth dimension" of money. It provides the denomination of credit/debt, and indeed, all money must be marked in this manner – in euros, dollars, rupees, etc. But money of account is not *primary* because denomination is not itself a full *concept of money.* The denomination "rupees" is not *money.* Rupee is a measure of credit/debt, and if we have a money token, denominated in rupees, held by a creditor, and pointing to a valid debtor – then and only then will we have money. *Money requires much more than money of account.*

---

21 A warning for upcoming chapters: we must be careful not to conflate this Keynesian distinction between "money of account" and "money proper" with the distinction between credit (as promise to pay) and money (as actual payment). Keynes is distinguishing between, on the one hand, the idea of denomination, the *concept* of a dollar as measure, and on the other, the thing that "answers to that concept," the "stuff" that we have in our hand and recognize as corresponding to such a measure. This is the difference between the concept of length (under the name "meter") and the thing we say *has* length (as measured in meters). But this means that the Keynesian "primary concept" precedes anything purporting to be money. In contrast, the money/credit distinction depends on an argument that some things *are* (that is, they successfully perform *as*) money, while some are not. This second distinction operates only on one side of Keynes's division; it centers on the question whether the money stuff really is money. I return to the money/credit distinction repeatedly over the next four chapters.

As much as Keynes helped his readers to avoid the dead end of functionalism, he put many of them on the wrong track by suggesting that as long as we have the "title" for money, we necessarily have a complete concept of money. By invoking the two levels, Keynes lets us see that the being of money – the moneyness of money, as Ingham helpfully puts the point – cannot lie within the money thing, what Keynes calls "money proper" (Ingham 2006: 270; Ingham 2004a: 8; Ingham 2018: 841). But we will not, we cannot, find that being in the idea of a dollar or a euro, and too many of Keynes's readers (even the best of them) have often taken this route as a shortcut. That is, they variously assert or assume that denomination itself, what Keynes called the "title of money," can stand in for a theory of money, can "be" the concept of money.

As I have shown both here and in the Preface, most authors who try to give an account of money cannot resist the temptation to simplify their narrative. This tendency explains both the money theory binaries – commodity versus claim; orthodox versus heterodox – and the efforts to find a plain slogan that serves as a kind of trump card – money is metal, money is fiction, money is money of account, money is the ledger.[22] However, for better or worse, money is just not that simple. We need instead to grasp money in its complexity, which means both to get a sense of how complex it can be but also to provide some handholds for dealing with that complexity – for making sense of money *as* complex. Such is the task of the following chapter.

---

22 For quite some time I myself was under the spell of this last watchword. Yet, while the ledger of credits and debts proves crucial to our understanding of both the money array and our efforts to track concrete money practices – by "following the money" as it moves across balance sheets – the ledger or spreadsheet that tracks credits must not be confused with money itself.

Chapter Two
The Matrix of Money Theories

1 Money Sources

The critique of functionalism and its attendant metaphysics, along with the broaching of broader ontological questions, clears the page so that we can begin to draw a matrix for categorizing and organizing the wide variety of theories of money. The goal is to clarify and indeed simplify, but without resorting to reductivism. We are aiming for a middle ground between, on the one hand, an unmanageable survey of each and every individual theory of money and, on the other, the simplistic notion that there are really only two theories of money.

Anyone who struggles to understand money and then strives to explain it to others will be tempted to remind readers of the previous failures on this front – failures by much more famous thinkers. Keynes's so-called (by him) "Babylonian madness" provides the best-known example: the benefit of late nineteenth-century advances in history and anthropology allowed Keynes to see how badly "classical economics" (also his term) got money wrong. Keynes conceived of *A Treatise on Money*, his first major scholarly work, as a fundamental break with that paradigm. In one way or another, Keynes largely abandoned that project – "recovered," shall we say – and moved on to the work that made him the most famous economist in the world, but he therefore left much of the dominant paradigm fully intact.[1]

Less famously, but more substantively important for our purposes here, Schumpeter failed to finish his money book because he never got "his ideas on money straightened out to his own satisfaction" (Earley 1994: 342).[2] Nonetheless, Schumpeter never abandoned this project, on which he was arguably still working at the time of his death, in the form of his unfinished *History of Economic Analysis* (*HEA*).[3] This text, in all of its repetitive, messy, yet still incomplete 1,300 pages, pro-

---

1 Ingham categorizes Keynes's first book as "heterodox work" and then describes the *General Theory* as "Keynes's own *rapprochement* with orthodoxy" (Ingham 2004a: 27). We might say that Ingham came to write his "money book" (originally intended as one short chapter of a different book) due to his own affliction of money madness (Ingham 2004a: viii).
2 James S. Earley credits Arthur Smithies (in personal correspondence with Earley) with this line, which eloquently captures Schumpeter's lifelong difficulties in understanding money. At the start of his major book on money, Ingham quotes this line as one he stumbled across part way through his own struggle with the topic (Ingham 2004a: 5).
3 Schumpeter spent the last nine years of his life working on this book, one that was itself meant to update work he published nearly four decades prior (Schumpeter 1956 [1917/1918]; Schumpeter

https://doi.org/10.1515/9783110760774-006

vides the richest resource for understanding the complicated history of theories of money, and also for constructing a workable conceptual framework that can make sense of such theories, past and present. My project goes back to Schumpeter, thereby in many ways bypassing, but not discounting, the profoundly important and much more recent work of Ingham.[4]

The drawbacks of Schumpeter's book appear obvious: now seven decades old; repetitious, scattered, and unwieldy; reaching no decisive conclusions. Nonetheless, I wager that the costs are worth it in the end. Schumpeter's analysis proves consistently rigorous, and it comes as close to comprehensive as one can possibly imagine; Schumpeter cites and discusses literally dozens upon dozens of sources that go unmentioned anywhere else in the literature (even in Ingham, whose text has an impressive and thorough bibliography). Moreover, the open-ended nature of Schumpeter's investigation – the very fact that he is not presenting a theory he has already "straightened out" but rather exploring the texts through a far-reaching method of discovery – makes this work a much more valuable source for mapping the terrain of money.

1954). After his death in January 1950, Elizabeth Boody – an economic historian, specialist in East Asian economics, and Schumpeter's wife from 1937 until his death – spent three months *locating* the various draft manuscripts of the work, only at that point realizing "it was nearly completed" (Boody Schumpeter, in Schumpeter 1954: xxxiv). Boody Schumpeter then spent the last three years of her life attempting to edit the manuscript pages into a finished book, but she died in summer 1953 before the project was complete. At that stage, some of Schumpeter's Harvard colleagues took over, and the book was finally published in 1954. Even with all this post-mortem work, the text is still a mess, but it is also, so far as I can tell, far and away the very best history of theories of money available – covering more ground in greater depth than anything else.

4 In my opinion the single most important contemporary author on money is without doubt Ingham. In Chapter 4 I engage in more detail with the substance of his historical and theoretical arguments, but here I want to make a narrower point about the way Ingham's work *frames* the question of "how to do the theory of money." Despite the sophistication, rigor, and breadth of his work, most readers will come away from it with the impression that there are two theoretical choices: orthodox or heterodox. In this chapter I disprove such an idea, by demonstrating the breadth of theoretical possibilities. Relatedly, while Ingham is not a historian, his work often implies a certain history of theories of money, and here the narrowing of choices to two does not do justice to the historical terrain of money theory. As a contemporary theorist of money, Ingham has no peer. But as an introductory overview to the history of theories of money, one is better off dealing with messy excerpts from Schumpeter's unfinished colossus. Finally, and this is my sharpest criticism of Ingham, he uses a misreading of Schumpeter (a misreading that was originally Ellis's) to legitimate an overly narrow framing of the history of money. I detail this last point just before my final section of this chapter, below.

Reading *HEA*'s sections on money[5] reveals the breadth and depth of money theory, while consistently demonstrating variety; no one can come away from close study of this text still clutching the tenet that there are only two theories of money "worthy of the name." As one traverses the mountainous terrain of his arguments, even Schumpeter's apparent self-contradictions become an asset because his reader comes to understand that the various positions or choices on money do not always or easily line up. The orthodox/heterodox framing of theories of money makes it seem as if there is only one choice: to buy into the orthodoxy, or reject it for the heterodoxy. Such a notion is belied at every turn by Schumpeter, who himself develops a unique set of positions on money, combining elements that, according to the dominant framing, are simply not supposed to go together. Schumpeter's reader therefore bears witness to the multiple and multiplying variety of theories of money.

2 Money Choices

Schumpeter divides his history into three periods: everything before 1790; 1790 – 1870; and 1870 to Schumpeter's present.[6] His overarching concern, however, lies with the nature of economic *analysis*, not with the history itself, so rather than dig into historical context for each period to show its uniqueness, Schumpeter approaches them all with the same set of options. I will adopt and modify this framework in order to create a money-theory matrix. The matrix is formed by combining responses to three sets of binary options. Any theory of money must pick one or the other of each of these options, and the cumulative set of choices will itself tell us much of what we need to know about the overall theory. First I will give a gen-

---

5 The book has three distinct chapters on money, ranging across almost 1,000 pages, and of course the reader can find numerous other discussions of money in passages nominally devoted to specific thinkers, theories, or economic episodes.

6 Originally Schumpeter chose 1870–1914 for his final period, but in published form those headings were changed to "1870 to 1914 (and later)" to reflect the fact that as he continued to work on the book during the 1930s and 1940s, he frequently referred to contemporary writings. And no reader of the text can fail to see that, throughout, Schumpeter is writing a "history of the present" in the Foucauldian sense that he reflects on the past as a way to grasp the present state of thought. For example, Schumpeter opens the section on money for the period up to 1790 with a long discussion of Keynesian aggregate monetary analysis. He takes it as obvious that the difference between Aristotle's real analysis and Quesnay's monetary analysis matters not for its own sake but for how it illuminates or reshapes contemporary (1930s) arguments. This may explain why over the years Schumpeter came to redefine the project as a history of economic *analysis*, not economic *thought* (see Boody Schumpeter, in Schumpeter 1954: xxxi).

eral description of each of the three options, before then turning to the combinatorics.

Real or Monetary Analysis

Schumpeter sees the history of theories of money as somewhat cyclical – from long periods of dominance of *real analysis* to "interludes" of viability of *monetary analysis*.[7] Real analysis[8] posits that all economic activity can (and usually should) be described strictly in terms of goods, services, and human choice. Money is not essential to economic activity, and reference to money is not required for economic analysis. Rather, "money enters the picture only in the modest role of a technical device that has been adopted in order to facilitate transactions" (Schumpeter 1954: 264). Real analysis describes money as *neutral* because it is nothing more than a secondary covering – "veil," "garb," and "epidermis" are just some of the metaphors used – a mere appearance for the real economic body (Schumpeter 1954: 264; cf. Schumpeter 1956: 150). Real analysis therefore always implies and often explicitly asserts that unless money introduces an unneeded and undesirable distorting impact, the real economy functions on the same principles as a so-called "barter economy." A pure commitment to real analysis could lead logically to the very rejection of a theory of money (as an irrequisite element of investigation), but to the extent that the "practical convenience" of money as a "technical device" makes it a ubiquitous part of economic life, it may prove necessary for the real analyst to deal with money. He or she does so by subtracting money from economic analysis and by attempting to minimize money's disturbances of real economic activity.

Schumpeter depicts monetary analysis not as its own positive project but as a negation of or departure from real analysis – a series of rejections of real propositions. First, money cannot be neutral because even casual study of economic history shows that money has fundamentally shaped that history (from gold rushes to

---

7 Real analysis (from Aristotle to the Scholastics, from Ricardo to Fisher) dominates history, but monetary analysis breaks through from time to time – for example, in the period of the French physiocrats (eighteenth century) and again with the rise of Keynesianism (twentieth century). Schumpeter's presentation implicitly suggests that real analysis is the norm and thus persists unless disturbed by a particularly important thinker. Real analysis provides the default baseline, while monetary analysis only survives when attached to a name such as Quesnay or Keynes.

8 The real/monetary dichotomy must not be confused with or mapped onto the real/nominal distinction. In the former, "real" means *non-monetary*. In the latter, "real" refers to a *type of monetary measure* (i. e., inflation-adjusted). From the perspective of *real analysis*, all prices ("real" or "nominal") remain monetary, *not real*, phenomena. See Schumpeter's own (much longer) footnote on this point (1954: 264n2).

modern banking practices) (Schumpeter 1954: 265). Second, in the form of incomes, savings, and prices, money becomes foundational to modern economic analysis and forces us to admit that modern economic life cannot be modeled on barter. Third, aggregate or macroeconomic analysis necessarily uses money terms as its fundamental variables; here the very "matter" to be grasped is monetary (Schumpeter 1954: 266). Fourth, any view of economics as structured by spending and saving decisions must necessarily be prosecuted along the lines of monetary analysis. Adding up, we can describe both a *weak* and a *strong* version of monetary analysis. The former sees monetary analysis as *unavoidable* and therefore indispensable given the monetary nature of modern economic activity. The latter insists on a description of money and the monetary as essential to the economic.[9]

Commodity or Claim

Schumpeter helpfully crystallizes the commodity theory of money by articulating its core commitment to "theoretical metallism." This he distinguishes from "practical metallism": many who advocate "sound money," or paper money's convertibility to/backing by a designated commodity (with intrinsic value), do not themselves hold to the fundamental tenets of theoretical metallism. In his early article on money, Schumpeter says metallism is the particular name for a general "commodity theory of money" (Schumpeter 1956: 157). Consistent with this, in his later work he defines metallism in terms of the commodity:

> By Theoretical Metallism we denote the *theory* that it is logically essential for money to consist of, or to be "covered" by, some commodity so that the logical source of the exchange value or purchasing power of money is the exchange value or purchasing power of that commodity, considered independently of its monetary role. (Schumpeter 1954: 274)

Schumpeter's insight lies in his capacity to see the theoretical problems that a commodity theory purports to solve – namely, the deeply complex question of the "value of money" (Schumpeter 1956: 157). The commodity theory of money "answers" the question by displacing or ignoring it: if money is a commodity then the value of money is the value of that commodity expressed as an exchange ratio with other commodities (the goods that it buys). This structure entails a nec-

---

9 Schumpeter himself accepts the weak thesis, but he would never endorse the strong. And this is perhaps exactly why he is trapped between real and monetary analysis (or forced to seek a synthesis), because he knows monetary analysis is unavoidable, but he cannot allow that it is essential.

essary distinction between money, which has intrinsic value as a commodity,[10] and credit, which is nothing more than some form of promise to deliver the designated money (i. e., the specified commodity) (Schumpeter 1954: 1053).

---

10 The commitment of a commodity theory of money to "intrinsic value" may confuse, or raise the critical hackles of, students or close readers of thinkers such as Menger and Jevons. As I noted earlier, Menger and Jevons are credited as co-discoverers of the theory of marginal utility, and each wrote a book detailing and defending a commodity theory of money. Central to marginalism is the claim, announced in one of Jevons's subheadings, that "Utility and Value Are Not Intrinsic." Jevons purposively conflates utility and value, arguing that they are not physical properties but "only accidents of a thing arising from the fact that some one wants it" (Jevons 2011 [1875]: 18). On the basis of such quotes, readers of Jevons could reasonably protest that he rejects "intrinsic value." But Jevons is not consistent: a dozen pages later he explicitly affirms that money "should itself *possess value*," clarifying that he means "substantial value" (Jevons 2011: 32, emphasis added). Building on this foundation, Jevons asserts that a "standard coin" (one with validated metallic content of a measurable weight) "is one of which the value in exchange *depends solely upon the value of the material contained in it*" (Jevons 2011: 67, all emphasis added). At just this point in his discussion, Jevons seems to realize that his account of commodity money has tied him to a notion of intrinsic value that his broader marginalist position rejects, so he follows up immediately with this:

> It has been usual to call the value of the metal contained in a coin the intrinsic value of the coin; but this use of the word intrinsic is likely to give rise to fallacious notions concerning the nature of value, which is never an intrinsic property, or existence, but merely a circumstance, or external relation. To avoid any chance of ambiguity, I shall substitute the expression, *metallic value*. (Jevons 2011: 66)

Hence: money as a commodity does *not* have "intrinsic value," but it *does* have "metallic value." If ever one needed an example of a distinction without a difference, Jevons has provided it here. The bottom line is that despite Jevons's protestations to the contrary, Schumpeter's account logically holds: the metallist theory (i. e., the commodity theory) depends on positing an intrinsic value to money (as commodity). A close reading of Jevons's misreading of Gresham's law powerfully validates such a summary. Gresham's law states that "bad money" (token money that does not have "full-weight" metallic content) will drive out "good money" (proper "standard" money of full weight) because the "full-weight" coins get withdrawn from circulation, melted down, and sold for their (intrinsic) metallic value, while the light coins continue to circulate as tokens that represent greater "value" than they in fact contain. Jevons's commodity theory of money can only respond to this historical and empirical fact by trying to insist that *all* coins be of "standard" weight. As I noted in the Preface and will explore in more detail in later chapters, a much more lucid account of Gresham's law emerges when we note the difference between commodity-gold and money-gold. Gold is taken out of circulation when its commodity value exceeds its money denomination, and for this reason the proper action (of the sovereign, or the central banker) is precisely the opposite of that suggested by Jevons and other "sound money" advocates: to make certain that the nominal money value *exceeds* the commodity value, thereby removing any incentive for hoarding commodity-gold. Rulers throughout history have always done just this, thereby performing in practice a powerful critique of the commodity theory.

Despite the availability of evidence to the contrary (Innes 1913; Innes 1914), Schumpeter repeatedly (but still falsely) asserts that the history of money appears to provide confirmation of the commodity theory. Here he echoes, and perhaps contributes to, the emerging standard narrative of money found in Menger and Jevons: "The historical origin of money certainly lies in the value of the money commodity" (Schumpeter 1956: 157; cf. Schumpeter 1954: 276). Notably, however, Schumpeter also radically departs from that narrative, as the line from above ends as follows: "*but its essential nature lies elsewhere*" (Schumpeter 1956: 157, emphasis added). In methodological arguments that resonate in important ways with those of Marx, Schumpeter insists on distinguishing historical origins from necessary logical relations (Schumpeter 1956: 157; Schumpeter 1954: 276; Marx 1977 [1859]: 24). Importantly, then, the structure of Schumpeter's presentation of theories of money (the "raw material" out of which I build my matrix) creates space to separate arguments about money's history from those concerning money's nature. Finally, in terms of the history of thought, Schumpeter rightly sees the metallist theory as dominating – from Smith and Ricardo to Jevons and Menger.[11]

Much as monetary analysis begins with a critique of real analysis, so the claim theory of money stakes its territory with a refutation of theoretical metallism. Taking gold as the representative commodity, the claim theory exposes metallism's fundamental error as a failure to distinguish commodity-gold from money-gold (my terms, not Schumpeter's). Schumpeter shows that metallism has no way of accounting for some practical facts about money that we frequently observe, even under a gold standard: 1) irredeemable paper money continues to circulate; 2) old metallic money (no longer coined) continues to circulate "above par" (i.e., at an exchange-value higher than that of commodity-gold); 3) making gold into money alters (increases) the value of gold. Schumpeter admits that commodity-gold will be worth as much as money-gold, but this does not serve as proof that money-gold's value is essentially the intrinsic value of commodity-gold:

> The assertion that metal as money [money-gold] depends on the value of the metal as a commodity [commodity-gold] is correct only in the sense in which it is also correct to say that the

---

11 Despite its length and massive coverage of authors, Schumpeter's book contains no detailed and explicit discussion of Marx. Instead, one finds dozens of offhand references to Marx, many of which betray the fact that Schumpeter has clearly read Marx, in some cases deeply. One of the most stupendous of these seemingly throwaway lines appears in the discussion of metallism: "For more than a century" after Smith, metallism "was almost universally accepted – *by nobody more implicitly than by Marx*" (Schumpeter 1954: 276, emphasis added). A full unpacking of this claim would constitute a separate project.

value of the metal as a commodity [commodity-gold] depends on the value of the metal as money [money-gold]. (Schumpeter 1956: 158)[12]

One might press Schumpeter here for more specificity: What is the mechanism by which the commodity value *depends* on the money value? The answer, under a gold standard, is straightforward: the mint price provides precisely this mechanism. The mint price must always remain higher than the price of the metal in industrial markets (otherwise, once again, coins would be melted down to sell to industrialists, so no metal would be supplied to the mint). Innes similarly observes that the only reason gold has been so valuable is that states hoard it – not because of any intrinsic properties of gold as an industrial commodity (Innes 1914: 164).[13]

Schumpeter's logic illuminates a crucial point: if commodity-gold and money-gold are not the same thing, we can never derive the nature of money from the nature of a commodity. Put differently, even when it is a commodity that comes to serve as money, this does not prove that money *in its nature* is a commodity. Moreover, closer observation reveals the opposite: that in its role as money, money-gold is something quite other than commodity-gold.[14] This leads Schumpeter to perhaps the strongest refutation of the commodity theory that one will ever find in the history of economic thought:[15]

---

12 Cencini reaches the same conclusion with a distinct argument that he draws from an innovative reading of Smith: "The use of a particular commodity as money is always possible, of course, but this is not the point. The important argument is that money cannot be identified with the commodity to which it is linked, whether it be gold, paper, or electrical impulses" (Cencini 1988: 11).
13 The so-called end of the gold standard was not the end of states hoarding gold, so Innes's general insight still applies to the most recent century as well.
14 This logic helps to explain historical cases that consistently confuse metallists – namely, instances in which commodity-metals (copper, silver, gold) abound, but *money* is nowhere to be found. Ingham provides a brilliant explication here of Max Weber's work on money in China. From the mid-sixteenth century onward, China had plenty of commodity-silver, but this led only to the "chaos of bullion barter and myriad exchange rates" (Ingham 2015: 177). As nineteenth-century Chinese government officials themselves understood at the time, China remained "a nation with no money" (Lau 2006: 1; quoted in Ingham 2015: 176). Put perhaps too simply (and in my language, which is not quite that of either Ingham or Weber), the problem was not a shortage of silver but a lack of banks.
15 It is worth noting that the basic distinction that drives this argument – that between commodity-gold and money-gold – had already been keenly observed outside of economic thought. In his famous account of "truth" as a "mobile army of metaphors," Nietzsche almost offhandedly gives the following as his example of a "worn-out" metaphor: "coins which have lost their image and now can be used *only as metal, and no longer as coins*" (Nietzsche 1979: 84). Here Nietzsche suggests that the "truth" of money rests on a metaphor, which again gives the lie to metallists – because if the coins were really just metal, they would never have been money.

Money is not a commodity – not even when it happens to consist of a valuable material. For as soon as the latter is used as money, it must necessarily cease to fulfil its role as an economic good; and as soon as a piece of money made of valuable material is diverted to use as a good, e. g., for jewelry, *it ceases to be money.* As long as a material is money, it satisfies no wants and can never be the object of subjective use-value appraisal, and therefore *as money can never have value of its own.* (Schumpeter 1956: 161, emphasis added)

Rejecting the commodity theory of money poses a dilemma: How do we explain money's "value"? Schumpeter argues, first, that in a technical sense money has neither use-value nor exchange-value. Money is not value; it is a type of *power.* For Schumpeter, money's "purchasing power" arises independently of any question of value.[16] Of course, we realize that money "exchanges" for commodities and in this sense surely seems to have an exchange-value. Schumpeter's explanation functions by way of a crucial metaphor: "We can speak of the exchange value of money *only* in the sense in which we can speak of the value of a theatre ticket in exchange for the seat to which it gives title" (Schumpeter 1956: 162, emphasis added).[17] No one would suggest that the theater ticket has any intrinsic use-value: if I take the ticket home with me, it immediately becomes completely useless. And though I may well hand over the ticket upon entry to the theater, this is not an example of exchange in the barter-economy sense; after all, the ticket-taker does not *use* the ticket but simply tears it in two. We are not swapping two commodities with use-values because we each want what the other has; I am exercising my claim to the seat, and the ticket-taker is recognizing that claim as valid. If money is not a commodity, which for Schumpeter it is not and cannot be, then money can only be a *claim* – a ticket or voucher. This basic point needs to be amplified (and clarified) along a number of dimensions.

First and most importantly, the claim theory at least erodes and at most completely undermines the distinction between money and credit. As we saw above,

---

16 "The point is that money not only has no use-value, but also, as a consequence, cannot have exchange value in the same sense as commodities" (Schumpeter 1956: 162; cf. Marx 1973: 142). To develop this point in the language I use in the text above, we can say that when a commodity performs the service of money, money-gold's purchasing power is not based on commodity-gold's value. Quite the opposite in fact: commodity-gold's value (exchange-value with other goods) rises to the level of money-gold's purchasing power. Crucially, if money-gold's purchasing power falls below a threshold of commodity-gold's exchange-value, then at that stage gold ceases to be money (it becomes a commodity, likely hoarded or exported for sale). This is why the metallic content of money-gold remains irrelevant as long as the exchange-value of commodity-gold is propped up by the purchasing power of money-gold. Metallic content only becomes a "concern" when the exchange-value of the commodity, as metallic content of the coin, exceeds the purchasing power of the coin as money.

17 For more on the "price" of money, see Chapter 6.

that distinction is drawn on the basis of the difference between money as a commodity and credit as a claim on future money, but if money itself is no more or less than a claim, then a sharp distinction proves impossible. Whether or not we call one "money" and the other "credit," both are conceptually similar as "claims." The money/credit dichotomy can be replaced with varying "levels" of money, with a "natural hierarchy," or simply with better or worse credits (Innes 1913; Mehrling 2012). This issue will center my argument in Chapter 5.

Second, given that the claim theory is a credit theory of money (Schumpeter 1956: 163), it comes as no surprise that Schumpeter argues lucidly and continuously for an endogenous theory of money in which banks "create deposits in their act of lending" (Schumpeter 1954: 1080). If money is a ticket whose "value" is actually the *power* of redemption for goods and services, then money can and will be created as an internal part of the process of economic activity (rather than being produced externally as a commodity, and then brought into "the economy" exogenously). In short, the "exogenous versus endogenous money" debate does not manifest as a fourth and distinct "money choice"; rather, it maps directly onto the commodity versus claim choice.

Third, the core of claim theory must be rigorously distinguished from the particular form it has been given by "state theory" (Knapp 1924 [1905]). Schumpeter himself could not have been more adamant about this distinction, which makes it ironic that the difference between claim or credit theory, on the one hand, and chartalism or state theory, on the other, seems to have been lost or erased by contemporary commentators – who frequently read not only Schumpeter but also Innes, Macleod, and others directly into the tradition of Georg Friedrich Knapp (Ingham 2004a).[18] I will take this point up in Chapter 4.

Finally, for Schumpeter the claim theory implies that we can bring monetary and real analysis together by viewing contributions to production as leading to "money incomes," which are themselves nothing other than "receipt vouchers" that authorize a claim on some portion of the product (Schumpeter 1956: 155).[19]

---

18 Even in his early article, Schumpeter goes so far as to suggest that despite the utter falsity of commodity theory, Knapp's state theory might prove to be the "worse aberration" (Schumpeter 1956: 161). In *HEA*, a book in which Schumpeter strives throughout for a voice that conveys disinterested neutrality, the short portion of the text devoted to Knapp takes on a sharply critical tone otherwise reserved for Smith. Schumpeter also officially marks his distance from Howard Ellis, and especially Ellis's treatment of Knapp, which he describes dryly as "a more generous appraisal of Knapp's performance than I feel able to present" (Schumpeter 1954: 1056; Ellis 1934). This matters in relation to contemporary surveys of money (especially Ingham's), which tend to rely on Ellis yet simultaneously suggest that Schumpeter can be folded into this same state money tradition.
19 Schumpeter ultimately wants a synthesis of real and monetary analysis, and he sees this as made possible by developments and advances in monetary theory that he identifies as early as

The Quantity Theorem

As the above sections make clear, Schumpeter articulates some of the most forceful and lucid arguments *against* commodity theory and *for* claim theory, and he recognizes much more clearly than his contemporaries the limitations of a blind devotion to either real analysis or monetary analysis. (Schumpeter was surely no Keynesian, yet he took Keynes very seriously.) I argue that these are Schumpeter's most important and lasting teachings on money, the ones we still need to learn today. Nevertheless, Schumpeter himself emphasized neither of those contributions; instead, he focused most of his energies on his own distinct elaboration of the so-called "quantity theory of money."

Schumpeter insists on a set of terminological clarifications – sadly, ones that again seem to have been erased by later commentators. First, Schumpeter repeatedly demonstrates why it is wrong to refer to the quantity *theory* of money: "The quantity theory is only a monetary theorem which in itself says nothing about the nature and value of money" (Schumpeter 1956: 163; cf. Schumpeter 1954: 297). He elaborates this point in his early article by explaining that one cannot compare the "claim theory" with the "quantity theory" because the latter is not in fact a proper theory of money at all. A "theory," as the quote above suggests, would have to give answers concerning the essential nature of money and its economic "value." A "theorem," as the *OED* indicates, is a non-self-evident statement or proposition, demonstrable by evidence or argument. Schumpeter's central aim is to prove that not only the commodity theory but also the claim theory can support the quantity theorem. He takes the former as obvious, and then sets out to prove the latter. Indeed, as his contribution to money theory, broadly construed, Schumpeter aspired not to articulate a new theory of money, not to prove the

---

his 1917 essay (Schumpeter 1956). At this stage Schumpeter expresses the confidence of a young man when he asserts the truth of real analysis: "It is clear that the function of money in the economy is in principle of a merely technical nature" (Schumpeter 1956: 150). By the end of his career (in *HEA*) he sounds much more ambivalent: while describing the various levels of monetary analysis, he simultaneously tries to show how real analysis can accommodate the challenge that monetary theory poses. The trick is to allow real analysis to "admit" a dimension of monetary analysis. One might say that at the end of his life he still chooses real analysis, but without the confidence. *HEA* tacitly implies the necessity of such a synthesis without ever pulling it off. Yet the reader can see Schumpeter pushing toward this aim, suggesting its inevitability and hoping for its realization. Schumpeter, then, wants to overcome the dichotomy by subordinating monetary analysis to real analysis. As will become clearer in Chapter 3, Section 1, my own treatment of this dichotomy takes the form of a deconstruction (or *negative* dialectics) – that is, displacement rather than synthesis.

quantity theorem, but to demonstrate the compatibility of the claim theory with the quantity theorem.

In the context of driving home this central point, Schumpeter writes the following, which both Ellis and Ingham after him use as fundamental framings for their own approaches to money: "There are only two theories of money worthy of that name: the commodity theory and the claim theory. The basic ideas of these two theories are not compatible" (Schumpeter 1956: 163; quoted in Ellis 1934: 3; quoted in Ingham 2004a: 6).[20] Of course it is absolutely true, as we have seen above, that Schumpeter sees the commodity and credit options as incommensurable; as essential propositions about the nature of money, these two cannot be reconciled. Yet it would be a serious mistake to draw from this argument – as both Ellis and Ingham do – the idea that in the broader sense there are only two developed theories of money. A full-blown "theory of money" will have to choose not just between commodity and credit, but between real and monetary analysis, and between affirming or rejecting the quantity theorem.

Read in total, Schumpeter's writings consistently demonstrate the *variety* of money theory, and the last thing we should take from him is the notion that money theories boil down to two. Most damningly, we do not even need to turn to Schumpeter's wider writings to make this point as we can see it in the very same sentence from which Ellis quotes (and Ingham repeats). Ellis leaves out the remainder of the sentence, which concludes as follows: "although in very many cases they lead to the same results" (Schumpeter 1956: 163). In other words, read in context, Schumpeter's point was to show that both commodity theorists and claim theorists can affirm the quantity theorem; Schumpeter used the idea of "two theories of money" *as foil* for his unique version of claim theory – a version supporting the quantity theorem. So far from splitting theories of money in two was Schumpeter that his 1917 article aims to *reconcile* claim theory with the mainstream position (on both real analysis and the quantity theorem).

As if he were writing a rejoinder to Ellis and Ingham avant la lettre, Schumpeter states: "The view that we are dealing with two standpoints which differ *toto caelo*, which lead to completely different results and are irreconcilable, is ... superficial" (Schumpeter 1956: 149). Ingham's favored Schumpeter quote (from Ellis) does not quite say what either Ellis or Ingham suggests. It is also worth noting that Schumpeter writes this line in 1917, very early in his overall career, more so in terms of his time spent specifically studying money. Whether he held firmly

---

20 Ellis cites Schumpeter's original article in German (1917/1918) and offers a translation very slightly different from that which appears in the 1956 version I am using. Ingham quotes directly from Ellis.

to the idea of "two and only two" theories of money in 1917, it is doubtless the case that he did not hold to it at the time of his death in 1950.

That (important) digression aside, we can return to a succinct outline of the quantity theorem. Schumpeter first clarifies that the *theorem* must not be confused for the earlier "*equation* of exchange." Schumpeter credits John Briscoe (1694) with being the first to write down such an equation (Schumpeter 1956: 299).[21] By the nineteenth century this equation had become commonplace, especially in English political economy – from John Stuart Mill to Alfred Marshall and the Marshallians. As a sort of algebraic construction, the equation of exchange can be rearranged in varying forms, but it is standardly written as MV = PQ. M represents total money supply; V, velocity of money; P, the price level; and Q, the total quantity of transactions. While many writers have assumed that MV = PQ is an *identity* – true by definition – Schumpeter is at pains to reject this notion: the symbols on the left side of the equation represent distinct concepts and can be captured by different statistical measures than the variables on the right side.[22]

Irving Fisher's work provides a breakthrough, says Schumpeter, because it uses the equation of exchange to derive the quantity theorem. Fisher constructs the essential proposition by rewriting the equation of exchange with P as a *function* of the other variables: $P = f(M,V,T)$.[23] And fundamentally, P is a function of M, since in the short run V and T will be relatively fixed. At its core the quantity theorem is a causal claim, asserting that "the price level is ... passive and determined," while money and its velocity "are the active and determining elements" (Schumpeter 1956: 183). In the most succinct form, the quantity theorem states that M→P.

As a precisely stated theorem, the "choice" for a theory of money proves quite simple: affirm or deny. To affirm means to insist that changes in the money supply

---

21 Schumpeter points out that in his classic statement of the quantity theorem, Fisher actually gets the history of the exchange equation quite wrong. Fisher primarily credits Newcomb (1885) and Edgeworth (1887) while also mentioning Mill and Ricardo (Fisher 1911: 305). In addition to giving credit for the discovery to Briscoe (more than a century before Ricardo), Schumpeter points out that Newcomb, in fact, never wrote down the equation of exchange, while Edgeworth was but one of many Marshallians who affirmed it (Schumpeter 1954; 299, 833, 1065).

22 It is true that if we know three of the variables we can derive the fourth, but this, for Schumpeter, shows that the equation expresses an equilibrium condition, not a tautology (Schumpeter 1954: 1062; cf. Schumpeter 1956: 183).

23 Since P varies directly with respect to M and V, and inversely with respect to T, Fisher's formula transforms back into the standard equation:

$$P = f(M,V,T)$$
$$P = MV/T$$
$$PT = MV$$
$$MV = PT$$

lead to changes in the price level, though of course this can occur through a whole host of different (and incompatible) mechanisms – depending on other elements of one's broader theory of money. To deny could either mean to reverse the causality (changes in PQ themselves cause changes in MV, i. e., the money supply adjusts to price changes) or to reject any kind of causal claim whatsoever (perhaps the whole mechanism is affected by distinct systemic forces, perhaps the very concept of a "money supply" is ill-conceived).

Schumpeter's first aim is to raise the quantity theorem to greater prominence, both in relation to theories of money and vis-à-vis the wider body of economic analysis. For Schumpeter, no theory of money can be complete without including a position on the quantity theorem (for or against) and an explanation of that position. Schumpeter thereby insists that the quantity theorem cannot and must not be reduced to a mere outgrowth of commodity theory. Of course, the commodity theory naturally affirms the quantity theorem: as a commodity, money is subject to the same laws of supply and demand as any other commodity; hence an increase in the money supply leads to a decrease in the "price" of money, which is only another way of naming the inflation phenomenon (all other commodities cost more in relation to the money commodity).

But this does not mean that claim theory will reject, or even that it can eschew, the quantity theorem. Hence Schumpeter's second goal: to show that the quantity theorem can be affirmed by a variety of different theories of money. This project takes multiple forms in Schumpeter's writings. In his early article we see it in his explicit effort to develop a claim theory argument that affirms the quantity theorem.[24] In *HEA* it appears in extensive discussions of the dominant (Keynesian) monetary analysis, and Schumpeter's resistance to the notion that the quantity theorem should be relegated to real analysis or an anti-Keynesian position. Here is just one representative quote from dozens of passages spread throughout the text: "The monetary theory of the twenties and thirties is much more under quantity theory [*sic*] influence than is generally realized" (Schumpeter 1954: 1067). To reiterate the main point: like the previous options (real versus monetary; commod-

---

24 Schumpeter's project is distinct (perhaps unique) in attempting to articulate a *different* mechanism to support the quantity theorem. I exclude the details of this long and sometimes convoluted argument, which Schumpeter never got right to his own satisfaction. In basic terms, Schumpeter tries to use a circular flow model to theorize monetary incomes as claims to goods. Following Fisher, Schumpeter's model excludes savings and tax payments so that money (claims) earned equals money (claims) spent. Given this restrictive (and unrealistic) assumption, Schumpeter can conclude that an increase in the money supply (understood as claim tickets) will necessarily lead to an increase in prices – since all money will be spent on a fixed amount of goods (Schumpeter 1956).

ity versus credit) the choice to affirm or deny the quantity theorem operates independently. Schumpeter's unfinished – indeed, undecided[25] – project on theories of money has the chief advantage of mapping out these distinct options.

3 The Matrix

My reconstruction of these three "money choices" out of Schumpeter's writings does not in itself develop a theory of money (neither Schumpeter's nor my own) but rather provides a map, a matrix of various theories of money. We can produce an initial sketch of that matrix simply by combining all possible choices to produce a typology. Here are the sets of binary options:

A = Real	B = Monetary
1 = Commodity	2 = Claim
x = Quantity – Yes	y = Quantity – No

From these choices we can derive eight possible types. The following table lists those combinations along with some representative thinkers or theories:

A1x	*Orthodoxy* – Petty, Hume, Menger, Jevons, Fisher
A2x	Schumpeter, Fisher and Wicksell (according to Schumpeter)
A2y	Innes, Cencini, Value-form reading of Marx
A1y	Benjamin Anderson, Standard reading of Marx (Mandel)
B1x	Smith (according to Schumpeter)
B2x	Hawtrey, later Keynes and Keynesianism (according to Schumpeter)
B2y	*Heterodoxy* – Macleod, early Keynes, Knapp, Wray, Ingham, Mehrling*
B1y	De Brunhoff's reading of Marx, Quesnay, John Law, Smith (according to Cencini)

I will not attempt to develop a detailed account of each type listed here, nor to defend rigorously the choice of representative names.[26] The aim of this exercise is to

---

25 In a line that expresses his ambivalence about his own contributions, Schumpeter insists in this same article that "it is in no way my purpose to defend the quantity theory [*sic*] as such" (Schumpeter 1956: 163).

26 This matrix fundamentally (perhaps constitutively) excludes a purely sociological approach whereby money is "meaning," "language," "institution," "ritual," or "form of life." Such an ap-

present the matrix of money theories itself; the fact that some readers of certain authors on the list would make the case for moving them from one category to another only reinforces my main point about the *variety* of theories of money.

The starting place for surveying this matrix must be the two types in which all three choices line up – namely, A1x and B2y. The former gives us the putative orthodox theory of money: committed to real analysis in which the money commodity is no more than a neutral veil; insistent on a sharp distinction between money and credit; and at least implicitly, but typically explicitly, supporting the quantity theorem. The list of thinkers across the history of economic thought who putatively fit in this category would be very long indeed. The latter gives us a pure form of the so-called heterodox theory: starting with monetary analysis as primary, rejecting the commodity theory for the claim theory, and subsequently refusing to support, or explicitly refuting, the quantity theorem. From the start we can see that "heterodoxy" must be "so-called" precisely because it proves to be but one of seven different theoretical types that offer an *alternative* to the orthodox account.

Here I repeat the name "heterodox theory" or "heterodox tradition" strictly because these terms have now themselves become standard in twenty-first-century writing on money (Ingham 2004a). Yet it does not require a Derridean to deconstruct this orthodox/heterodox binary because anyone can see that an enormous amount of the terrain of money theories lies beyond these two "pure types." The word "heterodox" means "not conforming to orthodox standards," yet the money matrix makes plain that there are numerous types of theories of money that don't fit the mold of strict orthodoxy. Moreover, the characteristics of a supposedly heterodox theory of money, as they have been delineated by both Ingham and post-Keynesians, are distinct and particular. Numerous major theorists of money over the years have rejected orthodox tenets without fitting into the B2Y type. And notice that some really "big names" fall outside these two pure types – for example, Smith, Marx, and Schumpeter. Even this very crude typology should

---

proach takes us from Georg Simmel to Michel Aglietta, with Wittgensteinians and everyone else in between. These important theorists and analysts of money as social form and ritual find no place within this matrix because their approaches ultimately do not result in a theory of money in an economic sense; they are all sociological or political explanations of money that subsume money into the social or political sphere. As the reader can see, some names appear in multiple locations depending on the stage of their career or their particular interpreter. In the case of Mehrling – work that I cite throughout this book and discuss most directly in Chapter 6 – I can see no other plausible location on the matrix to place his work (the location is not all that debatable). However, while Mehrling's work is crucially important, it develops not a "theory" of money but rather a "money view" (as he puts it) of economics based on a close phenomenological study of banking and money markets (hence the asterisk).

serve to disabuse us of the narrow notion that there are only two theories of money.

I should emphasize that this matrix is by no means exhaustive: by including questions beyond the primary three, one could easily expand the matrix. More importantly for my purposes here, the matrix is also not determinative. That is, the matrix provides a typological map, but its coordinates are relative: any A2x theory will differ from a B2x theory on the basis of a fundamental disagreement about the nature of economic analysis (real or monetary). But this does not mean that all A2x theories are the same. Schumpeter wished to claim Fisher and Wicksell for this category that he himself fits in, but Schumpeter's articulation and rigorous defense of claim theory dramatically exceeds anything one will find in those other authors. Indeed, much of Fisher's writing appears compatible with commodity theory, which is perhaps why he is often placed into the orthodox type. Moreover, the arguments that support any particular choice can take significantly different form. Here are just a few important examples:

1) *Real* can mean substantialist (physicalist), or it may merely refer to economic practices and actions; *monetary* can mean money as *distinct* from credit, or it can denote money *as* credit.
2) *Commodity* can indicate only metals or it can include any commodity; *claim* theory can refer to both state theory and credit theory.
3) The quantity theorem can be understood to posit a strictly causal or merely relational link; rejections of the theorem can maintain the significance of the exchange equation, or blow up the entire paradigm.[27]

To reiterate, this matrix does not itself serve as, provide, or stand in for a theory of money – it only offers a map. But the work of mapping proves important in its own right: it leads to a very different understanding of the history of theories of money; it opens up possibilities for developing new theories; and it provides a basic tool for situating any such theory in relation to others in particular or to the broad history of theories in general. Hence it offers us a better way to do the history of theories of money. Finally, the matrix provides the starter kit for building a theory of money since one can always initiate the process by answering the fundamental questions, thereby locating one's own theory on the matrix.

---

27 Earley's work on Schumpeter's struggle with his own theory of money provides numerous examples of these subtle differentiations (Earley 1994).

Chapter Three
Money "Is" Credit

1 What Is Economic Exchange?

It is easy for opponents of the orthodox theory of money (type A1x) to criticize the commitment to real analysis, because when taken to a certain extreme, the choice for real analysis precludes the very possibility of developing a theory of money: "There is no analytical place for money at all" (Ingham 2001: 307). If the core element of economic activity is the act of exchange, and if that act can be theorized in its pure form as *barter* – the swapping of one commodity directly for another – then money could never be more than a secondary phenomenon. All of the descriptions of money as a "technical device" that overcomes inconveniences and all of the discounting designators of money – as "neutral," a "veil," or "skin" – derive from this primary commitment to economic exchange as non-monetary. Indeed, in a powerful sense what makes the analysis "real" is exactly the fact that it can be carried out sans money.

But this problematic also vexes those who choose "monetary" over real analysis, because so many of them continue to presume the validity of a classical account of economic exchange as not involving money (e. g., Wray 1998). Accordingly, their preference for monetary analysis always seems like something of a *concession* to practical constraints or requirements. In other words, it is only because our economy today remains so intertwined with money, banking, and finance that it proves impossible to do real analysis. These theorists choose monetary analysis only because they are forced to do so. A close reader of Schumpeter catches repeated glimpses of this logic as his tacit critique of Keynesianism.[1]

My own theory of money starts with a reconceptualization of economic exchange as *fundamentally* monetary (Macleod 1889; Hawtrey 1919).[2] I build this ar-

---

1 Schumpeter's lifelong voyage to arrive at a coherent theory of money breaks apart on these same shores: he could never reconcile his own fervent commitment to real analysis (to economic exchange as non-monetary) with his highly sophisticated understanding of banking, credit, and money as claim. He clutched to the circular flow model as a lifeline, but that model's assumptions proved untenable and therefore could not save him.

2 As I discuss in Chapter 4, both Wray and Ingham defend the argument that money is prior (both logically and historically) to market exchange. Here I turn that argument inside out, which does not mean to invert it. That is, I do not revert to the economists' story of *homo economicus* as the naturally exchanging creature – the argument that Wray and Ingham are rightly refuting. Rather, I offer an utterly different conceptualization of exchange than the one proffered by classi-

https://doi.org/10.1515/9783110760774-007

gument from three distinct but overlapping planks. The first is a set of claims about history and historical development, and harks back to Chapter 1's discussion of capitalist social orders as both historically contingent and unique in their economic form. In a technical sense "economic exchange" does not exist in pre-capitalist social orders, so this category really only proves intelligible if we confine ourselves to the horizon of capitalism. This is not to deny that societies without money have surely existed, but it is likely that they were much rarer than economics textbooks would lead us to believe, and in any case these were just as surely non-capitalist social orders. So while it's fair to say that one could conduct an economic analysis of those societies, the investigation would necessarily focus on production, distribution, perhaps in-kind taxation, and maybe even on forms of trade between those societies and their neighbors. None of this, however, would be a study of *economic exchange*. As a rigorous concept, economic exchange only becomes central to the analysis of capitalist social orders because these societies' mode of production places the capitalist use of markets at the center of a system that circulates money and commodities for the sake of profit.[3] For this reason I circumscribe my argument by applying the concept, *economic exchange*, only to capitalist social orders. Yet this should not be taken as an arbitrary limitation (this move is not cheating) precisely because the category of economic exchange belongs to capitalist economics to begin with.

The second plank, supported by the first, is the work done in history and especially anthropology, to explode the myth of barter. After all, at its bedrock foundation the argument that economic exchange is *real* (i.e., non-monetary) depends on the existence of barter as the direct exchange of one commodity for another, $C \rightarrow C$.[4] Indeed, the preponderance of pure orthodox accounts of money (A1x),

---

cal political economy and the neoclassical paradigm – a conceptual account in which neither money nor exchange can be said to precede the other.

3 This crucial point is completely obscured or erased by the common move, in both classical political economy and neoclassical economics, to *project* economic categories back across time, rendering them utterly transhistorical. Hence Smith and Ricardo's ridiculous discussions of hunters and gatherers *exchanging* bows and arrows with one another; hence the constant invocations by economics textbooks of imaginary moments in early or pre-history that always look surprisingly similar to twentieth- and twenty-first-century capitalist social orders.

4 The *economic model* of barter as taught by economics textbooks: 1) has never existed as an actual practice in pre-capitalist social orders; 2) has never existed *within* (internal to) capitalist social orders (except where they break down – for example, in prisons); 3) only ever comes to be in the interstices of capitalist societies, and in the absence of a common money. At the same time, however, we can see that $C \rightarrow C$ (as the direct exchange of *equivalents*, $C=C$) is in fact brought to a certain level of actual existence in the world – namely, through and within the capitalist value-form. In a feudal society any $C \rightarrow C$ is only ever a random swapping of goods for their use-value; "they are not

along with the overwhelming majority of contemporary economics textbooks, all begin with a story of barter, which serves to indicate the grounding of the project in real analysis.

When it comes to the topic of barter, David Graeber accomplishes a monumental task, by: a) surveying the writings of economists on the topic and revealing it as myth-making; b) synthesizing, and presenting in simplified form, the massive anthropological literature that time and again disproves the economic narrative; c) doing all of this in an accessible, popular, and widely read text, thereby exposing a broad audience to the effects of the myth of barter and the specific reasons why it is false. Graeber's reading of both classical political economy (especially Smith) and contemporary textbooks nicely exposes the trope of asking the reader to "*imagine* an economy something like today's, except with no money" (Graeber 2011: 23, emphasis added). He then shows decisively that the historical record simply does not support these accounts of barter: "There's no evidence that it ever happened, and an enormous amount of evidence suggesting that it did not" (Graeber 2011: 28).[5] Finally, in a crucial argument that dovetails with our first plank, Graeber surveys the record to show that the actual historical examples of barter all come *after* the development of monetary societies, and usually follow the emergence of capitalist society. Barter is not what pre-monetary societies do to carry out real economic exchange; barter is what monetary societies do when they find themselves in emergency conditions, without access to a common money (Graeber 2011: 40).[6] Without barter[7] as its basis, the standard account of economic exchange

---

equal values" (Marx 1981: 447). But in the capitalist circulatory system, the movement of M→C→M' (money→commodity→more money) brings about and includes within it the *equalization* of commodities for one another. The closest we therefore come to the reality of barter (not as concrete practice, but ontologically) is within a capitalist social order. We can add this to the long list of reasons why the opening chapters of *Capital* are *so* hard to read: Marx illuminates this point about barter, but he includes no historical context. This fact tempts readers to take him as signing on to the myth of barter itself. The better reading is to see that Marx is showing us that *barter is only made real under capitalism.*

5 The same historical evidence that militates against the theory of barter also undermines any commodity theory of money – see my discussion of Innes below.

6 In Chapter 5 I more fully develop the concept of money space, which helps to explain what it means to have money "in common." But the point here can be made simply: the *absence* of money is not an absence of money tokens but a lack of common debtors. Individuals (or representatives of societies) that engage in barter with one another will quite likely each have money – that is, tokens of denominated credit held on a solvent debtor. What they lack is credit denominated in a shared money of account, held on a debtor recognized as viable by both of them. In this context, Ingham has recently drawn a subtle but crucial distinction between barter and payment in kind. Usually when monetary systems break down, barter is still unnecessary. Rather, a society can use commodities, denominated in a money of account, as "surrogates" for money. Russia in the early

falls apart; this opens up the possibility of entirely reconceptualizing economic exchange.

One reason why the commodity theory of money has proved so seductive and enduring is that it allows for the introduction of money and monetary phenomena while preserving the traditional account of economic exchange. It provides a framework in which the theory of money remains an intrinsic element of real analysis. If money is by its very nature a commodity, then there is no ontological difference between barter, C→C, and monetary exchange, M→C. In both cases one commodity is exchanged for another. The locus classicus for the pure type of the orthodox theory of money is Jevons and Menger, both of whom commit thoroughly to real analysis by essentializing money as a commodity (Jevons 2011 [1875]; Menger 2009 [1872]).

It is in this context, and as the third plank of my argument, that I turn to the work of Innes. I read his particular version of the credit theory of money as itself a redefinition of economic exchange. Innes's work has already been acknowledged – first by Wray, then by Ingham and Graeber – for its insights, its untimeliness, and its possible influence on Keynes (Wray 1998; Ingham 2004a). Even so, I am not convinced that Innes has yet been read for the truly radical and potentially paradigm-shifting nature of his work. Ingham naturally folds Innes into the "heterodox tradition," but this may do more to obscure the distinct nature of Innes's contribution. It's true that Keynes seems to be the only economist to have read Innes's 1913 and 1914 articles, yet in his opening lines Keynes casually dismisses the entire credit theory of money as a "fallacy" (Keynes 1914: 419). Schumpeter's massive and seemingly comprehensive *History of Economic Analysis* does not mention Innes, most likely because Schumpeter never read him. I make Innes a primary resource for radically rethinking economic exchange, arguing that his conception of money as credit[8] strikes at the very root of the real/monetary binary. In order for Innes's

---

90s, Ingham rightly argues, did not revert to barter (i. e., to the swapping of commodities at ratios negotiated on the spot); instead they used either rubles or dollars to denominate payment made in kind (Ingham 2020: 107).

7 I draw *only* from Graeber's work on the myth of barter, which is clear, powerful, and illuminating. Graeber's account of money, on the other hand, has fundamental problems. It overemphasizes the role of Smith; misrepresents the Sumerian money system by emphasizing the *weight* of silver, when what mattered most was the *number* of barley grains (see Ingham 2021: 7–8); reifies the distinction between money and credit; elides the distinction between state money and credit money; and confuses the absence of a common money space with the absence of physical cash (Graeber 2011: 24–25, 38–41).

8 Though his work has been repeatedly noted as foundational to the "credit theory of money" (a language I echo in this chapter's title), Innes himself emphatically underscores a point I made back in the Introduction: *credit* and *debt* are two names for the same thing:

thinking to play this central role, we must read his work beyond the interpretive frames previously imposed on it.

Innes opens his first of two articles on money by neatly summarizing the basic account of commodity theory, including the historical narrative in which first commodities – "cattle, iron, salt, shells, dried cod, tobacco, sugar, nails, etc." – and then intrinsically valuable metallic coins served as money, all while "Emperors, Kings, Princes, and their advisers vied with each other in the middle ages in swindling the people by debasing their coins" (Innes 1913: 377). He responds decisively:

> Modern research in the domain of commercial history and numismatics, and especially recent discoveries in Babylonia, have brought to light a mass of evidence which was not available to the earlier economists, and in the light of which it may be positively stated, that none of these theories rest on a solid basis of historical proof – that in fact they are false. (Innes 1913: 379)

Innes goes on to provide ample evidence against the commodity theory, beginning with Smith's famous examples of "commodity money." Innes proves that Smith's "nails" (in a Scottish village pub) and "cod" (in Newfoundland) were not examples of commodity money but of payments in kind (Smith 1869 [1776]). Such payments were made in designated moneys of account – "pounds, shillings and pence."[9]

[T]he word "credit" … is simply the correlative of debt. What A owes to B is A's debt to B and B's credit on A. A is B's debtor and B is A's creditor. The words "credit" and "debt" express a legal relationship between two parties, and they express the same legal relationship seen from two opposite sides. A will speak of this relationship as a debt, while B will speak of it as a credit. (Innes 1913: 392)

Innes's theory of "credit" is thus always and simultaneously a theory of "debt."

9 Just as it continues to celebrate the genius of Smith, so does modern economics cling to potential (Smithian) examples of commodity money. Tony Lawson's arguments about tobacco in colonial America serve as perhaps the most "live" current example. He repeatedly asserts that "throughout most of the colonial period, Virginia, and indeed Maryland and North Carolina, used tobacco as (commodity) money" (Lawson 2019: 181, citing Lawson 2016; cf. Lawson 2022). As evidence, Lawson observes that in 1619 the Virginia legislature "'rated' tobacco at three shillings per pound," that in 1642 the same legislature made tobacco legal tender, that businesses in Maryland and Virginia often paid taxes in tobacco, and that North Carolina used tobacco as means of payment up until the American Revolution (Lawson 2016: 981; Lawson 2019: 181). In both instances Lawson cites the same two sources, Scharf (1967) and Breen (2001). But these are *odd* sources to provide in an attempt to support an argument that hinges mainly on Virginia legislative acts in the first half of the seventeenth century: the Breen book centers on tobacco farmers in Virginia, but it covers only the eighteenth century, while the Scharf book is a history of Maryland that begins in 1660. Not only can neither source substantiate Lawson's claim, they do not even address the relevant period. If one undertakes one's own research by following some of Scharf's sources, particularly

Where Smith believes he has located commodity money, Innes shows that "he has, in fact, merely found – credit" (Innes 1913: 378).

We can begin to unfold Innes's credit theory by working through his two best-known quotes. First, "The eye has never seen, nor the hand touched a dollar" (Innes 1914: 155). This line has typically been read through the Keynesian framework that I discussed in Chapter 1. This means that readers of Innes – many of them Keynesians of some sort – take him here to be indicating the primacy of money of account. As we previously discussed, for Keynes the dollar is *only a name*, merely money's "title," while any particular form of money thing would be understood to "answer" to this title. Ingham draws from Keynes's twofold account a deeper distinction between "money" (the money thing) and "moneyness" (the proper concept). Moreover, Ingham argues that "moneyness is conferred by money of account" (Ingham 2004a: 48). Notice that Ingham here advances Keynes's argument significantly since he suggests not merely that the money thing must "answer" (must be specified in a money of account) but that money of account itself *confers* moneyness to the money thing. And Ingham freely attributes this idea to Innes: "Money of account is logically anterior" (Ingham 2004a: 38, citing Innes 1913).[10]

Streeter (1858), one is likely to reach a very different conclusion than Lawson. In the early seventeenth century, colonial Virginia and Maryland found themselves with multiple but inconsistent moneys of account, inadequate access to credit and credit expansion, and a dearth of financial institutions (i. e., banks). Under these emergency conditions, economic actors commonly reverted to payment in kind (tobacco) – payments still very much denominated in extant moneys of account (hence the need to "rate" tobacco at a given price in shillings). The best contemporary source I have found on this topic is Dror Goldberg, who carefully details the relevant Virginia history from 1585– 1645, a messy case from which I draw the following conclusions, listed roughly chronologically. In the absence of functioning banks, and to resist having Virginians be taxed in money they did not have, the Virginia legislature passed a law making it legal to pay in kind, in tobacco. They understood this as a stopgap, that they were allowing payment in kind in the absence of money, not trying to make tobacco money; thus there was no golden age of tobacco money but rather a period of chaos characterized by see-sawing and conflicting legislative acts (e. g., some acts *outlawed* payment in tobacco), all seeking an elusive monetary stability. From early on Virginians understood the need for financial institutions that could expand and contract credit: first they attempted to create a clearinghouse bank; later they proposed an entire coinage system, including a mint; finally, in 1645, they simply wrote credit money into law by allowing tobacco IOUs (Goldberg 2015). As with Smith's cod and nails, tobacco was never money. (See also Feinig 2022: 35–37.)

10 In a related vein, one relevant to the context of this section, Ingham also suggests that "economic orthodoxy" has focused so intently on a model of exchange as exchange of *commodities* that its adherents have rendered themselves blind to the significance of money of account. Consistent with the prioritizing of money of account in his reading of both Keynes and Innes, Ingham wishes to posit money of account as a "precondition" for any "model of multilateral market exchange" (Ingham 2000: 24). As I elaborate in the sections and chapters that follow, in one sense Ingham's point

However, as I indicated briefly in Chapter 1, taking "money of account" as the primary concept of money is an illicit shortcut – and projecting that argument onto Innes unnecessarily limits the richness of his text. When Innes says that a "dollar" has never been seen or touched, he indicates something much more theoretically significant than the basic concept (important though it may be) of denomination. Indeed, Innes himself finds the idea of measure or standard "not so extraordinary"; he does not deny the necessity of money of account, but neither does it impress him. The point of saying that a dollar cannot be touched is *not* to say that dollars are money of account (and therefore that moneyness is to be found in money of account). Rather, Innes wishes to contrast the intangible dollar with that which does have a practical reality: "All that we *can* touch or see is a promise to pay." True, there must be *some* denomination, but Innes asserts that the particular denomination is inconsequential: "What is stamped on the face of a coin or printed on the face of a note matters not at all" (Innes 1914: 155).[11]

Dollars are not things, according to Innes, but neither is "dollarness" equal to "moneyness." We cannot ponder the measure of denomination in its philosophical abstractness and fool ourselves into thinking that we have therefore unraveled the mysteries of money. Innes's aim is not to underscore the impalpable nature of "the dollar" but to direct our attention to concrete money practices. After saying that denomination does not matter, Innes strikes his keynote:

> What does matter, and this is the only thing that matters ... : What is the obligation which the issuer of that coin or note really undertakes, and is he able to fulfill that promise, whatever it may be? (1914: 155)

Neither "a dollar" nor "dollarness" nor even "dollars as money of account" provides a proper answer to the question "What is money?" Any adequate explanation or theory of money must address itself directly to these "promises to pay" and "obligations of debtors."

We must interpret our second quote from Innes (this one more famous) in precisely this context. That line states that "credit and credit alone is money," a claim that should serve as the starting point for any credit theory of money (Innes 1913: 392). Notice in this formulation that while Innes forwards "credit" as the very definition of money, he does so in a way that distinguishes this concept

---

holds: there can be neither money nor genuine economic exchange as understood within the neoclassical model of economics without denomination (money of account). But perhaps he overestimates the difficulty in establishing money of account, and thereby overvalues its importance.

11 In an important sense the denomination can be *anything* whatsoever – dollars or euros, rupees or pesos, goats or wizards. I detail this argument in Chapter 5.

of credit from the amorphous idea of counting in units of an abstractly denominated value. Any credit is concrete, because it is always nothing less than a *promise* to pay that thereby involves the *obligation* of an *issuer.* In other words, there can be no credit without a specified debtor – the obligated party, the party with responsibility to the agent holding the credit. And Innes stresses that credit therefore immediately raises the question of the debtor's ability to keep her or his promise – "this is the only thing that matters." There can be no credit without a debtor, so we must therefore directly inquire as to the liquidity and solvency of the debtor.

This brings us to Innes's extended critique of Smith. Much less discussed (if at all) in the small literature on Innes, I submit that it has just as much potency as the earlier lines. Antedating Graeber by a century, Innes refutes the barter myth and rejects a commodity theory of money. But he goes even further, making it possible to reorient our understanding of the most basic of economic acts – a sale. Innes quotes at length from the most famous passages in Smith's *Wealth of Nations* – those that depict the bartering brewer, baker, and butcher, who all agree that choosing one commodity and using it as money would solve their problems (Smith 1869). I now quote Innes's response at length:

> Adam Smith's position depends on the proposition that, if the baker or the brewer wants meat from the butcher, but has ... nothing to offer in exchange, no exchange can be made between them. If this were true, the doctrine of a medium of exchange [commodity money] would, perhaps, be correct. But is it true? Assuming the baker and the brewer to be honest men, and honesty is no modern virtue, the butcher could take from them an acknowledgement that they had bought from him so much meat, and all we have to assume is that the community would recognize the obligation of the baker and the brewer to redeem these acknowledgements in bread or beer at the relative values current in the village market, whenever they might be presented to them, and we at once have a good and sufficient currency. A sale, according to this theory, is not the exchange of a commodity for some intermediate commodity called the "medium of exchange," but the exchange of a commodity for a credit. (Innes 1913: 391)

This argument provides the foundation for a new and distinct account of economic exchange.[12] Exchange is not the swapping of two entities of the same kind (both commodities) but the mutual substitution of two utterly distinct kinds (commodity

---

12 The move I make here resonates with but remains distinct from the arguments of the nineteenth-century "banking school," whose members argued, as Ingham nicely phrases the point, that "a monetary transaction was not an *exchange* of commodities – precious metal for goods; but, rather, the *settlement of the debt* with a credit" (Ingham 2020: 31). The banking school attempted to *prioritize* "monetary transactions" vis-à-vis "commodity exchange," while I am trying to deconstruct the dichotomy.

and credit).[13] Accordingly, the distinction between real and monetary analysis breaks down entirely; "real" economic exchange *is monetary through and through.* Within capitalism, we can reach one of two conclusions: that there is no such thing as real analysis (in the sense of analysis sans money) or that real analysis *is* monetary.

Either conclusion makes it hard to position Innes in our matrix of money theories; in some sense, it shakes the foundations of the entire matrix. Innes testifies definitively against the commodity theory of money (2), and he withholds support for the quantity theorem (y). But where does he stand on real analysis versus monetary analysis (A or B)? In constructing the "heterodox tradition," Ingham naturally situates Innes within that pure type (B2y), suggesting that Innes chooses monetary over real analysis (Ingham 2004b: 242). The post-Keynesian strain of heterodox economic thought does in fact opt for monetary analysis – in much the way that Schumpeter describes the early Keynesians of his own day. Ingham reads Innes as a precursor to today's heterodox theory, which grows out of, even if it strenuously criticizes, a neoclassical paradigm fully committed to real analysis.[14] Authors in the B2y type therefore choose monetary analysis in just the way I described in Chapter 2: as a practical consideration given the "financialized" nature of the modern economy.

I contend that this is a limited, potentially inaccurate reading of Innes, who must instead be distinguished from the pure type of heterodox theory (B2y). In Chapter 2 I foreshadowed my interpretation of Innes by placing him initially in the A2y category. Put simply, writing outside of academic debates and seventeen years before Keynes's *Treatise*, Innes does not purport to be engaging in a "monetary analysis" that would be distinct from the real analysis of a commodity economy. Instead, he simply offers a new way of doing "real analysis." In this chapter I

13 One might pause here to ask how such a substitution is possible in the first place. Metallists need not address the question – for them, money is a commodity – while so-called heterodox theorists (especially the post-Keynesians addressed in the following chapter) have failed to take the question seriously. Here again we observe the acuity of Konings's point that heterodox theorists have ignored something important about the orthodoxy (Konings 2018: 17). In this case, a metallist theory of money, *while nonetheless false*, at least has the advantage of explaining why money and commodities would seamlessly substitute for one another. An adequate answer to this question would, I suggest, need to combine the full credit theory of money as developed in this book with the insights of a value-form analysis of capitalism (see e.g., Arthur 2004; Heinrich 2012; Chambers 2018; cf. Ingham 2020: 44).
14 For his part, Wray reads Innes as a fellow traveler with Knapp – that is, a state theorist in credit clothing – marking both as precursors to later Keynesian and post-Keynesian monetary analysis. As should be evident at this stage, one aim of my reading of Innes, which I call on throughout the book, is to pry him out of the frame built by Ingham and Wray.

push past the binary choice "real or monetary"; my reading of Innes directs us toward a new conception of economic exchange and thereby advances us beyond the real/monetary binary. To be more accurate, we need to expand or move outside the matrix to a position marked C2y, where "C" denotes a displacement or overcoming of the real/monetary dichotomy.[15] Innes's theory exemplifies category C by showing that there can be no non-monetary economic analysis.

The monetary is real.[16] To defend this principle means to insist upon the absolute primacy of money to all economic relations (at least under capitalism). We cannot juxtapose the monetary to "the real," and thus our "monetary" analysis cannot and must not be (as it was and still is for many Keynesians) a concession to practical reality. This redefinition of the basic principle of economic exchange as the swapping of money for a commodity has a host of important implications. It renders money and commodities co-constitutive of economic relations; commodities cannot ground economics, and they cannot be hypostatized as existing in nature.

Moreover, arguing that economic exchange is the exchange of commodities for credit opens up a space to bring in and take seriously what Mehrling dubs the "money view." The money view studies political economy not from the perspective of the neoclassical paradigm of economics, nor from the perspective of business school finance theory, but from the on-the-ground perspective of bankers, central bankers, and those who work directly in money markets (Mehrling 2011). Contemporary capitalist economics depends entirely on these markets, in which trillions of dollars of denominated value are traded every day. Crucially, these are not markets in goods and services, but, as the name plainly states, markets in money. Here we have the exchange of credits for other credits – the swapping of IOUs. The standard definition of economic exchange as C→C has no choice but to dismiss, mar-

---

15 If space and time permitted, I would advance a similar argument about Cencini's incredibly rich and sadly neglected theory of money. I placed Cencini in the A2y category for the same reason I did Innes: Cencini does not choose "monetary" analysis but rather sees the monetary as real. Cencini also belongs in the newly created C2y category. Cencini's broader argument hinges on the attempt to prove that money is real, just not in the same way that commodities are real (Cencini 1988). John Milios also offers a reading of Marx and endogenous money that suggests a similar move beyond real/monetary. As Milios puts it, "the only economic theory *inherently formulated as a monetary one*, is Marx's value theory" (Milios 2002: 2).

16 In the previous chapter I suggested that Schumpeter's struggle to clarify his theory of money hinges on his attempt to synthesize real/monetary analysis while affirming the quantity theorem. In the language used here, Schumpeter was pushing toward category C, but he wanted a theory of type C2x. However, as I show below, once you make the monetary "real," it becomes impossible to affirm a causal relation of M→P. Schumpeter's lifelong project thus failed out of necessity: he was aiming for an utterly untenable theory of money.

ginalize, or explain these markets as epiphenomenal. Our redefinition of economic exchange instead avows the importance of markets in money, and can even widen its ambit to include what we might call "financial exchange," M→M – a task I take up in Chapter 6. Here we can underscore the following point: by making economic exchange primary, by making money and commodities co-constitutive of "the economic," we create a space in which "barter," if and when it occurs (extremely rarely), would also be "economic," but so would financial exchange when it occurs (constantly).[17]

This major conceptual shift has implications for the entire theory of money. C2y is not just a version of B2y; rather, it operates in a different dimension, such that the "C" has an impact on the meaning of the "2" and the "y." The next two sections take each transformation in turn.

2 A True *Credit* Theory of Money

As briefly discussed in the previous chapter, one doesn't have to dig too deeply into the literature on money to find references to the distinction between a "monetary theory of credit" and a "credit theory of money" – a turn of phrase first coined by Schumpeter (e.g., Schumpeter 1954: 686; see also Ingham 2004a: 38; Mehrling 2000: 397; Wray 2004: 224). Unfortunately, many references to this framing remain too close to the surface: they limit the scope of the distinction to particular arguments about exogenous versus endogenous money creation, or to recapitulations of the generalizing dichotomy orthodox/heterodox.[18]

---

17 I engage Mehrling's money view in later chapters of this book, but throughout it I constantly keep in mind Mehrling's fundamental point about the importance of liquidity. Markets are not natural; they are made. And while they are made *possible* by legal structures, by cultural, social, and political institutions, they are quite literally *made* by dealers who offer both to buy and to sell at any time. A "market" only exists because dealers post two sets of prices – "bid" (the price at which they will buy) and "ask" (the price at which they will sell). The market is founded on this liquidity provided by the dealer. Mehrling shows that both economics and finance ignore liquidity or assume it away (as a "free good"). Even though I lack the time and space to explore these issues, I contend that the theory of money as credit, which I develop here, itself points toward the crucial importance of liquidity. Note that the "dealer function" is constitutive of markets, even before one considers complications like monopsony or monopoly powers that would otherwise be thought to "distort" said markets; there is nothing there to distort before a dealer, providing liquidity, makes it. Thanks to Henry Scott for his constant and justified advocacy of the money view.

18 Ingham frequently leverages this distinction as support for the assertation that there exist only two *incompatible* theories of money (Ingham 2004a: 9). I outlined my critique of that account in Chapter 2; here I merely add that Ingham's broad framework swallows up the subtlety of Schumpeter's distinction and blocks from our view the critical work that can be done with it.

Schumpeter's point was not to create broad categories or to divide the world of money theories into two. Rather, the distinction emerges as the result of a *deft critique* of early work on money. In a series of passages devoted to the theory of credit in the period 1790–1870, Schumpeter observes that most writers on the topic were jurists. Thus they tended to define money as *legal tender*; credit instruments were themselves only claims to (legal) money. This leads them to begin with coins and bank notes (what they frequently call "currency"[19]) and "build up" to an analysis of "credit." Schumpeter sees such approaches as unsurprising, reasonable, yet nevertheless wrong:

> Logically, it is by no means clear that the most useful method is to start from the coin ... in order to proceed to the credit transactions of reality. It may be more useful to start from these in the first place. ... A credit theory of money is possibly preferable to a monetary theory of credit. (Schumpeter 1954: 686)

Schumpeter is not marking out neutral categories but rather advancing a sharp attack. Theorists of this period "failed ... to develop a systematic credit theory of money"; they were unable to grasp the nature of either money or credit because they were confined by "the strait-jacket of the monetary theory of credit" (Schumpeter 1954: 687). Schumpeter's detailed account of the history of economic thought

---

19 In contemporary usage, "currency" has two distinct, but almost never *distinguished*, meanings:
1) It denotes concrete bank notes as issued by a commercial or central bank. This is how the term operates in nineteenth-century money debates: the word "currency" is shorthand for "bank currency" and refers specifically to bank money (see Schumpeter 1954: 686–700).
2) It references national moneys of account (pounds, dollars, etc.), as in "domestic currency" versus "foreign currency," with the latter term driving the meaning.

Failure to distinguish these two meanings elides the quite profound differences between concrete money tokens, issued mainly by commercial (but also central) banks (1), and the general money of account of a particular (national) money space (2). In both popular discourse and in today's money literature, one regularly sees discussions about "dollars" as "currency." This common usage badly conflates money proper (the $20 bill as a specific token of bank debt) with money of account (dollars as denomination). By collapsing the difference between "dollars" as general denomination and specific dollar-credits issued by a bank (or by any other debtor), the term "currency" subtly underwrites a state theory of money – because it suggests that "currency" (as a general synonym for *money*) is largely a state concern. For these reasons, I generally avoid using the term, with the main exceptions being historical cases (such as the one in the text here) and discussions of foreign exchange (as exchange of one "currency" for another).

Currency's etymology traces to the mid-seventeenth century and indicates "the fact or condition of flowing." The term's application to money appears less than fifty years later and refers to the fact of coins and paper bills being passed from person to person. (See "currency" in the *Oxford English Dictionary*).

nicely throws Innes's work into relief. Schumpeter argues that writers from the period before 1790, such as Boisguillebert and Cantillon, "might have set the writers of 1800 – 1850 on the right track" had anyone but read those early works.

Instead, the weight of the money-first approach was so heavy that when an author tried to reject it explicitly, "they remained so completely outside the pale of recognized economics" as to be unintelligible to the field (Schumpeter 1954: 687). Schumpeter here refers directly to the work of Macleod. If the narrative seems hyperbolic, we need only remember that the basis for Keynes's first-line dismissal of Innes is nothing less than the simple (assumed) fact that Innes "is a follower of Mcleod [sic]" (Keynes 1914: 419). Macleod's work is so "outside the pale" that Keynes can refuse even to engage with a credit theory of money in his review, merely by identifying Innes as a reader of Macleod and an advocate of such a theory. One wonders what Schumpeter might have said about Innes, had he read him; far from being a mere follower, Innes actually advances precisely the fully "developed" credit theory of money that Schumpeter calls for. Innes provides the core principles for a rigorous credit theory, one that must be carefully distinguished not only from later post-Keynesian ("heterodox") writings but also from both Macleod and Knapp.

Schumpeter is right: in the context of the emerging neoclassical paradigm of the time, Macleod's *Theory of Credit* (1889) reads like it was dropped from another planet. Almost the entire first half of the book (running to some 148 pages) consists of a "Definition of Terms," a project through which Macleod redefines nearly all the terms of economics by drawing almost randomly from sources throughout Western history. Nonetheless, the core claim of the work can be summarized simply: credit is just like money; it has the same basic nature and performs the same basic functions (Macleod 1889: 276). Iconoclast though he may be, Macleod begins by working within the genre established by Walker – money is the functions it performs – but then goes on to demonstrate the failure of this approach to distinguish money from credit in any proper sense. Credit instruments perform all the same functions as "money." Schumpeter is right again: this is, indeed, an effort to develop a much more robust theory of credit by refusing to "start with the coin." Nonetheless, I argue that Macleod comes up short, because he never lets go of the distinction between money and credit. While he insists that credit is of the "same nature" as money and that it can do what money does, he also contends that credit is "inferior in degree" (Macleod 1889: 276; cf. Mehrling 2012). Macleod expresses this difference in terms of time: the holder of money "may keep it as long as he pleases," while "credit is always created with the express intention of being ... extinguished" (Macleod 1889: 276 – 277).

Innes goes well beyond Macleod, arguing not that credit is *like* money but that *money is credit*. When Innes writes that "credit and credit alone is money" he refuses any effort to distinguish money and credit, either by kind or degree.[20] This does not mean, however, that we cannot make ordinal distinctions between various *types of money*; it does not mean all money is the same. Money is credit/debt. As such, money always and immediately involves two parties: creditor and debtor.[21] If I hold money in my hand, I hold a credit against some other entity. They, in turn, owe me a debt. It therefore matters a great deal how legitimate or reliable that creditor is. As Innes puts it, "a first class credit is the most valuable kind of property" (Innes 1913: 392). But the difference between a first-class credit and a second-class credit (let alone "junk" credit) is nothing more than a slide down the scale of money forms. This hierarchical ranking of money cannot be made to reflect Macleod's purported distinction between money that we can hold indefinitely and credit that must be extinguished. Because money is credit, it is always temporal and temporary: it always points toward future "redemption" of the credit, even if such redemption never comes. Rather than redeeming the credit with our debtor, we almost always transfer the credit instead (by spending the money). That is, money is *circulated:* when I make a purchase I transfer my claim on a debtor to someone else, who then holds a claim on my previous debtor. In a sense then, contra Macleod, credits need not be temporary because their redemption can be indefinitely deferred. On the other hand, and again contra Macleod, money is never good indefinitely because my money always depends on my debtor. Bank runs and hyperinflation are just two of numerous examples that undermine the idea of holding money as long as we please. As money, my credits always remain subject to destruction or disappearance. Money is that thing which allows its holder to extinguish a debt, an act that may itself destroy money.[22]

In vainly trying to preserve a money/credit distinction, Macleod remains rooted in a long tradition that has always adamantly insisted on the difference be-

---

20 The rest of this paragraph provides a short rehearsal of an argument I defend in greater depth in Chapter 5.

21 It can be easily demonstrated that the most basic exchange of money for a commodity, if paid for with bank-deposit money (check, ACH, direct debit, etc.), actually involves: five parties (buyer, seller, buyer's bank, seller's bank, central bank); two types of money (commercial bank money and central bank reserves); and seven sequential (sometimes instantaneous) steps through which the commodity and monies move. Hyman Minsky was probably the first to underscore (and popularize) the crucial point that when banks pay one another they need credits on some other bank located further up the hierarchy of money (Minsky 2008: 258).

22 Whether money is destroyed hinges on the relation between the payee and the debtor: paying off my mortgage with bank deposits and paying my US taxes with US Federal Reserve notes both destroy money, but a person buying something on Craigslist with cash (again, US Federal Reserve notes), or one company buying out another (by purchasing all shares of public stock), does not.

tween a mere *promise to pay* (credit) and an *actual payment* (money). For any commodity theory, maintaining such a distinction proves trivial: only the commodity is actual money, and anything else is credit because it promises future payment in the form of the commodity. Here we see clearly for the first time a crucial issue that animates much of the discussion in Chapter 5: by thoroughly rejecting the commodity theory's insistence on positive, intrinsic value, the credit theory puts enormous pressure on the money/credit distinction.

Indeed, even at this stage of the argument we can already indicate that without grounding in a commodity theory, the money/credit distinction can never truly hold. If money is credit, then *when we pay in money, we pay in nothing less than another promise to pay.* For example, if you make me a loan denominated in USD, then at the time of the loan's creation, we could say that you hold a credit (my promise to pay you), not money. Yet at the time of payment, precisely what I give to you is another form of credit: if I pay you with a check, then my *payment* is the *transfer of credit* I hold against my bank. I am no longer obligated to pay you, my bank is. And when you deposit that check into your bank account, you are again only transferring the credit in the sense of swapping out your debtor: first I owed you; then my bank owed you; and now your bank owes you. The so-called "actual" payment that would constitute money never actually arrives, but is always deferred.

To grasp money as credit means always seeing money as a social relation in the specific sense of the *money array.* There is no positive, intrinsic value to money; there is only, as Schumpeter emphasizes, a *claim* on some future product. But as Innes helps us see, that claim cannot come from the ticket alone; the ticket is only ever a receipt that confirms our relation to our debtor. Of course we must verify the authenticity of the ticket, but doing so does not verify the money. The latter requires us to prove the legitimacy and solvency of the debtor.[23]

To forge a ticket (whether it be coin, paper bank note, or a credit default swap) is to commit fraud by claiming to hold a credit (to have a legitimate relation to a debtor) that one does not in fact have. But this has nothing to do with the validity or reliability of money. Forgeries are not "unsound money"; they are not money at all. Any question of the relative "soundness" of money only arises *after* the legiti-

---

23 As I show in detail in the next chapter, to theorize money as an array entails resisting the tendency to conflate the idea of money as fundamentally *relational* with the notion that money is a social *institution*, one chosen by society or its leaders. "Verification" also cannot be carried out at the level of society itself. That is, the existence of the "institution of money" (a phrase often favored by post-Keynesian thinkers) does not itself legitimate any *particular* money claim. The institution can persist while particular forms of money (credit) fail all the time. We obscure the nature of money as credit when we describe it as an institution.

macy of the claim has been settled. The "quality" of money concerns only the reliability of the debtor. It therefore matters not how much gold or silver is in a coin; if it has the proper stamp, it is money (because it is a denominated claim of credit/debt).[24] Commodity-gold must be assayed for its metallic purity because the buyer buys a specific quantity (measured in weight) of gold.[25] Money-gold need not be assayed or even weighed; as token or claim, we must only verify that it is not a fake.[26]

Whether credit money proves to be a "first-class" credit depends on the debtor, the issuer of the coin or paper or spreadsheet entry. Innes puts the point this way: "The value of a credit depends not on the existence of any gold or silver or other property behind it, but solely on the 'solvency' of the debtor, and that depends on whether, when the debt becomes due, he [the debtor] in turn has sufficient credits

---

24 This point chimes with Schumpeter's critique of the commodity theory of money, elaborated in the previous chapter. Schumpeter shows that paper money, old money, and coins "below par" all continue to circulate in a properly functioning monetary system. We can now add to this point: money fails when we lose faith not in the token itself but in its issuers.

25 Christine Desan's otherwise illuminating history of money in England frequently founders on a lingering belief in "commodity money," in particular on a failure to see that the mint price is precisely what establishes the difference between commodity-silver and money-silver. Desan argues that the mint "charged users for money creation" in that "users pay for money at the mint." She allows her work to be underwritten by metallist theory when she assumes that because a minted coin of £1 denomination has less metal in it than £1 worth of metal bullion, that this means the mint must be "charging" the individual (Desan 2014: 8–9). This account ignores the fundamental fact that the £1 coin is not a commodity; it is a token of denominated value. As such, it absolutely must, of necessity, have less metal in it than £1 worth of commodity metal. If it had the same or more, then it would fail to function as money. All of this means, contra Desan, that the existence of the mint price *props up* the market value of commodity-silver. Silver as a commodity is only *worth* as much as it is because the mint stands willing to pay such a high price for it in money. The mint overpays for commodity-silver, and its overpayment influences the market rate. Moreover, the quantity of silver in the money token is mostly irrelevant (to everyone other than silver miners); as long as the token remains money-silver, it simply is not commodity-silver. This also means that there is no lower bound to the amount of commodity-silver contained in the money-silver token. It's true that should the money system itself collapse such that the money token fails to circulate, then the holder of a coin may treat it as commodity-silver. At that point they will hold less total commodity-silver than they did back at the start (i. e., when they sold their original commodity-silver to the mint). But under these circumstances it makes little sense to describe this difference in metal as a "charge" because in this context we have no viable money of account with which to measure value. People brought bullion to the mint not to turn it into less bullion but to turn it into money.

26 The denomination of money-gold is usually stamped on the face of the coin, but even in cases of coins without such stampings, the denomination is fixed by the mint, the sovereign, or by custom (not determined by weighing the coin). Everyone knows that the smallest US coin is worth $0.10, though the coin itself only contains the colloquial "one dime" on its reverse.

on others to set off against his debts" (Innes 1913: 393).[27] My bank deposits are credits at my bank, who is my debtor, and my credits remain good up until the point that my bank itself either becomes insolvent or runs out of liquidity.[28]

A rigorous credit theory of money affirms what Mehrling helpfully names "the hierarchy of money," a concept that raises the crucial relation between a credit theory of money and a state theory of money (Mehrling 2012; cf. Minsky 2008). That is, at some point as we move up the hierarchy, it is likely (or in modern societies, inevitable) that we will encounter state money – that is, government-issued

---

27 As Mehrling lucidly argues, we must always be careful to distinguish between liquidity and solvency, but we often find it hard to do so because mainstream economics consistently ignores and elides questions of liquidity – often assuming that liquidity is just a given (Mehrling 2011: 59). The distinction is simple to draw definitionally but often hard to keep separate in practice. Solvency describes a condition in which total assets exceed total liabilities (when liabilities exceed assets, the result is insolvency). If we conceive of any economic agent (bank, firm, household or individual) according to their balance sheet of assets and liabilities, then that agent is *solvent* if the former are greater than the latter. Solvency is a measure of stocks, in the sense that we must count up total assets and liabilities. On the other hand, liquidity is a measure of flows; specifically, it is a measure of periodic (usually daily) flows of money (understood in some sense as "cash" – for more on this, see Chapter 6, Footnote 14). An agent remains "liquid" as long as their daily incoming flow of cash (or available strategic stock that can be *liquidated* – hence the term) exceeds their daily outgoing flow of cash. A healthy financial entity will obviously be both solvent and liquid, while a bankrupt institution will be both insolvent and illiquid. The tricky situations occur when an agent is: 1) *simultaneously insolvent and liquid* or 2) *simultaneously solvent and illiquid.* In the first case, an insolvent bank, dealer, or firm can remain in business long enough to return to solvency so long as they can make their money outflows line up in time with their money inflows. In the latter case, despite being solvent, if they fail to have adequate daily cash flow to pay current commitments, they will still be in trouble. Hence Mehrling's mantra: "illiquidity kills quickly." Obviously these two conditions are related: solvent institutions will find it much easier to get access to loans needed to meet liquidity constraints; illiquid agents will find that the value of their assets gets reassessed based on their funding problems, and this fact could lead to their becoming insolvent. But Mehrling's main points are: 1) liquidity cannot be subsumed under solvency, and 2) in most circumstances, liquidity matters more than solvency.

The first use of the term "liquidity" in the economic sense appears in Hawtrey's *Currency and Credit* (1919). Written a decade prior, Innes's credit theory of money contains a fascinating section wherein he articulates the newer concept of liquidity (i. e., having "immediately available credits at least equal to the amount of his debts immediately due and presented for payment") using the older language of "solvency" (Innes 1913: 394). In other words, Innes understands the primary importance of the concept of liquidity, which he describes clearly, even if at the time he lacked the terminology to name it.

28 To repeat: when I use my bank credits to pay for something (say, to pay a friend my share of the costs of dinner), this involves: my bank debiting my deposit account (they now owe me less); my friend's bank crediting his deposit account (they owe him more); my bank transferring central bank reserves to his bank (see Minsky 2008: 231; also cited in Wray 1998: 35).

debt that circulates in and helps establish the primary money of account – dollars, euros, etc. Recent post-Keynesian work at various times asserts or assumes that state theory is a natural development out of credit theory. Ingham grounds much of his project on the earlier work of Ellis, who, in surveying *German Monetary Theory*, places Knapp and his followers at the center of the narrative. Ellis, however, makes a subtle distinction between "orthodox nominalism" and "state theory," one that later writings tend to elide (Ellis 1934: 42; cf. Ingham 2004a; Ingham 2004c).

It proves crucial to articulate the *relation* between the credit theory and the state theory, but I argue that we must magnify, not minimize, the differences. I again take my cues from Schumpeter, who very early on sounded a prudent warning that seems to have gone unheeded by contemporary writers. In his 1917 article on the quantity theorem, Schumpeter was already worried about Knapp's state theory taking up all the air available in the anti-metallist camp. Schumpeter is emphatic: "A sharp distinction must be drawn between 'nominalism' and 'state theory.' The nominalist idea has received in the latter a special form which is not essential to it, and which exposes it to objections that would otherwise not apply" (Schumpeter 1956: 161). Both in this article and at much greater length in *HEA*, Schumpeter positively rails against Knapp. This critique is essential for at least three reasons:

1) It helps to correct the historical record, showing that there was never a direct line running from Innes and Knapp to Keynes, Schumpeter, and today's post-Keynesians (without that lineage, the very idea of a heterodox tradition must be scrutinized). Quite the contrary, when we look closely at the enormous quantity of writings on money between 1870 and 1940, we uncover a contentious dispute *within* the claim theory (or "nominalist") category.
2) It allows me to refine and augment my particular presentation of the credit theory of money, a specific variant of claim theory that rejects a hard money/credit distinction while resisting appropriation by state theory.
3) It shines a bright light on contemporary political debates over money, especially as they crystalize around modern money theory (MMT); Schumpeter's withering appraisal of Knapp reads like a powerful and important attack on MMT, avant la lettre.

Schumpeter aims to warn his readers, to prevent them from concluding – as both Knapp and his followers (as well as advocates of MMT today) often insist on doing – that Knapp's state theory is the only alternative to a standard, commodity theory of money (Knapp 1924: viii). Schumpeter cannot control his outrage: "*This absurd claim was widely accepted*" (Schumpeter 1954: 1057). The notion that rejecting commodity theory leads straight to an embrace of state theory – this idea so appalls

Schumpeter that he avers we might be better off sticking with commodity theory (a *false* theory, according to Schumpeter) than taking up state theory.[29]

When it comes to the relation between money, on the one hand, and the power of the state, specifically the power of law, on the other, Schumpeter conceives of two viable theses a writer could proffer: 1) the state can *declare* what counts as legal/legitimate/viable "pay-tokens"; 2) such state declarations "will *determine* the value" of those tokens. Schumpeter says thesis 1 is true but boring, while thesis 2 is interesting but false (Schumpeter 1954: 1056). The former fails to offer any real challenge to metallism: that money as legal tender is established by state law tells us nothing directly about the inherent nature of money. The latter *would* provide such a challenge (if state edicts constitute money's value, then surely money is not a commodity), yet that thesis is untenable (Schumpeter 1956: 160).[30]

To his detriment, says Schumpeter, Knapp pursued neither thesis. Knapp eschewed the question of money's "value"; instead, he constructed an ontology of money, developed out of its factual existence as a "creature of law" (Knapp 1924: 30, 1; cf. Schumpeter 1954: 1056). It will perhaps come as a surprise to those who have read Wray or Ingham but not Knapp to learn that the last builds his entire project on top of a standard commodity-theory story of money. Knapp takes the Mengerian narrative as his starting point: "We observed the fact that in human society a definite commodity, or, more accurately, a definite material grew into a means of payment" (Knapp 1924: 25). Knapp's question simplifies to the following: How do we understand the nature of money when debts measured in material value get *transformed* – through historical development and the growth of the modern state – into legal tokens? Knapp does not just tacitly presuppose the commodity-theory narrative; he explicitly adopts it (Knapp 1924: 35).

It would therefore be hard to overestimate the distance that separates Knapp from Innes. Knapp embraces the standard (yet already outdated) history of coinage as a series of metallic standards of weighted value – the very history that Innes takes as his chief critical target. In this context we can better hear Schumpeter's plaint: Knapp offers no deep or rigorous challenge to the core tenets of metallism, and what he does provide in terms of the nature of chartal money turns out rather empty. Schumpeter formulates his most forceful charge against Knapp in the shape of a repeated and extended analogy:

---

29 Schumpeter stresses that the only good explanation for the enduring influence of Knapp is that he (over)simplifies the choices for a theory of money (Schumpeter 1954: 1057). Over this chapter and the previous one, I trace some of the enduring legacy of this oversimplification, which, as I show in the next chapter, we see in contemporary contributions to the theory of money.
30 For a much more generous and productive reading of Knapp, see my discussion of Ingham's development of Weber's interpretation of Knapp (Chapter 5, Section 4).

Money is as little and in no other sense a creature of the law than is any other social institution[,] such as marriage. ... Marriage [is] regulated by law[,] and to that extent [its] concrete form [is a] creature of the prevailing legal system. *But no-one can explain marriage by this legal system.* Rather, the relevant legal provisions themselves are comprehensible only on the basis of the social nature and the social functions of the relations and modes of behavior which these legal provisions regulate and which, to be sure, never exist without them, but also never exist only through them: the essential nature of marriage relations explain the legal provisions which regulate them, but the legal provisions do not explain the essential nature and causes of marriage relations. Similarly, money transactions are regulated or shaped by the legal system, but as an object of regulation they retain a separate existence apart from the legal system itself and can be explained only by their own nature or by the inner necessities of the market economy. (Schumpeter 1956: 160–61, emphasis added; cf. Schumpeter 1954: 1056–57)

The power to regulate a complex social institution is not the power to create that institution, to literally bring such social relations into being. More to the point, identifying the state power to regulate money does not give us insight into the nature of money itself.

In today's hierarchy of credit money, state money indeed plays an absolutely central role. Sovereign government debt is always one of the highest forms of money, and in the case of US sovereign debt, it is also a form of world money – with US Treasury bonds playing the chief role of Innes's first-class credits, otherwise known as a high-quality liquid assets (HQLA) (Pozsar 2018). Nevertheless, we cannot think that admitting the significance of state money and the role played by states (and today, central banks) brings us directly to a deep understanding of the ontology of money. Knapp's own work proves otherwise: he fails to offer an alternative to metallism's singular ontology; instead, he substitutes the legitimacy of sovereign legal decree (chartal tokens) and sovereign taxation powers for the validity of metallic content.

This extended critique of Knapp opens up large holes in the heterodox lineage, and perhaps gives us some explanation for the staying power of both the commodity theory and the so-called orthodoxy. To put the point bluntly, I am trying to show that heterodoxy bet on the wrong horse: of the many varieties of claim theory (type 2), Knapp's is the weakest by far. Worse still, contemporary reconstructions of a so-called heterodox theory of money tend to erase the gap between Innes and Knapp, to reduce everything down by forcing it into a "non-orthodox" crucible. Despite never mentioning Innes himself, Schumpeter warns strongly in advance against just this move. Indeed, Schumpeter's own defense of claim theory proves far more rigorous and tenable than Knapp's work. Yet those warnings have not even been heard – much less heeded – perhaps because Schumpeter's perduring commitments to both real analysis and the quantity theorem mean that he cannot be made to fit into the pure heterodox type.[31]

Schumpeter shows that a viable claim theory will not only distinguish itself from Knapp and the tradition his work founds but also decisively oppose that tradition. Schumpeter's challenge to Knapp serves to sharply contrast state theory with credit/claim theory. From here we can zoom in and focus, by pointing out the detailed differences between Schumpeter's claim theory and the particular theory of money as credit that I develop from Innes. The chief variance in the two arguments lies in the context of the presentations. As I have shown above, Innes effectively replaces the theory of barter with a distinct theory of economic exchange involving a commodity and a credit. We can thereby understand Innes as offering: 1) an alternative to the commodity theory of money (i. e., the credit theory of money) and 2) a distinct account of economic activity itself.

Schumpeter, as I detailed in the previous chapter, rejects commodity theory directly and entirely: "Money is not a commodity" (Schumpeter 1956: 161). But he does not plant claim theory in new ground, beyond the fields of neoclassical economic thought. Rather, Schumpeter derives his claim theory from the mode of economic analysis that had become standard in the early part of the twentieth century: "The basic process of economic life is clearly a *circular flow* of production expenditure and consumption uses within each economic period" (Schumpeter 1954: 150–151, emphasis added). This "continuous and automatic" process circulates goods and services, and each individual's share (whether worker or capitalist) of the product "depends upon the market value of his personal or material contribution to production" (Schumpeter 1954: 152). The circular flow model is a form of real analysis, sans money. To describe the model in monetary terms means to define money as *money income,* which is nothing other than "the monetary *expression* of the goods consumed" (Schumpeter 1954: 153, emphasis added). From these apparently simple assumptions (widely shared across neoclassical economics, then and now), Schumpeter produces his unorthodox theory of money: "Since money income is acquired on the market for the means of production only to be spent on the other market for consumer goods, *the essential nature of money is obviously correctly described by the analogy of a 'claim ticket to goods'*"

---

31 Ingham sometimes tries to pull off this impossible feat. He continually points to Schumpeter as a resource for the heterodox theory, going so far at one point as to name Schumpeter as an alternative to "the orthodox quantity theory of money" propounded by Fisher (Ingham 2004a: 160). But this is to ignore: the extended praise Schumpeter gives to Fisher; the extra lengths to which Schumpeter goes to suggest that Fisher himself might be understood as a claim theorist; and most of all Schumpeter's lifelong project to prove the compatibility between claim theory and support for the quantity theorem (Schumpeter 1954: 1081; Schumpeter 1956: 163).

(Schumpeter 1956: 153–154, emphasis added). This is an impressive accomplishment: Schumpeter successfully derives the claim theory from a standard textbook account of the circular flow model – "Money is a claim ticket and receipt voucher" (Schumpeter 1956: 155).

This general conclusion, and the fundaments of a claim theory of money, prove completely compatible with Innes's credit theory of money. Both agree that the claim or credit has no metallic or commodity basis, that even if a commodity is used to produce the credit token, the purchasing power of that claim (its power as a credit) has no footing in the commodity's use-value. But the key difference also proves clear: Schumpeter's account remains tethered to the circular flow model. Doubtless this explains both Schumpeter's commitment to real analysis (his theory of money starts with no money present) and his support for the quantity theorem. Indeed, this model authorizes Schumpeter to make the crucial assumption that all money is spent each economic period (no savings) specifically so that he may conclude that an increase in the "supply" of money (more tickets) will necessarily lead to a rise in prices (Schumpeter 1956: 163). More speculatively, Schumpeter's commitment to a version of claim theory grounded in this larger economic model may itself offer the best explanation for his lifelong failure to perfect his theory of money: the circular flow model cannot but constrain the potentially radical implications that the claim theory of money otherwise entails.

Removed from that model, Schumpeter's basic notion of money as claim complements (if it does not merely repeat) Innes's assertion of money as credit. The accounts of Innes and Schumpeter blend together nicely to refute the commodity theory. Innes's work has the advantage of generality, in the sense that his ontology of money can be used to develop a more sophisticated account of money and value under capitalism. Meanwhile, Schumpeter's theory remains trapped within the context of a capitalist social order that it *assumes* but for that reason cannot *explain.*

3 Beyond the Quantity Theorem

By the time we reach the third row in our table of money choices, we have already placed enormous pressure on the money theory matrix. This makes it possible to dispense with any extended discussion of the quantity theorem and instead merely indicate why the theory of money we are developing can largely avoid it entirely. In general terms we may say that by committing itself to (1) the idea of the real as monetary and (2) a deep understanding of money as credit, the theory developed in this chapter unravels the very problematic in which the quantity hypothesis would be raised. In other words, it's not just that the causal relation, MV→PQ, proves false, but that the variables themselves cease to make sense ontologically.

This argument starts with our redefinition of economic exchange. The quantity theorem incorporates a framework of real analysis as the direct exchange of goods and services. That is, fundamentally the quantity theorem poses the question: What happens to economic exchange when an economic order experiences monetary fluctuations? More precisely, what happens to the circulation of commodities when the "supply" of money changes? As I detailed in the last chapter, the quantity theorem is developed from the much older exchange *equation:* MV = PQ. By presuming that M and Q can symbolically express money and commodities – separately and on opposite sides of the equal sign – the equation itself tends to presuppose real analysis, and it remains thoroughly embedded in the traditional framework of economic exchange. Yet a capitalist social order turns out to be precisely the sort of system that calls such simple assumptions into question.

I want to emphasize a more straightforward and, I think, uncontroversial claim: the exchange equation assumes traditional economic exchange at the most fundamental level since it posits the existence of commodities and prices (PQ) as distinct from money (M). Put differently, every argument in support of the quantity theorem relies on the traditional, real-analysis conception of economic exchange as the swapping of two commodities.

Let us take two contrasting examples. First, the standard metallist account, which holds that an increase in the supply of the money commodity leads directly and inevitably (definitionally) to a decrease in the "value" of money. This decrease in money's "value" necessarily entails a decrease in the purchasing power of money, which is just another name for inflation. Second, Schumpeter's account, which combines a claim theory with the circular flow model, assumes that all issued claims (money) must be used (spent), and thus concludes that increases in money income must drive up prices. Both arguments obviously affirm the quantity theorem (attesting that M→P), but we can also observe a much deeper connection between them. In each of these cases – indeed, likely in *all* arguments supporting the quantity theorem – we always find *one mass confronting another mass*, such that the increase in the money mass relative to the commodity mass leads to a rise in prices.

However, none of this makes any sense at all – that is, the very terms become unintelligible – if we reject the standard account of economic exchange and substitute the account derived earlier in this chapter. In other words, if exchange involves the swapping of a commodity for a credit (money), then there is no longer reason to believe that an increase in credits will have any *necessary* impact on the prices of commodities. *Money is not a mass.* The existence of more credits (or fewer) has no inevitable effect on price levels whatsoever. The reason is deceptively simple: one can hold more credits without spending them.[32] If Jeff Bezos and Tim Cook have millions more dollars in their account at the end of the month than they did at the beginning, this phenomenon in itself does not *directly* shape price levels. Moreover, under capitalism one often strongly desires to hold credits without spending them.[33] To understand money and capitalism today we must often see the movement of credits as *separate and separable* from the movement of goods and services, just as we must at other times grasp the links and connections between them.

For clarity, let me state plainly that the theory of money I have started to develop, when faced with the "yes or no" question of the quantity theorem, can only and unequivocally respond in the negative. At the first level, I reject the quantity theorem and affirm the basic idea, which can be traced back to the currency debates, that to the extent we wish to suggest any causal relation, it operates in the opposite direction: not M→P, but P→M. If we seek to track the movement of price levels, we must start with the basic economic activity of buying and selling commodities. The fundaments of supply and demand prove much more helpful here than the quantity theorem: more buyers and fewer sellers will, ceteris paribus, drive prices up (and vice versa). The "quantity of money" – which can only be measured in the total amount of credits and debts – will generally respond to those movements in prices. Put otherwise, money is created (endogenously) in a boom and destroyed in a bust.[34] The above positions are not new or unique. They can be traced back to classical political economy (Quesnay, Law), were developed in thinkers like Minsky, and are advocated forcefully today by representatives of MMT and other post-Keynesians. I seek not so much to advance those positions as to displace the entire quantity theorem framework.

---

32 This is a lesson that was learned by central bankers during the GFC, which repeated American experience in the 1930s: sometimes expanded availability of money-credits manifests not in increases to economic activity (much less prices) but merely in "expanding bank reserves" (Mehrling 2011: 42).

33 Keynes, of course, understood this phenomenon to a certain extent, and described it in the language of "liquidity preference" (Keynes 1936). Unfortunately, Keynes's original presentation of the concept lent itself to appropriation by a model that reconciled this notion with "supply and demand" of money, making many Keynesians and post-Keynesians into supporters of the quantity theorem. I explore the issue of liquidity, and Keynes's unique understanding of it, in some depth in Chapter 5.

34 To investigate the nature of that value destruction requires something more than a theory of endogenous money creation. It also requires a thoroughgoing rejection of any trace of positive money value, which makes it possible to see that value can disappear instantaneously precisely because money, at one and the same time, both *has no* value and is the *form* that value takes.

This chapter has begun to elaborate a new theory of money. My account uses the previous chapter's money matrix as a guide, but also places that matrix under significant torsional pressure. Hence my own location on the matrix actually lies outside of it, or at least requires its expansion. My theory is of the variety C2y:

1) It deconstructs or displaces the real/monetary binary by redefining economic exchange as the swapping of a commodity for a credit, therefore insisting that *the monetary is real.*

2) Going back to Innes, it details a theory of money as credit, resisting any ontological money/credit distinction while also distinguishing the credit theory from state theory (sharply) and from a claim theory linked to the circular flow model (more subtly).

3) It rejects the quantity theorem, and goes further to dispute the entire ontology implied by the exchange equation.

Each of these particular positions is not wholly unique when considered in the context of today's best money theories. Indeed, many theories of money today – often catalogued under the broad entry "heterodox" – complement and elaborate the positions I have staked out in this chapter. Heterodox theories prosecute a vigorous critique of theoretical metallism, consistently reject the idea that money is a commodity by nature, refute the notion that money is a "neutral veil," and dismiss the austerity politics attendant to supporting the quantity theorem.

In order to draw out the novelty and distinctiveness of my theory, the next chapter will probe the limitations and weaknesses of the dominant theories of money circulating today. Ultimately, the main and best representatives of this "heterodox tradition" develop theories of money that still retain traces of positive value; such accounts reject commodity value as money's basis but tacitly smuggle in a substitute. More specifically, while numerous theorists today attest that all "money is credit," they refuse the idea that all credit is potentially money; instead they opt to hold the line, by drawing a firm (if shifting) distinction between money and credit. In Chapter 5 I advance a more radical argument, by demonstrating that ontologically we cannot tenably distinguish "credit" from "money"; there is only one ontological "substance," and we can call it *money-credit.* First, in Chapter 4, I address the dominant voices of money theory today, and show how and why they remain unwilling to affirm the most radical and also most salient claim, one articulated in distinct ways by thinkers as diverse as Schumpeter and Marx: *money has no value.*

Chapter Four
Money Theories Today

The previous two chapters aimed to map the matrix of money theories in broad terms, and then to locate a thoroughgoing credit theory of money on that matrix (or slightly off it, as the case may be). The goal was to give the reader a wider sense of the diversity of historical theories of money, and then to use that context to provide clarifying contrast for the particular flavor of credit theory I am beginning to propound. While surveying a broad range of thinkers and theories, and in an attempt to make the previous presentation as lucid and succinct as possible, I have largely eschewed engagement with contemporary debates – both theoretical and practical, as Schumpeter might say. This chapter turns to the two most important writers on money over the past twenty-five years, Randall Wray and Geoffrey Ingham. The work of the former has inspired the most significant new policy ideas on money since Milton Friedman's monetarism. The writings of the latter have served as the starting point (and often the ending point) in the study of money for a generation of students – at all levels and across a variety of fields.

I intend neither to summarize their oeuvres (each of which proves sizable) nor to definitively refute their theories or positions. My own work on money would never have been possible were it not for the writings of Ingham, and I certainly would never have read the central source for my own theory were it not for Wray's rediscovery of Innes. I agree with each author much more than I disagree. Nonetheless, my differences with their work matter to just the extent that tracing them allows me to provide a fine-grained account of a more thoroughgoing credit theory of money. A critical engagement with Wray and Ingham enables me to augment, hone, and clarify the specific contours of my theory and to make plain its distinctiveness.

As I have now indicated on multiple occasions, I simply cannot accept the idea that there are only two theories of money – orthodox and heterodox. Such a framing does no justice to the complexity and diversity of the history of money theories, while it also tends to obscure some crucial insights from past thinkers – insights we need for theorizing money today. Therefore, I eschew the notion that to theorize money outside the terms of the neoclassical mainstream (orthodoxy) means to contribute to a heterodox tradition. As I suggested in Chapter 2, a better path for thinking money in the twenty-first century can be traced by drawing out the differences *among* heterodox thinkers. I do that here through circumscribed encounters with Wray and Ingham. My ultimate aim: to show that a more far-reaching and thoroughgoing credit theory provides a distinctive account of money. Such a theory, in turn – and to put it in the most straightforward terms – helps us

https://doi.org/10.1515/9783110760774-008

make better sense of the economics and politics of money today. From the 2008 crash, to crypto, to the global health and economic crisis brought on by COVID–19, we do better with a radical credit theory of money than with a state theory.

1 Money and Credit Redux

In standard accounts of money, from classical political economy through the neo-classical paradigm, we can easily locate a fundamental – indeed, ontological – distinction between money and credit. I described this idea briefly in Chapter 3: credit is nothing more than a *promise* to pay, while money is the medium of exchange or means of payment *itself.* Any commodity theory of money insists on differentiating money, which possesses positive intrinsic value, from agreements or contracts that specify terms according to which such positive value will be delivered at some future date. In the previous chapter I noted that Macleod's effort to question this sharp distinction between money and credit – by carefully demonstrating that credit instruments could perform all the exact same functions as money – rendered his work unintelligible to the economic establishment of his day (and of ours). But I went on to argue that Innes's essays afford a deeper conceptualization of money *as credit/debt,* and as such, I suggested that a more incisive and insightful theory of money would need to do away with or deconstruct the money/credit distinction.

This is not at all the path taken by today's leading lights of money theory.[1] In saying as much, I am not denying or deprecating the fact that Wray himself discovered the lost writings of Innes, nor forgetting that Wray's work brought Innes to the attention of Ingham. Certainly both Wray and Ingham affirm at various points Innes's fundamental idea, which I advance in the previous chapter: money is a

---

1 By no means do Wray and Ingham advance the *same* theory of money. While both slot comfortably into the B2y matrix location, and while each insists that modern money is state money, when analyzed closely their differences prove dramatic. Wray is a post-Keynesian economist (a student of Minsky) who turns to money theory in a focused effort to support a specific policy proposal – a national jobs guarantee, or the state as employer of last resort. Wray always tethers money to macroeconomic models of national spending and saving. Ingham is a Weberian sociologist who stumbled upon money theory as a genuine intellectual puzzle and pursued it to its furthest ends. Wray tends to think of economics as a universal discipline that studies transhistorical forces (produced by the actions of *homo economicus*), while Ingham insists on historicizing the emergence of capitalism as a distinct social order, and grasping capitalist money as a unique invention of such a social order. My aim in the text is not to deny or elide any of these important differences but to use the points of overlap between Wray and Ingham as a foil to sharpen my own theory and clarify its distinctiveness.

form of credit/debt (Wray 1998: 34; Wray 2004: 238; Ingham 2004a: 46; Ingham 2004b: 225). However, both authors – each in his own way – insist on a distinction between money and credit.

Wray, for his part, does not belabor the point but rather writes as if it were obvious to his readers that money and credit are different things. To flesh out this idea we can look at an edge case, as found in Wray's authored chapter within the volume on Innes that he himself edited (Wray 2004). Even here, in a section titled "The Credit Theory of Money," Wray repeatedly invokes the distinction between money and credit. As he puts it, during economic expansion, "newly created *credits* create new claims on *money*," while a credit/debt clearing system functions "without the use of money." In this context, Wray draws a stark dividing line between a "credit theory of money" – which he attributes to Schumpeter (and also to Innes) – and a "'pure credit' approach with no place reserved for money" (Wray 2004: 238, emphasis added). For Wray, the latter is an obvious mistake; Schumpeter, he declares, "is not guilty of propagating" such a theory. Twice, Wray repeats that Innes and Schumpeter "reject a 'pure credit' approach" (a phrase that Wray always presents with the included quotation marks) because they maintain "a place for 'real' or 'lawful money'" (Wray 2004: 240, 242).[2] In acquitting Schumpeter and Innes, Wray makes the lesson clear: failure to reserve a place for money *as distinct from credit* would be a crime. A credit theory of money, Wray demands, must *stop* at a certain point so as to inscribe the line between money and credit.

Unlike Wray, who cannot countenance the notion of what he disparagingly names "pure credit," Ingham makes a series of arguments that directly address whether, how, and where to distinguish money from credit.[3] In his first of many attempts to capture the nature of money, Ingham separates himself from Wray and other post-Keynesians, whose views on money are trapped within the lan-

---

2 The role of "lawful money" as "real" money proves critical for Wray because in his account the ultimate and overriding money is always state money. Thus, while it may be possible for "credit" to be created endogenously and privately within a society, *real money* is always a "creature of the state." Blurring the line between money and credit (as a careful reading of Innes demands we do) would undermine Wray's entire project of theorizing money as ultimately *controlled* by the state – through spending, taxing, and monetary policy. I note here that this larger morphology, centered on state control, provides the perfect foil for the "crypto imaginary," the dream of money as utterly *untethered* from state control. See my discussion of bitcoin and crypto in Chapter 7.
3 Although Ingham regularly cites Wray over the years (e. g., Ingham 2012) and contributed to Wray's edited volume on Innes (Ingham 2004b), his first direct and sustained engagement with MMT comes in a forthcoming chapter in an edited volume, wherein he faintly but genuinely praises MMT's challenge to orthodoxy, especially as it requires MMT thinkers to "cross … disciplinary boundaries," while taking his distance from a number of the simplifications of the MMT model that pull it back into the gravity well of the neoclassical paradigm (Ingham, forthcoming).

guage of neoclassical economics; as he puts it here, "the conventional textbook distinction between 'money' and 'credit' is not merely anachronistic, but it is based on a conceptual confusion" (Ingham 1996: 509–510). As his theory of money develops over the years and as he engages critically with his interlocutors, Ingham will sometimes go so far as to offer a plain and direct denial of the dividing line: "The distinction between 'money' and 'credit' is false" (Ingham 2006: 266).

However, in a later restatement of his position, Ingham moderates his stance, less forcefully indicating that "the *absolute* distinction between 'money' and 'credit' is misleading" (Ingham 2012: 121, emphasis added). I italicize the word "absolute" because Ingham typically wishes to hold back from denying the distinction altogether. To the contrary, though Ingham embraces (more fully than Wray) Innes's primary thesis, he resists the corollary: "Whilst we may agree with Innes that all money is credit (or debt), it does not follow that the converse is true. *Not all credit (or debt) is money*" (Ingham 2004b: 185, emphasis added; cf. Ingham 2020: 41). Given Ingham's resolute refusal to accept the money/credit distinction as a base assumption, given his insistence that the distinction can never be absolute, and given his embrace of Innes's claim that all money is credit, we need to move slowly here and answer carefully the question "Why is not all credit money?"

As always, this conceptual question has both historical conditions and implications, and Ingham provides a rich and important account of the novel development of capitalist credit money as circulating (monetized) public debt.[4] Nonetheless, the historical account cannot substitute for a rigorous theoretical answer. Rather, as I suggested in my discussion of the theory–history relation in Chapter 1, each depends on the other. Attempting to maintain fidelity to Ingham's own texts, I reconstruct the conceptual argument by starting with Ingham's 2012 clarification of the 2004 money/credit distinction: "In this I have merely followed Simmel's clear, well-established and essentially sociological distinction between bilateral and multilateral, or 'private' and 'public,' relationships" (Ingham 2012: 128). In other words, *logically* we can distinguish between the *holding* of a credit, wherein party A holds a

---

4 This account is one of Ingham's most potent and perhaps his *unique* contribution to our understanding of money today. He summarizes the point concisely in a later essay:

> The social mechanism by which private debts are transformed into public money is one of the most important and distinctive elements of the capitalist system. ... Loans from banks to their customers are private contracts in which the banks create deposits for borrowers. In the act of spending, these private debts become public money. This is accomplished through institutions that have developed between states, public banks and banking systems since the sixteenth century in Europe. (Ingham 2012: 131)

For a critical engagement with this argument, see Chapter 6, Footnote 5.

claim (a credit) against party B (the debtor), and the *circulation* of that credit, wherein party A *pays* party C with that credit. In the latter case, party C thus *accepts the transfer* of the credit held on party B, as payment. Not all forms of credit can perform this latter action; only "money" can do so.

Drawing from Georg Simmel, Ingham is arguing that in my first case (party A holds a credit on party B), the social relations are "private" and "bilateral," whereas in my second case (party A spends the credit by transferring it to party C), the relations are "public" or "multilateral." In other words, the assertion that not all credit is money is meant to be deducible from the argument that not all private (bilateral) credit relations can function as public (multilateral) credit relations. In other texts Ingham offers the concluding step to this logic:

> Money is transferable credit. (Ingham 2006: 267)
> Cash [money] is "portable credit" that cancels a debt.
> (Ingham 2018: 846, citing Gardiner 1993)

On the one hand, the reasoning here seems hard to deny: not every IOU between two private parties can function as public money generally. On the other hand, the careful observer might spot the ghost of Francis Walker in the above quotations. That is to say, at the core of this demonstration designed to prove the claim "not all credit is money," we find functionalism. "Money is that money does"; hence that which functions as money is money, *not credit.*

But as with all functionalist arguments, we may have the tail wagging the dog because the last step in our deduction only returns us to the original question – *What is* "that which functions as money"? The answer is obvious: "Credit and credit alone is money" (Innes 1913: 392). Indeed, Ingham's definitional quotes above express just this essential point: "money" is a type or class of *credit.* Both putative definitions of money declare that money is credit – credit that functions in a particular way. Far from rigorously distinguishing money from credit, the argument merely shows that not all credit is the same. As I suggested in the previous chapter (drawing from Innes's account of "first-class credits"), and as I elaborate below, there can be no doubt that credits differ in quality; some can function in ways that others cannot. But we cannot bestow upon the name *money* the magical or alchemical power to alter the essential nature of some credits vis-à-vis others. The thing that functions as money remains nothing less, nothing more, and absolutely nothing other than credit. Therefore, to interpret it in its best light, we would need to reconstruct Ingham's "not all credit is money" assertion so as to widen the gap between, on the one hand, that *particular* claim, and, on the other, the money/credit distinction that runs like a red thread through the entire history of economic thought (right up through today's post-Keynesians), and which Ingham himself consistently and sometimes forcefully rejects (e. g., Ingham 2006: 266).

2 The Myth of Community Debt

In the following chapter I propose what I see as a more perspicacious move: to push past Ingham's claim here and instead to make a stronger, but still *negative* argument – namely, that ontologically we can never securely draw the line between money and credit. At the level of ontology there are not two entities, *money* and *credit*, but only *money-credit*.

To build up the underlayment for that argument, however, I first need to address – in this section and the next – the deeper reason why Ingham hangs on to a weak form of the distinction in the first place, and to show why both Ingham's sociological account and Wray's post-Keynesian, chartalist project repeat (in much more modest form) some of the same errors as the commodity theory of money. Faced with the absence of money's intrinsic value (as a commodity with use-value), both authors (more or less subtly) smuggle in a conception of positive value that rests on society or the state. By refusing to accept that *money has no value*, each ends up with an account that tries (but always necessarily fails) to ground money – that is, relations of credit/debt – in something larger or deeper. Wray and Ingham both wish to identify an independent source for money's existence (at the least) or perhaps even for its value (at the most). This move is directly tethered to, and expressed in, their commitment to some form of money/credit distinction. We can illuminate this phenomenon by first surveying the wide swath of Ingham's writings.

In positing a money/credit distinction, Ingham relies heavily on the sociology of Simmel, whose major work, *The Philosophy of Money* (2004 [1907]), appeared just two years after the ur-source for Wray's work – namely Knapp's *The State Theory of Money* (1924 [1905]). Over the course of his nearly thirty years of writings on money, Ingham has quoted one key passage of Simmel's work at least ten different times. Indeed, on a minimum of seven different occasions, Ingham quotes this passage at length (offset from the main text), and he always does so at a pivotal moment in his argument, because the Simmel quote is meant to provide the sociological grounding for a theory of money that Ingham always (rightly) sees as lacking in most economic accounts.

More importantly for our purposes, Ingham usually turns to this quote from Simmel in an effort to explain the money/credit relation or distinction. In earlier writings Ingham uses the quote to reject the distinction entirely (Ingham 1996:

525 – 26; Ingham 2006: 266 – 67). In later work Ingham uses Simmel to explain and justify the claim that not all credit is money. Here is the passage in full:

> [In a monetary system] the pivotal point in the interaction between the two parties recedes from the direct line of contact between them, and moves to the relationship which each of them … has with the economic community that accepts money. This is the core of the truth that *money is only a claim upon society.* Money appears so to speak as a bill of exchange from which the drawee is lacking. … It has been argued against this … that credit creates a liability, whereas metallic money payment liquidates any liability; but this argument over-looks the fact [that] … [t]he liquidation of every private obligation by money means that *the community now assumes this obligation to the creditor.* (Simmel 2004: 177; Ingham 2012: 128, text in brackets Ingham's, emphasis mine)[5]

Ingham's first essay on money provides the best context to begin unpacking this passage; it shows lucidly why he originally turns to Simmel to provide a richer so-ciological alternative to the exceedingly thin classical and neoclassical economic explanation of money as deriving functionally from a "natural" state of barter. Like all state-of-nature theories, the commodity theory of money proves thorough-ly *asocial* precisely because it derives "money" from, but also *within*, a pre-social (pre-political, pre-historical) state of affairs. Following the earlier lead of John Locke, both Smith and Ricardo assume that individuals in a state of nature will simply "agree" to the use of money. Menger's theory of money as the most "sale-able commodity" or Jevons's description of "the system of exchange, being one of perfected barter" merely augment and (perhaps) refine those early, crude argu-

---

5 The passage is also quoted at length in Ingham 1996: 526; Ingham 2000: 23; Ingham 2004b: 178; Ingham 2006: 266 – 67; Ingham 2020: 10; Ingham, forthcoming. It is quoted less fully in Ingham 2004a: 64; Ingham 2001: 319; Ingham 2018: 846. The quote in my main text above is the longest sin-gle version Ingham ever offers, but in an earlier essay (2000) he begins the quote later in the pas-sage and extends it for another nine lines. This is not the place to conduct an extended critique of Simmel, but it can be useful to note the incompatibility between the claims he makes here and the credit theory of money I am articulating. Describing the historical shift of a society toward a de-veloped monetary system, Simmel refers to "the community that accepts money" and paints a pic-ture of money as "a bill of exchange from which the drawee is lacking." My version of credit theory responds as follows. First, "the community" is never the one that *accepts* money. Speaking broadly and historically, we might say that some societies *use* money more than others, but the "accept-ance" of money in any such society can only ever be the acceptance by specific entities (individ-uals, households, firms, agencies, governments). Second, a bill of exchange with no drawee is like a check written without a bank; it is like a note or coin without an issuer – a credit without a debtor. This concise concept is nonsensical. A credit without a debtor is nothing at all. As I show below, the only way in which money could circulate as credit without a debtor is if the tokens themselves were somehow imbued with intrinsic value. For my own discussion of bills of ex-change, see Chapter 7.

ments (Menger 2009: 36; Jevons 2011: 31). These accounts make possible a perspicacious view of what Ingham means by "private" and "bilateral": the neoclassical
commodity theory purports to account for money in just these terms. And in his
1996 essay, Ingham directly contrasts Simmel with "Alfred Marshall's schoolyard
barter" (Ingham 1996: 525).

This context helps to clarify how it is possible that Ingham can read the Simmel quote as both undermining the money/credit distinction, and as expressing a
new version of it. On the one hand, if the point is to challenge a metallist theory of
money that asserts intrinsic value (as opposed to credit, a mere promise to pay),
then Simmel demonstrates that metallic money itself symbolizes at once a claim
(a credit) and an obligation (a debt). As Simmel puts it a few lines later, "Metallic
money is also a promise to pay" (Simmel 2004: 177; quoted in Ingham 1996: 526).
Hence Ingham's early conclusion that all forms of money "are essentially social,
and the conventional economic distinction between 'money' and 'credit' can
only obscure this principle" (Ingham 1996: 526–27).

On the other hand, if money depends on society, then strictly private, bilateral
credit relations would not be money. Despite quoting it so often, I wonder if Ingham has fully considered the strengths of Simmel's claims: the arguments in
this passage extend far beyond the anti-metallist critique for which Ingham initially uses them. Simmel argues not just that money (as claim or credit) entails complex relations between multiple parties, involving a wide range of practices, across
various social, political, and economic institutions. Rather, he goes much further to
assert that money is itself a *claim on society.* The implication appears to be that
with the appearance of fully circulating public monies, the credit/debt relations
of money become relations between the individual and the social totality. Making
this move is the only way to render coherent Simmel's claim that to hold money is
to hold a credit on (or against) *society,* and that "the community" itself "assumes
this obligation to the creditor" (Simmel 2004: 177). The argument surely supports
Ingham's later conclusions: within this framework, an IOU from my neighbor is
merely a credit on one individual, while money must be a special credit held
against the entire community; hence not all credit is money.

This brings us finally to the crux of the problem: in Simmel's account money is
not a particular quality of credit but a *unique kind;* in his own words, money is a
credit on society, a symbol of the community's obligation to the individual creditor.[6] At some point this line of argument ceases to be an account of money and

---

6 In the very different context of contemporary French sociology, Aglietta echoes this language:
"Money is the means by which society gives back to each of its members what it judges each of
them to have given to it" (Aglietta 2018: 65).

becomes a theory of society. Or, put differently, it takes a theory of social order and subsumes money within it: a society is defined by bonds of mutual obligation, and money is merely epiphenomenal. Again, if one seeks a source for the distinction between bilateral and multilateral relations, Simmel surely fits the bill. Yet, in terms of a theory of money, Ingham's otherwise impressive work is weakened, I think, by his over-reliance on Simmel's claims, which cannot not bear the weight of closer scrutiny.[7] The basic difficulty is that while the complex social relations of credit/debt, which are money, certainly depend on many other elements of the social order – norms of reciprocity and trust, expectations about the moral obligations of debt, patterns of exchange and distribution – these relations are not equivalent to, nor does their existence support, the significant suggestion that money is a claim on the entire community, on society.[8] That latter argument will not hold.

Money is always and only a claim on a debtor. Contra Simmel, the drawee on the bill of exchange (similar to the bank name on the check) must always be present. Without the drawee, the credit is not a "credit" because it is not a debt (because there is no debtor). The debtor can take many forms: an individual, a firm, a community organization, a sovereign nation-state, an international organization. But the debtor is always specifiable as such. The debtor is never "the community" or "society" writ large.[9] A claim on everyone would not be a *credit* at all, and any credit only remains a credit in light of the specific liquidity and solvency of the particular debtor. The difference between an IOU from my neighbor and a $20 bill is neither equivalent nor reducible to the difference between a credit against an individual and a credit against society. The credit I hold in the form of the $20 bill is not a claim against the community or its individual members; society is not my debtor. No, the $20 bill is quite clearly, explicitly, and in a certain sense *narrow-*

---

7 The fact that the key Simmel quote forces Ingham into changing his mind on money/credit already provides readers a clue that there is something amiss here.

8 In his essay in the edited volume devoted to Innes, Ingham sets up his favorite Simmel quote by suggesting that Innes "would have agreed with his contemporary, the sociologist Georg Simmel" (Ingham 2004b: 178). And in his recent book, Ingham weaves the famous Simmel quote directly into a paragraph that begins with Innes (Ingham 2020: 10). My arguments in this section, combined with my reading of Innes in the preceding chapter, indicate the extent to which such presentations subtly misrepresent Innes in limiting ways.

9 Ingham argues that "a money transaction differs from barter in that the burden of trust is removed from the participants in the actual transaction and placed on a third party – the issuer of money" (Ingham 2004a: 72). This is a valid distinction, but it only goes so far. And it certainly does not produce a qualitative difference – first, because the participants still must trust that the exchanged pay-tokens and goods are not fraudulent (just as they would in "barter"), and second, because whether I accept an IOU or cash from my neighbor, my "trust" is still *trust in the debtor.* Only the identity of the debtor has changed. For further discussion of trust, see Chapter 5.

ly a claim on the US Federal Reserve banking system, a claim itself supported by the United States Treasury and ultimately backed by the US government.[10]

We should assess the Fed as our debtor the same way we would assess any other debtor – in terms of solvency and liquidity. Regarding solvency, first we consider the Fed's link to the US Treasury, then we take into account the US government's monumentally significant power to tax, a power that enables them to render any citizen *their debtor* (a debtor to the US government). In crude terms, we could only imagine an insolvent Fed in the context of an insolvent US government.[11] When considering the Fed's liquidity, we note its power to generate central bank reserves instantaneously.

These facts make the Fed, other things being equal, a much better debtor to have – a much better entity against which to hold our credits, i.e., money. But it does not change the fact that the Fed is a debtor: perhaps unlike any other in some ways, but very much the same in most respects. The quality of my credit thus depends on the solvency and liquidity of the Fed[12] as a central bank.[13] Therefore my neighbor's obligation to the US government (in the form of her tax burden) must not be conflated with either her obligation to me (in the form of the IOU I hold against her) or the Fed's obligation to me (in the form of the $20 bill). In no case do we render tenable or even intelligible (other than in a vague and amor-

---

10 Discussions of money and the nature of debt typically assume that national currencies (coins and notes) are direct debts of national governments. That is, a £5 note is the debt of the United Kingdom, while a $20 bill is the debt of the United States. But that's not actually true. These national currencies are *bank money*, debts of the Bank of England and the US Federal Reserve, respectively. Yes, because those banks have direct support from their national treasuries, the notes are *effectively* debts of the national government, but the difference matters for both conceptual and practical reasons. Practically, US Treasury bonds (which are *direct* debt instruments of the US government) have a massively important role to play in money markets, especially when compared to Federal Reserve notes (see Chapter 6), and conceptually, we underscore here again the significance of bank money. The primary example of "state money" is nothing less than another form of bank money.

11 Given their taxation power, government insolvency usually goes beyond the balance sheet to include a crisis of legitimacy or power, but in the text I narrow the analysis to money terms.

12 Debts owed in sovereign-denominated monies are a special case in which liquidity concerns appear to be beside the point. As MMT frequently proclaims: the US government can always create US-dollar reserves at the click of a mouse. Nonetheless, government solvency remains a relevant concern because a government – like any other debtor – can always default. Moreover, some advocates of MMT tend to forget that most governments also owe debts denominated in foreign moneys of account. Under such circumstances the liquidity constraint is real.

13 It is worth noting that the US Federal Reserve is a banking *system*, not a single institution; that system nevertheless acts like a central bank.

2 The Myth of Community Debt —— **97**

phous way) the assertion that money is a claim on society. Simmel has merely hypostatized this "community obligation."

The problem described above might well be understood as an overreaction to economists' Robinsonades. Neoclassical economics rests on a theoretical foundation in which "economics" precedes "society." Exchange, trade, and money all emerge in a pre-social state of nature. In this framework, "man" is *homo economicus*, and it is he who founds – who literally creates through willful consent and contract – society (the gendered language belongs to the neoclassical scheme). In this context we can see that sociological accounts[14] such as Simmel's only invert this framework, offering a theory of society that develops the institution of money – including the concept of money of account and a system of valuation – organically, and separately from (if not prior to) economic exchange. In this counternarrative, the human being is a social animal but not an economic animal; society itself founds economics.

Ingham reaches for Simmel's thick sociological account of community obligations as an alternative to the neoclassical economists' myth of barter. He finds there a far superior theory of society, but a still inadequate theory of money. Both points must be emphasized. First, a Robinsonade is a fantasy, a mythical tale that certain societies tell, but it cannot even begin to be a theory of society. Simmel poses the question of society's very existence, and his response surely provides a deeper and more rigorous theory of society than any state-of-nature tale ever could. Second, I have a much narrower and sharper point: a theory of money cannot be *derived* from a theory of society, even if the theory of society is a very good one. I am not offering (and do not mean to imply) a critique of either Simmel's (or Ingham's) theory of society, which I would surely choose over a state-of-nature theory. But I am providing a critique of his theory of money, which I contend suffers precisely because it remains contained within, as a derivation of, that social theory.[15]

---

14 Another, quite powerful way of reading Simmel has been suggested to me by John Seery. On this take, Simmel's most salient point is neither "economic" nor "sociological" but philosophical – namely, as Seery puts it, that "capitalism turns *everyone* into a philosopher" (pers. comm.). In other words, all agents under capitalism must, to some degree or another, engage in the metaphysics of money and commodities most famously presented by Marx in volume I, chapter 1 of *Capital.*
15 Arguably my theory of money presupposes some sort of theory of society or social order, at least to the extent that I eschew Simmel's question, "How does society exist?" (For my own set of arguments on this topic, see Chambers 2014.) Thanks to Geoff Ingham for provocation and insights regarding Simmel.

3 Origin Stories: From Barter to *Wergeld* and Chartalism

The roots of this issue run deeper, and in tracing them we can again *link* Ingham and Wray and *contrast* their accounts with a deeper credit theory. Although they develop them in distinct ways, both Ingham and Wray proffer alternatives to the neoclassical narrative of barter as leading to the development of commodity money. Ingham turns to *wergeld* ("worth payment" or "blood money") – historical practices in which compensation was paid to the family of someone killed or injured – while Wray calls on ancient tax levies and the putative power of the state to declare a money of account (along with his own, thinner account of wergeld). I will show that across differences in both historical detail and the scholarly sources upon which they rely, these arguments insist on the possibility of the development of money *before* or *outside* economic exchange. They thereby smuggle in an untenable conception of money as positive value.

In London in 1970, Philip Grierson, the Cambridge University historian and numismatist, delivered the Creighton Lecture in History titled "The Origins of Money."[16] The text plays a singular role in Ingham's writings, as Grierson contributes *the* alternative source for the *concept of money*.[17] Grierson quickly surveys some of the examples (all European) of wergeld, including the minutely detailed and elaborate system of offenses and payouts, but the essential line reads as follows: "The conditions under which these laws were put together would appear to satisfy much better than the market mechanism, the prerequisites for the establishment of a monetary system" (Grierson 1978: 13).[18] The central idea here is that if we set out the theoretical "requirements" for an abstract money of account, wergeld seems more likely than *barter* to provide the historical explanation. As a hypothetical, that might well be true, but it's not much of a comparison since it pits history against *fiction*. Whatever else we might say about wergeld systems (and I remain skeptical that they tell us much at all), there can be no doubt that wergeld practices were real historical events, while the idea of pre-monetary societies with internal systems of barter has been repeatedly proven false.

---

16 In 1977 the lecture was published as a short standalone book by Athlone Press, and the next year it served as the lead article in the inaugural issue of the journal *Research in Economic Anthropology*.

17 Ingham typically follows Keynes in thinking that the primary "concept" of money is money of account. I have marked my distance from this notion in Chapters 1 and 3.

18 This passage is also quoted in Ingham 1996: 519; Ingham 2000: 25; Ingham 2004a: 91; Ingham 2012: 124.

The bogus comparison leads Grierson to conflate the mythical idea of "barter" with a distinct economic conception of "the market." We observe this starkly in his closing lines (which Ingham cites repeatedly): "Behind the specific phenomenon of coin is the more general phenomenon of money, the origins of which are not to be sought in the market but in a much earlier stage in communal development, when worth and wergeld were interchangeable terms" (Grierson 1978: 23; cited in Ingham 1996: 518–19; Ingham 2000: 36; Ingham 2004b: 163.). The logic here is faulty: just because money's origins do not lie in barter does not prove that money antedates "the market," at least if we take that term in a general sense as pointing to economic activity, to economic interactions and exchanges broadly conceived.[19] Indeed, within a model in which all money is credit (an idea Ingham himself consistently affirms), it makes no sense at all to suggest that we could have money relations that were separable from or prior to economic relations.

Yet Ingham flirts with just such a notion, and Wray positively embraces it. Each author in his own way tells a story in which money comes into being not just as a series of social relations but as a societal *institution* – an institution prior to and separable from economic forces and relations (Ingham 1996: 516; Ingham 2000: 26; Wray 2004: 245). Ingham draws this conclusion directly from Grierson, whom he takes as providing "very good theoretical grounds for arguing that the idea of money – that is to say, its logical origins as the social practice of accounting for value – originated outside the market" (Ingham 2000: 26). Elsewhere Ingham defines money as "constituted by social relations that exist independently of the production and exchange of commodities" (Ingham 2004c: 25). Here again, if the point is merely to refute the silly-yet-dangerous claims of neoclassical economics – which purports to found all social orders on primary economic forces – by insisting that money as credit/debt remains intimately intertwined with social, cultural, and political forces and relations, then obviously the claim can only be met with our assent. But Ingham's formulation seems much stronger than all this, and we must resist resolutely the notion that money is *constituted* by strictly *non-economic* relations. Doubtless the economic can never be isolated from society. Nevertheless, and at the very same time, monetary relations can never be generated and maintained independently from relations of exchange, production, distribution, and consumption (i.e., economic relations).

For his part, while Wray does cite Grierson and mention wergeld practices (Wray 1998: 49), he develops his own particular line of argument for the origins

---

19 If we interpret "the market" in strict historical and etymological terms, then we must admit that it was not invented until sometime in the early twentieth century, and therefore the list of things that antedate the market grows very long indeed (Rebrovick 2016).

of money. Unfortunately it goes even further than Ingham in propagating this untenable idea of money before the economic. Ultimately Wray roots the origins of money in the power and declarations of the state (this is the core idea of chartalism). Like Ingham, Wray takes as his point of departure an argument against the standard, neoclassical account, and like Ingham, his critique ultimately inverts its target. For Wray, money's origins lie entirely with the power of the state; he therefore bases his overall conception on the foundations of Knapp's state theory. The core claim here is best expressed in the opening line of Knapp's book: "Money is a creature of the law" (Knapp 1924: 1).[20]

As I made clear in the previous chapter, starting with Knapp proves problematic for many reasons, most of all because Knapp himself hardly questions the standard neoclassical narrative in which commodity money develops organically from barter practices. Knapp makes no effort to provide an alternative origin story for money, remaining perfectly content to work with the orthodoxy of his day.[21] Because he bases his account on Knapp's framework, Wray must graft onto it a distinct account of money's development. To do so, Wray follows Keynes in asserting that money of account must be primary, and that money of account can only be established by the state. The following are representative quotes:

> The state announces the money unit and may define its value.
> (Wray 1998: 49.)[22]

---

20 As a properly trained late twentieth-century economist, and a student of Minsky, Wray draws his primary intellectual and scholarly sources mainly from the very same neoclassical paradigm that he otherwise challenges. Wray therefore cites Lerner, who himself – in a line that truly gets at the essence of Wray's own approach – merely paraphrases Knapp as follows: "Money is a creature of the state" (Lerner 1947: 313; cited in Wray 2000: 58). Here it is worth noting that Wray repeatedly contends his argument does not hinge on legal-tender laws. In this context he also claims (falsely) that Schumpeter's critique focuses narrowly on such laws. When I say Wray rests his argument on Knapp's fundamental idea, I do not mean the narrow notion of legal-tender law. Rather, law for Knapp is but one example of the declaration and expression of *state power*. State taxing power, state monopoly of violence – these are Knapp's sources for money's existence and value. And they are Wray's as well. All of this explains how Wray gets from Knapp's famous line "creature of law" to the phrase quoted in Lerner above, "creature of the state" – a move that almost seems like an invisible edit or quiet translation. But the problem is the same in both instances, and Schumpeter's critique cuts to the heart of Knapp's claims about determinative state power. (Legal-tender laws are a red herring.)

21 This is not to say that the resources for such an alternative story cannot be found in the history of theories of money. Quite the contrary, in his *The Closed Commercial State*, Johann Gottlieb Fichte builds an account of what Stefan Eich calls "pure fiat money"; Fichte develops a money narrative with no basis in metallism (Fichte 2012 [1800]; Eich 2022: 77).

22 Wray's line paraphrases Knapp: "A proclamation is made that a piece of such and such a description shall be valid as so many units of value" (Knapp 1924: 30; quoted in Wray 2014: 5).

The state defines money. (Wray 2014: 18)
The state defines money as that which it accepts at public pay offices, mainly in payment of taxes. (Wray 2000: 48; cf. Wray 2012: 24)
The state determines the nominal value of money. (Wray 2000: 56)

In other words money (as money of account) can *only* be brought into being through the actions of a significant, central power.[23] Barter cannot create money – only the state can. This distinct account of money's origins leads Wray to conclude, even more forcefully than Ingham, that money somehow comes "before economics." Presented, ironically, in the midst of his reading of Innes,[24] Wray puts the point this way: "Once the state has created the unit of account and named that which can be delivered to fulfill obligations to the state, it has generated the necessary preconditions for development of markets" (Wray 2004: 245).[25] Where neoclassical economics locates the source of money in markets (modeled as the inevi-

---

23 This narrowly focused approach overlaps or aligns at times with the argument from Simmel drawn on by Ingham because it leads Wray to conclude that money is a "social institution," by which he means not merely that money relations are overdetermined by other social relations but that there is something substantive and "sticky" (my word) about money as a singular *institution*. Wray explicitly compares money with language, suggesting that money gets its value the way language gets its meaning (Wray 2004: 231). To simplify the response I develop in the text, we might say that while society itself may be formed by all sorts of institutions of trust and reciprocity, and while the ultimate viability of money may even be linked to those institutions, money is not an "institution" in any meaningful sense. In an otherwise penetrating analysis of the logic of speculation, Konings sometimes flattens money into an institution in the sense described here. He puts the point this way: "Money functions as one of the most unambiguous norms and predictable sources of control that we have in modern life, a uniquely objective fact, the social institution that we have least reason to question" (Konings 2018: 55). This claim, I suggest, says more about a certain societal self-understanding of "the money institution" than it does about either the ontology of money (which is always credit/debt, and therefore never an objective fact) or about the concrete money practices or movements of money markets (where traders almost never forget the riskiness and precariousness of all money).
24 In this same context, and apparently as an interpretation of Innes, Wray suggests that "the market, then, is not viewed as the place where goods are exchanged, but rather as a clearing house for debts and credits" (Wray 2004: 239). This, however, is a backward reading of Innes, who (as discussed in the previous chapter) redefines a sale as the exchange of money for *goods*. Wray has confused historically concrete *"fairs"* (the word Innes uses), which served as clearing sites for credit and debt, with the generic economic idea of "the market." It is true that monies can sometimes be swapped without the presence of goods, but those very swaps (clearing houses) themselves presuppose the existence of money, which does not arise through them.
25 Wray sometimes goes further and suggests that the state itself can determine the *value* of money (e. g., Wray 2000: 56). There is no space to address this claim in detail, but following Schumpeter, and consistent with my own theory, I do reject it entirely (see Schumpeter 1954: 1056).

table interactive creations of *homines economici*), Wray sees the state as the ur-source of money, which itself comes before and grounds "the market."

The fatal flaw in these accounts is that they attempt to meet the standard narrative of the discipline of economics on its own terms – that is, they seek to substitute a new theory of positive, intrinsic value for the old one. If wergeld systems or state proclamations *establish* money and its value, then we have achieved through societal explanations what orthodox theories sought to construct through the myth of barter. However, the problem with the neoclassical account – whereby the barter of goods leads naturally to a commodity theory of money – was never just *how* it arrives at positive, intrinsic value, but *that* it does. Tacitly, and surely unintentionally, Wray and (to a certain extent or at certain times) Ingham both replace the commodity "backing" for money's value with community or state "backing." The pure orthodox theory of money (A1x) has persisted for so long because it tells a comforting tale: it insists that money is *real*, that it has *positive value*, and that to hold money is to possess value directly. Wray and Ingham rightly refute the false logic and bad history of these types of theories, but they refuse to peer into the abyss[26] – to see that money has no depths, no value at all. We therefore witness in both of their cases an illicit positing of community obligations or state power as a kind of "backing" or support for money. This move serves to fill the void created when the theory of money as commodity with intrinsic value is rightly rejected. But the void cannot be filled.

Contrasting their accounts with my own development of Innes in the previous chapter, we can now observe that both Wray and Ingham – the closest readers of Innes we have to date – have both missed some of the insights to be found in or developed out of his work. Innes's account of the history of coinage repeatedly returns to the same conclusion: money is never "backed" by anything at all since money is only ever credit/debt.[27] If we think money is positive value, then we wind up having to admit there is no money, only ever promises to pay, along with actual clearances of debt or creations of credit. Understood radically as cred-

---

26 To be fair, Ingham does repeatedly look down, but he also frequently turns away.

27 We must distinguish between the idea rejected here, that all credit instruments are "backed" by commodities of positive, intrinsic value, with the separate but related question of the solvency and liquidity of the debtor. My bank does not hold gold bars in a one-to-one ratio with my deposits. But my bank does have assets (which theoretically could include commodities) that exist in some proportion to my deposits (which are liabilities for the bank). The bogus idea of *backing* – including the elision of the difference between "commodity money" (a myth) and commodities as assets on the balance sheets of financial institutions (a not uncommon practice) – has played a central role in the rise and fall of crypto. For more, see Chapter 7.

it/debt, money needs no backing because *money has no value.*[28] We do not seek "truer" money; rather, we seek higher-quality credits, which means we seek the most solvent, liquid, trustworthy, stable, and reliable debtors, against whom to hold our credits.

The best alternative to the myth of barter and its attendant origin story is in some sense no alternative at all. In order to understand money today, we must reject the specific barter origin story while also refusing the general requirement that we provide such an origin story in the first place.[29] Here Graeber's work offers a tonic, as he illustrates the point lucidly, simply, and somewhat humorously. Early in his book, Graeber quotes a representative example from an economics textbook. The text tells a simple tale of two people, Joshua and Henry, each of whom owns one good and wants another, but neither of whom wants what the other has (Stiglitz and Driffill 2000: 521; Graeber 2011: 23–24). This lack of a "mutual coincidence of wants" is meant to be the determinative defect of the mythical "barter system," a defect whose existence inevitably leads to the invention of money as the solution to this "problem."

A different way of describing what I see as the limitations of Ingham's and Wray's respective turns to the community, society, or the state as the foundation of money would be to say that they leave far too much of the barter myth intact (as Knapp himself explicitly did). By insisting that money is created prior to and independently from "the market," their narratives problematically suggest that economic relations are a late addition to a social order.[30] But what if money rela-

---

28 This conclusion can, of course, be reached without going through Innes. In Chapter 2 I quoted from Schumpeter's early essay, in which he defends the thesis that "money can never have value of its own" (Schumpeter 1956: 161). Here again we can also call on the work of Cencini, who argues the point directly: "The physical qualities of material used as money are totally irrelevant precisely because money cannot be identified with its physical substratum. *In itself, money has no value at all*" (Cencini 1988: 12, emphasis added). Finally, while defending this claim requires greater exegetical and hermeneutic work than I can here provide, in another context I would argue that Marx too grasped the same point: for him, money is the necessary form in which value must appear within a capitalist social order, but money is not itself value, nor does money *have* value.

29 It is plausible to read Hawtrey as taking such an approach. In his opening chapter he suggests that rather than imagining a state of nature with no social or economic development, and only then trying to tell a logical story about money's emergence from barter, we ought instead to imagine an advanced capitalist society *just as it is, only without the presence of money.* Hawtrey then proceeds to show, à la Macleod, that all of advanced economic activity can go on just fine as long as there are dealers in credit. There is no need for "money" in the sense of gold with metallic value, i. e., Menger's most saleable commodity (Hawtrey 1919: 1–16).

30 Sgambati has recently issued a similar critique of the strand of money theory that he calls "nominalism." Specifically, Sgambati contends that Ingham goes awry in making moneyness both "logically anterior and historically prior" to "the market" (Ingham 2004a: 25). According to

tions, which are nothing other than social relations of credit/debt, are inseparable from economic relations?

To pose this question is absolutely not to revert to a notion of "the economic" as the prior and natural ground for money's origin. Rather, it is to suggest that economic and social relations are always intertwined. We therefore need not posit an "origin" for money any more than we must posit an "origin" for society. Human beings have always lived in social orders of some sort. But if we must, for heuristic purposes, think our way through the problem of money's creation, we can tell a simpler, more logically powerful and compelling tale than either the myth of barter or the narrative of community obligation. Here's how Graeber narrates that story as an alternative to the economics textbooks:

> How could ... money come about? Let us return to the economics professors' imaginary town. Say, for example, that Joshua were to give his shoes to Henry, and, rather than Henry owing him a favor, Henry promises him something of equivalent value. Henry gives Joshua an IOU. Joshua could wait for Henry to have something useful, and then redeem it. In that case Henry would rip up the IOU and the story would be over. But say Joshua were to pass the IOU on to a third party – Sheila – to whom he owes something else. He could tick it off against his debt to a fourth party, Lola – now Henry will owe that amount to her. Hence is money born. Because there's no logical end to it. Say Sheila now wishes to acquire a pair of shoes from Edith; she can just hand Edith the IOU, and assure her that Henry is good for it. In principle, there's no reason that the IOU could not continue circulating around town for years – provided people continue to have faith in Henry. (Graeber 2011: 46–47)

This is not a substitute for detailed historical work on the emergence and transformations of money over time. But it captures a great deal more about the nature of money (as credit) than Simmel's notion of money as community obligation or Knapp's concept of money as state declaration. Graeber's story can be read as a playful elaboration of Innes's succinct (re)formulation of a sale as the exchange of goods for credit.

Crucially, Graeber's account – one that, as he goes on to show in his review of various anthropological accounts, squares with actual historical events – answers

---

Sgambati, Ingham wrongly "enforces an ontological separation between money and states" (Sgambati 2020: 422). Clearly I share this specific concern of Sgambati. However, I do not sign on to his Keynesian critique of nominalism. To my eyes, that argument goes off the rails because it rests too much weight on Keynes's notion of "liquidity preference," one of Keynes's weaker concepts, especially as mobilized in IS/LM theory. Briefly, Keynes deploys a sharp distinction between, on the one hand, "cash," which both earns no interest and is "riskless," and "securities," which are risky and earn interest (Keynes 1936; Sgambati 202: 425–28). As I show in the chapters that follow, such a distinction cannot hold because it's wrong on both sides: cash can be risky and earn interest, while bonds are a form of money.

to Ingham's question concerning how we get from bilateral to multilateral transactions, and it does so without recourse to community obligations or proclamations by a state power. Indeed, we can see in Graeber's text that the hard distinction between bilateral and multilateral was never tenable: *all it takes to cross
between the two is for one party to a bilateral arrangement to offer credits to a
third party, who then accepts them.* Innes documents such historical practices in
great detail in the form of the medieval use of tally sticks, which, while eventually
accepted by the state, were certainly not originally *issued* by the state (Innes 1913:
394). Wray fairly underscores the former point, but he problematically underplays
the latter.

Again, Graeber's fanciful narrative is not itself a theory of money or a full explanation of money's historical or logical origins. A skeptical reader can raise
many questions. For example, how do we deal with the problem of a standard
money of account, i.e., in what units will the credits on Henry be denominated?
More to the point, how is the transition to a standard money of account and the
implementation of a full monetary system brought about? We should not roman-
ticize Graeber's lighthearted account, and we must insist that monetary systems
are not just willed into being by a small group of individuals. On the other
hand, despite Wray's claims to the contrary, monetary systems are also not decreed into being by the state. As Innes shows, moneys of account develop historically in complicated and dynamic ways, and the emergence of a standard usually
depends on a dialectical interplay between social practices, customs, and traditions, on the one hand, and state actions, interventions, and regulations, on the
other.[31]

Wray and Ingham find themselves trapped in the dilemma of trying (even if
unintentionally) to provide an alternative account for the commodity theory's conceptualization of economic exchange. In their efforts to resist the false and dangerous notion that economic exchange naturally produces money as its logical (and
historical) outcome, they turn to the community and the state to provide a prior

---

31 This means that the most plausible scenario for the emergence of a new money of account
would likely involve the circulation of a private money that was then taken over by or incorporat-
ed into state money – through legal-tender laws, taxation, or the like. Note also that if by "standard" we mean something like the *stability* of monetary value, then we must immediately
admit that even the most advanced forms of state money cannot *solve* such problems, because
there quite simply are no enduring standards. States cannot set or maintain the "value of
money" because money has no value. And any particular money's purchasing power (a rough an-
alogue for "value" but not reducible to it) will always vary relative to the purchasing power of
other credits, i.e., other forms of money. The IOU from Henry might trade at a discount (less
than "par" – its face value) but so might any other form of money (see Mehrling 2016: 13).

substantive ground. In so doing they fail to see what was carefully demonstrated in the previous chapter: a credit theory of money completely undermines that theoretical structure, while also providing an immediate alternative account of economic exchange – one that is, to the core, thoroughly monetary. To avoid these traps we have to take a leap into the abyss that most "heterodox" theories carefully avoid: we have to refuse any definitive distinction between money and credit.

Chapter Five
From Money/Credit to Money-Credit

1 The Ontology of Credit

As we have seen over each of the previous two chapters, even the most apparently radical, "heterodox" theorists of money ultimately insist on maintaining the distinction so central to "orthodoxy" – namely, that between credit and money. The commodity theory asserts that credit is a mere *promise* to pay *actual* money; hence the two (credit and money) differ fundamentally in kind. Money is a commodity with intrinsic value; credit is a legal or social obligation. Therefore, ontologically money and credit are inherently incompatible. Wray's MMT purports to fully contest the commodity theory, yet he explicitly affirms the money/credit distinction, going out of his way to spurn the idea of a "pure" credit theory. Consistent with what Schumpeter calls a theoretical metallism, Wray insists that any tenable theory of money must maintain a place for "real" money. The case of Ingham proves far more complicated, as he first rejects but then later struggles to hold on to a money/credit distinction, albeit in a manner quite different from the traditional account.

In tracing Ingham's thought as he vacillates on this key issue, we further illuminate the contours of a thoroughgoing credit theory of money. We can start with the basic fact that, like Wray, Ingham also rejects entirely the orthodox account. Ingham consistently refutes any and all commodity theories of money, arguing instead that money in its "specific nature … is a token credit denominated in money of account"; for just this reason, money must be "ontologically distinguished" from commodities (Ingham 2018: 839, 844). At this stage, the argument maps out like this: for the commodity theory, money must be distinguished from credit because money and credit are different ontologically; for Ingham, ontologically, *money is credit*, and therefore distinct in its being from that of a commodity.

This raises the obvious question: If money is credit in its nature, how could we maintain a money/credit distinction (and why would we want to)? Ingham details an answer that emanates from his own extensive historical and sociological study of the emergence of capitalism. In the previous chapter I both quoted the takeaway line, "money is transferable credit," and glossed Ingham's basic argument: any credit can be created, held, and even repaid (destroyed), but not all credit can be transferred to and held by another party (or redeemed by them). Not all credit *circulates* (Ingham 2006: 267).

https://doi.org/10.1515/9783110760774-009

Ingham derives this argument from the key element in the story he tells about the emergence of capitalism: "It is the extensive *transferability* of debt and the creation of a hierarchy of acceptability that was crucially important in the development of the form of (circulating) credit money" (Ingham 2004b: 185, emphasis added). Ingham rightly insists that money can and has "undergone fundamental change during historical development" (2004b: 186). More succinctly, "Capitalism is founded on the social mechanism whereby private debts are 'monetized' in the banking system" (Ingham 2004a: 13; same line appears in Ingham 2004c: 26). Ingham traces this transformation to two key elements. First, bills of exchange begin to circulate widely, creating a commonly used "private money."[1] Second, a transformation occurs when sovereigns begin to borrow from their own merchant classes. These loans become "national debt," and the sovereigns' promise to repay forms "the basis for public credit money" (Ingham 2004b: 187). Money can be distinguished from credit, Ingham contends, because earlier historical forms of credit did not circulate (were not transferable) in the way that later forms of capitalist money do (and are).

Ingham remains quite clear that his defense of the money/credit distinction rests on, and even remains limited to, the historical register. He repeatedly sustains Innes's position that all money is credit, but supplements it with the assertion that "in order to understand the historical distinctiveness of capitalism, the admittedly confused distinction between money and credit should not be entirely abandoned" (Ingham 2004b: 213). He formulates the point concisely in his recent book: "All money is credit, but not all credit is money" (Ingham 2020: 41). I think we can best make sense of Ingham's desire to maintain the very distinction that he admits

---

1 Bills of exchange were arguably the most important money for most of the history of merchant capitalism, yet they were obviously *not* state money. Moreover, as I discuss in greater detail in Chapter 7, bills of exchange were very early derivatives; as such, they serve as stark evidence for the centrality of money markets to capitalism – from the very start. Ingham nicely underscores the importance of bills of exchange, and in his recent book he concisely and accurately describes them (Ingham 2020: 29; see Ingham 2015: 172–73). However, in earlier writings Ingham sometimes appears to mischaracterize bills as "*detachable* from any particularistic creditor-debtor relation" or as establishing money that is "anonymously transferable" (Ingham 2004b: 187, emphasis added; Ingham 2004a: 115). In these passages Ingham may mean only that as bills circulate more widely, the sphere of trust broadens, but at times he seems to echo Simmel's language about money as "a bill of exchange from which the drawee is lacking," and thereby to advocate the idea of *anonymous money* (Simmel 2004: 177). I thus feel the need to emphasize that such a concept is no more tenable historically (for Ingham) than it is theoretically (for Simmel). While the fact of "anonymous money" surely often *seems* to be true under capitalism, it is never in fact the case. Any and every example of money is a credit, and as such we can discern the debtor. Typically today the debtor is a bank or a central bank, but *there is never no debtor* at all. To hold a credit on an unknown debtor is not to hold a credit. Anonymous money is not money.

is confused by clarifying the difference between an ontological and an empirical approach to money. Innes's contention that all money is credit is an ontological argument (an argument about the being of money), one which Ingham supports, whereas Ingham's defense of a limited version of the money/credit distinction is an empirical claim (based on our observations of which credits circulate). As I show below: "transferability" *sounds like* an ontological concept, but as Ingham implements the idea, it serves only as an empirical definition.

The point can be thrown into clearer relief by returning once more to Innes:

> *Credit and credit alone is money.* Credit and not gold or silver is the one property which all men seek. … The word "credit" is generally technically defined as being the right to demand and sue for payment of a debt, and this no doubt is the legal aspect of a credit today; while we are so accustomed to paying a multitude of small purchases in coin that we have come to adopt the idea, fostered by the laws of legal tender, that the right to payment of a debt means the right to payment in coin or its equivalent. And further, owing to our modern systems of coinage, we have been led to the notion that payment in coin means payment in a certain weight of gold. Before we can understand the principles of commerce *we must wholly divest our minds of this false idea.* (Innes 1913: 392, emphasis added)

Innes was no philosopher, but throughout his two essays on money he develops the outlines of an ontology of money. Innes focuses primarily on the claim that *money is credit*, but here he indicates a significant second argument: *credit is all there is.* "Credit" provides the best answer to the question "What is money?" and when dealing with "the principles of commerce," we find nothing above or beyond credit.

Over the entire history Schumpeter covers, he sees but one or two thinkers who even dare to contemplate the notion of "the fundamental sameness" of all credit (Schumpeter 1954: 688; see Thornton 1802). But for Innes the point is plain: "A credit redeems a debt *and nothing else does*" (Innes 1914: 154, emphasis added). Innes refuses the money/credit distinction precisely because he sees money and credit as indistinguishable at the ontological level.[2] Again, most com-

---

2 I focus intently on Innes's writings here, for a number of reasons: his articles are some of the earliest to advance a credit theory of money; they are certainly the most lucid on the topic; and they are now well known by most interlocutors in today's money debates. However, I certainly do not mean to suggest that Innes was *alone* in pushing the case for money as credit (nor credit as money). As I noted in Chapter 3, Macleod's work appeared twenty-five years earlier. And Hawtrey, whose book appeared just six years after Innes's articles, makes a series of complementary arguments. On the particular topic of the credit/money distinction, for example, Hawtrey writes: "Credit and money are both equally media of exchange. Credit is often said to be a substitute for money. It would be just as accurate to say that money is a substitute for credit" (Hawtrey 1919: 15).

mentators on Innes come at this text from the perspective of his "theory of money," thus rightly reading him as defending the thesis that all money is credit. However, they rarely take heed of the other dimensions of the argument, and thus fail to note how far Innes truly pushes his case. Yet we need not read anything into Innes's text to see the ontological angle: *"All forms of money are identical in their nature"* (Innes 1914: 154, emphasis added). Innes was no fool; he was well aware, and indicates clearly to his readers, that not all forms of money (as credit) are the same; some credits are indeed much better than others. In practice we find that differences in forms of credit abound, but in terms of the nature of money, we can discern no differences at all. Here I am reading Innes not for his theory of money but for his *ontology of credit.*

I do so in order to link back to the key element in Ingham's defense of the money/credit distinction: transferability. The basic idea seems relatively straightforward: it names *the capacity to be transferred.* The entire point of the concept would be to determine if a credit has this capacity. Faced with a handful of credits, we sort them into two piles: the transferable credits have or partake of *transferability* – transferability is an aspect of their being; the non-transferable credits lack this aspect.

I contend that if we start with this simple framework, and then consider Innes's ontology of credit, we can only conclude that *every credit partakes of transferability* because every credit has the capacity, in the sense of latent *potential*, to be transferred. This is not to say that we can know in advance that a credit can or will transfer, but only to insist that we cannot know in advance that it will not or cannot. Any credit *might* be transferrable, though many (perhaps even most) will not actually transfer.

Ingham rightly shows that both historically, and in any given instance, some credits *actually* circulate and some do not. We can therefore make an empirical distinction between money and credit. We simply observe which credits circulate: those that do, meet the definition of money; those that do not, do not. But it would be illicit logically to conclude from this account that we can discern an *inherent* capacity for *transferability* in some credits and not in others. We cannot move from the empirical (ontic) fact that a particular credit has failed to circulate, to the ontological conclusion that such a credit permanently lacks the capacity for transferability – a capacity that some other credit (which does circulate) is taken to possess.[3] Just because I'm not currently swimming doesn't mean I can't swim.[4]

---

3 To make this move would be to assume that whether a credit circulates depends strictly on something intrinsic to the internal nature of the credit: only transferable credits (money) circulate,

2 Five Theses on Credit and Money

This argument now has a number of elements in play across multiple levels. To clarify, let me specify a series of theses, which I will then elucidate:[5]
1) Empirically and ontologically, all money is credit
2) Empirically, money is credit that circulates
   (credit that *is* transferred)
3) Ontologically,[6] all credit is *transferable*
   (might *potentially be* transferred)

---

while non-transferable credits (mere credit) do not. Below I demonstrate that this logic fails to capture the being of money, while also flying in the face of the history of money.

4 I use this metaphor as a rhetorical device – to try to drive home the basic point about transferability – not as a strictly formal analogy. That is, we might say that "transferability" is *unlike* "ability to swim" in that some human beings really cannot swim. Nevertheless, the primary point holds: we cannot tell who can swim and who cannot merely by observing who swam yesterday. Moreover, while at first it might seem theoretically possible to *test* for swimming ability, this too may prove impossible: some individuals who think they cannot swim (and would fail a basic test by refusing to get into the pool) might surprise themselves in an emergency situation, discovering an unknown ability to stay afloat; and some who would easily pass the pool test might panic in a crisis and drown. My metaphor here is not random, but rather a variation on the much older and well-established trope of *liquidity*. Modern bank stress tests are eerily like my example of the swimming test (with the same stark limitations). I discuss liquidity in more depth in Section 3 of this chapter.

5 My theses on money must be read in the context of the money array – creditor, debtor, and denominated token. The arguments of this section do not replace, but rather elaborate that wider project. Thus, for example, when I assert in Thesis 1 that "money is credit" this should not be understood as a new definition or theory of money, which would supplant my account of the money array. To the contrary, in the context of the broader theory, this thesis asserts that the *money stuff* is a token or symbol of credit, denominated in some money of account, held by a creditor as a claim on a debtor, while the name *money* describes this entire concatenation.

6 At this juncture I aim to raise ontological questions, in contrast to empirical questions – to consider the question of money's being, rather than stating facts about money things. The idea of posing ontological questions (concerning money) must be sharply distinguished from the project of developing a fundamental ontology. We do not need an ontology to ground the theory of money or to answer all of its questions. Rather, in developing that theory we can pose ontological questions, as well as historical, empirical, and other questions. In this section I go beyond the ontic to analyze money ontologically, but my theory is not an "ontology of money" – and these five theses must not be taken as derivations from a deeper ontology. In this I distinguish my project from Lawson, who makes social ontology fundamental. Lawson takes the being of money as *prior* to the question of its social positioning (Lawson 2016: 966). Regarding Lawson, I concur with Ingham's powerful response: "I cannot see how money as an anterior value can be securely established ontologically without recourse to a non-monetary theory of value" (Ingham 2018: 838). Wilkins and Dragos unintentionally affirm Ingham's critique when they favorably cite Lawson as support for their claim that "whatever is positioned as money must already have some form of value" (Wilkins

4) Ontologically, we cannot distinguish "money" from "credit";
   there is only one "substance" or thing – namely, *money-credit*
5) Ontologically and empirically, monies are always plural
   (there is a hierarchy of money)

Previous chapters have already made the case for Thesis 1 in detail (and it is not in dispute here). The foundations of the argument can be located in the prescient work of Innes, but many of the precepts are taken up and developed (if not fully embraced) by a variety of early twentieth-century writings (e.g., Macleod, Hawtrey, Schumpeter). Ingham, Wray, and other post-Keynesians regularly affirm this point even if they do not pursue it to its furthest conclusions.

Thesis 2 is my redescription of Ingham's defense of the money/credit distinction. Working within a credit theory of money, we can start with Ingham's definition of "transferable credit" and then *operationalize* that definition through empirical observation and categorization. That is, to make this conceptualization "robust," we need to gather data on which credits circulate and which do not – and then assess that data in some way. I affirm this basic thesis. But I insist that we circumscribe our understanding of it: "Money is credit that circulates" must be understood as an empirical claim, not at ontological one. To say money is transferable credit is to claim that we can know what is money and what is not by observing which credits circulate and which do not. If we weigh the (significant) bulk of Ingham's writings, we find that his only attestations of the money/credit distinction are backed by historical descriptions. Ingham has no ontological account that would differentiate money from credit, and like Innes, he refutes the commodity theory's bogus account (premised on the claim that money is a commodity while credit is not).

Nevertheless, nothing prevents us from exploring the following hypothetical, which we will call Thesis 2x: "Ontologically, money is transferable credit." This is little more than an ontological rendering of Thesis 2 (Ingham's thesis). The assertion seems plausible at first: if money in its being is *transferable* (has the capacity to be transferred), then Thesis 2x is valid. The problem is not that 2x is false but that it fails entirely to *distinguish* money from credit, as it says nothing about the ontology of credit vis-à-vis transferability. In other words, Thesis 2 entails a valid corollary: "Empirically, some credits do not circulate and therefore are not money." However, Thesis 2x cannot sustain its own corollary – "Ontologically, some credits

---

and Dragos 2022: 4). Moreover, in general terms, I reject this entire approach to money's "being" because for me the being of money cannot be understood apart from its "positioning," i.e., its dynamic historical becoming. I discuss this dialectical relation between theory and history in Chapter 1. Thanks to Rothin Datta and Ben Taylor for helpful discussion on this point.

are not transferable" – because there is no way to analyze the being of a credit and know in advance that it will not, cannot, circulate. This is why our third thesis (see below) directly refutes this corollary of Thesis 2x. Ultimately then, Thesis 2x proves empty, tautological; it describes an ontological feature of money but not one that distinguishes money from credit. Thesis 2 can only uphold a money/credit distinction if taken as a knowledge claim that we verify through historical or empirical examples.

Another way of expressing this crucial point would be to say that we can only ever distinguish money from credit post hoc. Money is credit that circulates in a particular way, but there is nothing in the nature of any specific credit that reveals *in advance* whether it will in fact circulate. And there is nothing in the nature of any specific money stuff that guarantees it will continue to circulate. My argument above may at first seem like nitpicking, but it turns out to have profound practical implications because, when we turn to the historical analysis and practical study of money and money markets (see Chapters 6 and 7), we find that what we call money is *never* guaranteed to circulate. Money that circulated yesterday may simply fail to circulate tomorrow; this is the nature of money.

This leads me to Thesis 3, the point at which my argument goes beyond any extant theory of money.[7] The core of the argument is straightforward: *ontologically*, all credits are *transferable* in the very literal sense that their being includes a *potential for transferability.*

Let me develop this thesis by starting with its ontological character. I loosely follow Heidegger in taking ontology as the inquiry into the being of beings, or as the study of being "itself." *Being is not a genus* (Heidegger 2000: 85). Being cannot be grasped as a *category* or *type* or *property* of an entity; those are all "ontic" descriptors – that is, "facts about things."[8] To ask after the being of a thing is not to find facts about its empirical existence but to pose the very question *of its existence.* For our limited purposes here in clarifying the ontology of money and credit, we can creatively appropriate Heidegger's notion of an "existential": an essential

---

7 The previous chapter showed that this move beyond the money/credit distinction proves a bridge too far for so-called heterodox money theorists. At the same time, I have also demonstrated that the effort to hold the line between money and credit leads even the most sophisticated and intelligent writers into a kind of cul-de-sac, sharing space with those theories on the matrix that see money as positive value. In trying to justify the money/credit distinction, they must resort to a hand-waving form of explanation in which money is an "institution" created and controlled outside of and before economic activity. In this chapter I deal only narrowly with the very best articulation of the money/credit distinction, in Ingham.

8 The phrase is a common gloss on ontic, drawn, it would seem, from a footnote in John Macquarrie and Edward Robinson's translation of Heidegger's *Being and Time* (1962: 31n3).

characteristic or feature of the being of an entity.[9] On the one hand, we can see that *transferability* (the capacity or potential to be transferred) is an existential of *all* credit. It is in the very nature of a credit as a relation of denominated debt between two parties that the holder of the debt *could try* to pass it on to a third party – and that third party *might accept it.* A credit that utterly refused this possibility would not be a credit at all.[10]

The argument for the existential of transferability as applying to all credits must be highly specified and narrowly circumscribed. My claim is not that we can know in advance that a credit will or definitively can circulate but that *we cannot know in advance that it cannot circulate* (hence my repeated use of "might" above). To say that transferability is an essential characteristic of any credit means that no credit can be ruled outside the bounds of possible transfer to another party. The fundamental nature of a credit is to remain permanently (potentially) transferable.

One might challenge my argument for transferability as an existential of all credit by pointing to the conditions of possibility for transferability itself. For example, a credit can only transfer if it is denominated in a recognizable money of account.[11] I have three responses to this line of argument. First, I readily affirm that some broader social conditions prove necessary for something like monetary circulation to be possible in the first place. This is one reason why I confine my

---

9 I say *creatively* appropriate here, just as I say *loosely* follow above, because I am drawing mainly on Heidegger's very idea of ontology, of the question of being (including its meaning). Most Heidegger commentary today still centers on his magnum opus, *Being and Time*, wherein Heidegger raises this question within the terms of the "ontological difference," the difference between Being and beings. Less attention is paid to the fact that in his later writings Heidegger argues quite directly that the proper approach to being is to go beyond or outside of the ontological difference (Heidegger 1972). Heidegger thereby indicts much of his earlier conceptual framework for tethering its account to *Dasein* – Heidegger's novel reformulation of "man" or the human subject as "there-being." The term "existential" comes from the framework of *Being and Time* and thus applies strictly only to Dasein, not to other entities. I am therefore intentionally misusing the term when I invoke it for the case of money, but in so doing I am also taking my cues from the later Heidegger, who insists that ontological questions be posed outside a framework of the human. Under the technical terms advanced in *Being and Time*, the determinations of the being of all entities that are not Dasein would be restricted to the rubric "categories." However, Heidegger himself does not develop such a rubric in *Being and Time*, and in his widely read lectures on metaphysics (published the year before *Sein und Zeit*), he explicitly reserves the concept "category" for the history of metaphysics that he hoped to escape (Heidegger 2000: 202).

10 We could imagine a contractual obligation that legally precluded transfer; perhaps we could call this a debt contract, but not a credit.

11 Sincere thanks to Geoff Ingham for pressing me on this point and for advancing the counterargument I address here.

arguments to capitalist social orders, which are precisely monetary social orders. Second, however, while those broad conditions might tell us whether something like "credit transferability" is even possible in a particular social order, they do not enable us to distinguish transferable credits from non-transferable credits (within that monetary order). Put differently, inquiring into the conditions of possibility for the existential of transferability might underwrite a distinction between monetary and non-monetary societies, but it will not support a money/credit distinction.

Third, and most importantly, on closer scrutiny it again proves impossible, ontologically, to isolate these supposedly "prior" conditions – that is, to render them properly *prior*. Even "money of account" will not hold up as a supposed prior condition to determine the existential of transferability, and for a very important reason. Undoubtedly a credit proves more likely to circulate if denominated in a recognizable money of account, but at the same time it is precisely the circulation of credits that can bring about a *new* money of account. Say we have three different credits in front of us: one for 10 "dollars," one for 20 "tethers," and one for 2 "stoats." The denominated money of account for the last credit, stoats, sounds ridiculous, and we might rightly assume it has very little chance of circulating. Nevertheless, there is no way to know in advance that credits denominated in stoats will not transfer to third parties. After all, just a few years ago we would have reacted the same way to tethers as we now react to stoats. And yet, over the course of 2022 between $64 billion and $85 billion worth of Tether bank money, putatively denominated in tether, *circulated*.[12] The paradoxical temporality of money-credit, in which the fact of circulating helps to establish the conditions that would seem to make circulation possible to begin with, helps to substantiate my claim for potential transferability as an existential of *all* credit.

On the other hand, the *guarantee* of transfer is *not* an existential of *any* credit. To conceive of a credit that not only *may* circulate but also is *assured* of circulating is, once again, to imagine something other than credit. Guaranteed transferability would amount to guaranteed liquidity – the idea that this credit can always and immediately be swapped for other credits or for commodities. But this notion of "guaranteed liquidity" is little more than a different form of the positive, intrinsic value that serves as the bedrock of commodity theories of money, and which claim theories must always reject. Hence a guarantee of transferability would mark the

---

12 Tethers, of course, circulate within a very small but still quite consequential money space. One might wish to question the validity of tether as money of account on the basis of the fixed exchange rate between tethers and dollars, but if fixed exchange rates invalidated moneys of account, we would have to erase or somehow invalidate the existence of many national currencies throughout history. For more on tethers, see Chapter 7.

limit of credit theory – the place where we are no longer dealing with a credit but rather with some entity of intrinsic value. Credit, of course, has no intrinsic value. Credit is always a claim on another party (the debtor), and this makes the guarantee of transferability impossible, because no debtor's liquidity and solvency can ever be perfectly assured. Just as a credit can always be offered to and accepted by a third party, it can also always be rejected.

Thesis 3 affirms both that all credit *can* circulate and that any credit can *fail* to circulate.[13] As an ontological category, transferability is inherent to all credits; it cannot be the element that allows us to distinguish credit from money in their respective natures. But if our ontology of credit reveals that all credit is transferable, this means that we must refuse any ontological distinction between money and credit. At the level of their being, there are not two distinct entities with different natures.

Put differently, what we take to be "credit" when drawing the money/credit distinction *might* in fact circulate in the future, while what we take to be "money" *might not* circulate. This leads me to Thesis 4: our efforts to hold the line between money and credit will always prove futile. In advancing my critique of the money/credit distinction over the years, I have found it perplexes, confounds, or even angers many scholars of politics and economics, yet the point comes naturally to money-market traders. Here's how one particularly reflective trader formulates the idea in terms of the balance-sheet assets that he trades: "Financial assets are money-like to the extent that you don't need money, and very much not money-like when you're desperate for cash" (Hobart 2022).[14] *"Money" is money-like credit.*

Ontologically, there are not two "substances" (money and credit) but just one. The existential that would mark money as distinct – transferability – is an existential of all credit. If at any given moment we analyze the structure and nature of a

---

13 Note that the empirical argument from above cannot intervene in or arrest this inherent undecidability. The empirical definition of money as circulating credit does not tell us much at first. If we want to really know what money is, we have to go out each day and observe, to see which credits circulate (we can place those in the money column) and which do not (those we will place in the credit column). At the end of each day, we can update these two tables, but as we do so we may notice that some items keep jumping back and forth between columns. Yesterday *that* was money and *this* was credit, but today they are reversed. This brings us to the elemental limitation of an empirical account of money: it cannot rigorously distinguish money from credit (conceptually, within the very account of the nature of money). At best, this sort of "theory" can only provide a starting point for empirical data-gathering and analysis.
14 For an unpacking of the latent concept "cash," see Chapter 6, Footnote 14.

handful of credits[15] of whatever form – from a friend's IOUs to a US Treasury bill – we will never be able to sort them into distinct "money" and "credit" categories.

Ontologically, the being of "credit" is indistinguishable from the being of "money." Both appear here within quotation marks because the ontological argument pushes us to see that at the level of being, there is only one entity. I propose to call this entity *money-credit*.[16] In coining the term I replace the slash mark that would *separate* money from credit at the empirical level with a hyphen that links the two at the ontological level. Anything we call "credit" possesses the existential of transferability just the same as that which we call "money." There is nothing but money-credit. And, to return to the language just above, *all money-credit may or may not circulate.*

Taken together, Thesis 4 and Thesis 2 expose a profound contradiction between the empirical account (where a money/credit distinction can be maintained by observing the success or failure of credit circulation) and an ontological account (where everything is money-credit – so no such distinction can hold). Crucially, this is not a contradiction to be overcome or undone. Not in the least, because this contradiction forms the basis for the inescapable possibility of capitalist financial crisis: we keep successfully distinguishing money from credit, and thus money freely circulates, right up to the moment that the distinction collapses and circulation ceases. A deep understanding of money today requires bringing together the empirical account and the ontological account, while recognizing that they cannot be reconciled.

To spell this point out, let us see what happens if we attempt to align the two accounts. Empirically, money is credit actually transferred in practice/history – credit that does, in fact, circulate. As I suggested above, the only apparent way to make the ontology of money support this distinction would be to include in our ontology of money the existential that we have named "guarantee of transfer" (while excluding this existential from our ontology of credit). But rather than al-

---

15 In developing this argument we must carefully (though not starkly) delineate *credit* relations. Not all relations of obligation and responsibility are relations of credit. For example, we may have moral or social debts to friends, to family, and to the wider community, the very existence of which itself rests on a certain basis of (some degree of) mutuality and co-commitment. But not all forms of owing, or even of what we call *debt* in ordinary language, should be understood as credit/debt for the purposes of a theory of money. As the concept of the money array indicates, a credit/debt in the monetary sense must specify more or less clearly both the parties (creditor and debtor) and the denomination.

16 Specifically, the money token is money-credit, but this also means that the wider money array pivots around this symbol of money-credit. In other words, the money array is itself the money-credit array: creditor, debtor, and denominated money-credit.

lowing us to support an ontological distinction between money and credit, this requirement of the argument would force us into a very different conclusion – namely, that *money does not exist.* In other words, if, ontologically, money is that which includes the existential "guarantee of transfer," then there *is no money* – there is only credit – because nothing is guaranteed to transfer. This is one way, quite radical yet thoroughly plausible, of reading Innes.[17]

Unsurprisingly, and for a host of both conceptual and practical reasons, I eschew this conclusion. While the paradox of developing a theory of money that concludes "there is no money" might grab people's attention, overall it would be less than helpful in understanding money. Therefore I defend the primary thesis that ontologically we cannot maintain the position that money is transferable credit; ontologically we cannot distinguish money from credit because in their being money and credit are the same (they are money-credit).[18]

Finally, Thesis 5 returns to less controversial waters, and like Thesis 1, this claim holds on both the ontological and empirical levels. We know in practice that not all money-credit is as good as any other money-credit. Some credits are of higher quality than others: some seem more sound, some seem more liquid, and some help to diversify a portfolio of other credits. Yet this conclusion is not strictly empirical: it is in the very being of credits to be of differing quality; for this reason it is in the very nature of monies to form an (always shifting) hierarchy. In his second, less cited article, Innes points out that when different credits are issued in the same money of account, they are effectively issues of *different dollars:* "Everybody who incurs a debt issues his own dollar, which may or may not be identical with the dollar of any one else's money" (Innes 1914: 154). We can formulate the point more forcefully: "a" dollar is not a thing. The "thing" is a token of credit/debt denominated in dollars, and some tokens will be *better* than others – more stable, more liquid, or wielding more purchasing power – even if they have the exact same denomination.[19]

---

17 Such a conclusion can also easily be drawn from a study of the history of money and money markets – even the highest forms of money sometimes cease to circulate – and thus, in some important sense, *cease to be money.* For more on this point, see Chapter 6.

18 It might be worthwhile at this point merely to remind the reader that my ontological arguments are always restricted to the particular historically developed social order that is capitalism. I obviously draw repeatedly on the historical evidence of past societies' technical uses and practices of money, but I refuse to speculate about the ontology of pre-capitalist money. I discuss this methodological point in more detail in Chapter 1.

19 As setup for the conclusion I quoted above (that everyone who issues debt issues their own dollar), Innes offers an example that brilliantly illuminates *how* different "dollars" can be:

Money can never be singular because money is always a claim on a debtor, and debtors are always multiple and of differing quality (i.e., different degrees of solvency and liquidity). There is never money, but always only monies – even ontologically. Hence the inevitability of the money hierarchy. When we refuse the money/credit distinction (there is only money-credit), we must never forget that not all money-credit is the same. Thesis 5 must always be kept sharply in mind when considering the implications of Thesis 4: to refuse the money/credit distinction is not at all to level the differences between various forms of money-credit. There are always different dollars.[20]

Before moving on, it is worth noting that this argument could easily be construed as overly abstract or narrowly terminological (the differences often seem semantic), yet the stakes are quite high and therefore worth foregrounding. The history of money – both theoretical and practical – has been marked by a series of efforts to draw the line between money and credit, and each has been in the service of a broader effort to maintain some sphere in which money has stable value. Yet all of these arguments have failed.[21] The argument here indicates why they were always doomed to fail – precisely because money has no value and thus can never be a guarantor of value. The nature of money as credit and the ontology of credit show us that the "value of money" (money's purchasing power) can always disappear at a moment's notice. And every financial crisis demonstrates the same point. There is never any place, nor any time, where money exists as

---

Suppose that I take to my banker a number of sight drafts of the same nominal value. ... For the draft on the Sub-Treasury and for that of the bank in the city, my banker will probably give me a credit for exactly the nominal value, but the others will all be exchanged at different prices. For the draft on the New York bank I might get more than the stated amount; for that of the New York merchant, I should probably get less; while for that on the obscure tradesman, my banker would probably give nothing without my endorsement, and even then I should receive less than the nominal amount. All these documents represent *different dollars of debt*, which the banker buys for whatever he thinks they may be worth to him. (Innes 1914: 154, emphasis added, punctuation altered for clarity)

20 There is all the difference in the world between higher-quality and lower-quality credits, and if we wish to reserve the moniker *money* for only the higher-quality forms, then there may be no harm in that. But in trying to grasp money conceptually, we must resist the temptation to reify the semantic distinctions of everyday discourse. We cannot pretend that the dividing line is ever clear or fixed, and we absolutely must remember that it can shift or seemingly disappear at any moment.

21 Put differently, whenever a person, an institution, or even a larger society seems overly confident that it has fixed and preserved the money/credit distinction, that it has found credits with guaranteed transferability – that is the moment to worry. Contemporary readers might be reminded of the algorithmic stablecoins that blew up in 2022: their promise was precisely the guarantee of fixed, stable value.

money and *not* as credit. In practice we can surely distinguish circulating money from non-circulating credits, but no *theory of money* will ever be able to draw a rigorous, tenable conceptual distinction between the two.

3 Liquid Goat Money and Illiquid US Treasuries

In a certain sense, ontological arguments must by definition separate themselves from daily lived experience in order to ask properly the question of *ontos* (being) as distinct from ontic questions (related to particular beings). But such separation can and should be temporary, and it must not lead to a divorce from practical reality or concrete concerns. I explore the ontology of money and credit because an ontic approach proves incapable of adequately accounting for both the nature of money and the *practices* of money today. Thus, having worked through the conceptual argument (and the five individual theses) in defense of this overall framework, I want now to contour further these arguments, by building out two examples.

To help make the case that all credit can become money and all money can revert to credit[22] (and thus that there is only money-credit), I draw examples from opposite ends of the money hierarchy. The first case explores the lowest-quality credits imaginable, so as to demonstrate that even here credit can be/become money. The second turns to "first-class" money, but proves that even there the credit nature of money can reveal itself in a flash (i.e., a crash).[23]

Starting at the bottom, let us assume that I offer my neighbor some food today in exchange for a future credit. That credit takes the specific form of an IOU, signed by my neighbor, for "1 goat."[24] In holding the goat IOU, I hold a credit; my neighbor

---

22 The phrase "revert to credit" works within the terms established in the preceding section: empirically, money is credit that circulates, so when it ceases to circulate it *reverts* to its merely credit form. In practice, "reversion" would serve as a euphemism for a bank run or an all-out financial crisis. If your debtor becomes illiquid your *money* turns into worthless *credit* held on a failed or failing institution. Ontologically, of course, there is only ever *money-credit*, but the empirical question cannot be ignored because it matters a great deal whether that money-credit circulates.

23 These exemplars lack parallelism: one is an empirical case from very recent history; the other is utterly hypothetical (and ahistorical), a stylized heuristic device. The ontological account is not restricted to the empirical example, and thus the hypothetical proves significant because it serves to illuminate both future possibilities and *potentiality* as such.

24 Ingham rightly challenges a minor tendency in orthodox accounts (commodity theories) of money to explain money's emergence from a prior state of barter through the introduction of IOUs (in his case, pig IOUs). The orthodox idea is that, first, there is barter; then, at some stage of development, the party who lacks a commodity to barter instead provides an IOU as substitute;

is my debtor (the denomination is "goats," and the quantity is 1). I may also hold a US $20 bill. The latter is not qualitatively different from the former: the $20 bill is also a credit; my debtor is the US Federal Reserve banking system (the denomination is "dollars," and the quantity is 20). It should go without saying that these are very different credits, but that important fact, addressed in Thesis 5, must not be allowed to distract us from the essential validity of Thesis 4: there is no difference in kind. Both the goat IOU and the $20 bill are money-credits.

To repeat, there are vast practical differences between these two credits, but we can explore those differences in a way that underscores their ontological sameness. To elaborate this point let us analyze my "goat credit" more closely. I can exchange it for a goat from my neighbor, but can I use it to buy milk at the corner store? Probably not.[25] But why not? What exactly prevents this credit from circulating widely, from circulating as *money*?[26] The answer has nothing to do with its

---

finally, the IOU "could be held by the co-trader and later handed back for cancellation on receipt of a real pig," and thus the IOU would be "money." Ingham dismisses this nonsense, pointing out that money must be a *transferable debt* (denominated in money of account) and not just a claim on a specific commodity (Ingham 2004c: 25). Just to be clear: my story in the text above also starts with an IOU, but it is not preceded by barter, it does not support a commodity theory of money, and it *does* seek to explain the idea of transferable debt.

25 This would be Ingham's point in his critique of the orthodox theory: the goat IOU is a credit but not money, because: 1) the debt is denominated in a specific commodity (goats), not in an abstract money of account, and 2) the credit/debt is not transferable (Ingham 2004c). As I show, however: *if* in fact the credit circulates (which is not a given, but always possible), then in so doing it will render "goats" the money of account. And at precisely that moment, just as with gold, commodity-goats and money-goats will become two distinct entities. Moneys of account have often been denominated in commodities – a fact that in no way proves the validity of a commodity theory of money. If debts are actually paid in the commodity (rather than in the denominated credit), then they are not paid in money, but this is largely beside the point (as it is a question of assets that render the debtor solvent, a question that persists whether or not the money of account purports to be commodity backed). The initial denomination of the credit does not matter as long as it remains quantifiable in discrete units. (As discussed previously, "I owe you love and support" is not a *credit*.) Whether it be goats (a real animal, possibly a commodity) or dragons (a mythical creature, an utterly abstract idea), the crux of the issue pivots on the same question: Do credits denominated as such circulate from hand to hand? I imagine that the idea of owing someone 47 dragons will sound bizarre to many readers (and this is why I use goats in my example in the text), but as Innes would remind us, *the idea of owing someone 47 dollars is not one bit less fantastical.* "The eye has never seen, nor the hand touched a dollar" (Innes 1914: 155).

26 Geoff Ingham has suggested a different answer than the one I give in the text. He proposes an ontological distinction between *personal and impersonal trust.* This would be a fundamental difference between the trust I have in my neighbor (personal) and the broader social trust I have that the credit could circulate to other parties (impersonal). Without this impersonal trust, credits cannot circulate (Ingham 2022, pers. comm.). It seems to me that such a distinction may tell us some-

nature (as a credit) and everything to do with the *quality* of the credit. Few people will want to hold credits denominated in goats; fewer still will wish to hold credits against my neighbor. But these significant practical facts do not change the nature of the credit; they do not alter its ontological existence as money.

And we can easily imagine an example wherein the practical conditions look quite different: perhaps I reside in a small community populated by numerous goat herders and dairy farmers. These folks might be quite keen to take and hold goat credit, not only because it could have direct purchasing power for them but also, and more importantly, because they know that others in the community will also value such credits. Therefore I could use the credit when in need of another goat (by cashing it in with my neighbor), but I could also exchange it with a different neighbor for some other good entirely (because that neighbor too will be happy to hold goat credit). Moreover, it may be that in such a small, tight-knit community, a large number of people know my neighbor (either personally or by reputation) and therefore know that she is both an upstanding member of the community and one who possesses a healthy household balance sheet with excellent cash flow (and healthy goats, of course). In other words, as a debtor she is solvent (her assets exceed her liabilities) and liquid (she has available money on hand, daily). Given all of this, we were wrong to assume at the outset that I could not buy milk at the corner store with my goat IOU. Quite the contrary, the grocery store owner is likely to have dealings and interests in the various local goat businesses. He may be more than happy to "cash" my goat IOU and give me store credit, allowing me to buy not just milk today but groceries and supplies

---

thing important about the difference between monetary societies and non-monetary societies: the former require some degree of impersonal trust. But my concern here, as throughout, lies only with monetary societies, and within such societies there must already be some degree of such impersonal trust, because some credits do, in fact, circulate as money. The condition of impersonal trust fails to ground an ontological distinction between money and credit. After all, impersonal trust is a condition of the social order itself, not of any particular credit. Properly directed, trust in money should always be trust in the specific debtor on which the money-credit is held. That said, Ingham's point raises a separate set of important and complicated issues: sometimes trust in money is misplaced, precisely because the holder of money does not consider the debtor. Put in Ingham's language, individuals may be fooled because their "impersonal trust" (their trust in societal institutions) prevents them from seeing the risky debtor in front of them. This seems to be part of the explanation for significant investment in crypto shadow banks that promised guaranteed, high yield: these were incredibly risky, uninsured, and unregulated investments, but many individuals who put their money in them thought of them as safe investments like bank certificates of deposit. I offer this as further evidence against Simmel's thesis that money is a claim on society; when your crypto shadow bank goes bankrupt and loses all your money, society will not pay you back (even if it was society you trusted to begin with). For more on crypto, see Chapter 7.

for weeks to come. As Innes says, a sale is the exchange of goods for credits. The goat IOU from my neighbor is exchangeable credit; it is money.[27]

Obviously this example is stylized, but nothing in it requires altering the nature of the goat credit, and following through on the logic allows us to see the extent to which (and context in which) all credit has the potential to circulate. Furthermore, the example makes clear that if money is circulating credit, the issue before us is not where to draw a line between credits that "count" as money and credits that do not, but how to locate the specific *money space* in which such credits do in fact "count."

The concept "money space" can be thrown into relief by comparing it with one of the constitutive elements of the money array – namely, denomination. All tokens of credit/debt must be denominated in some money of account, and we might say this creates a kind of *virtual space* in which those tokens can circulate. However, I distinguish between, on the one hand, the logical requirement that any money token be denominated, and on the other, the domain in which it circulates. My concept of money space is not abstract or virtual, but quite concrete. Money space is that area in which credits circulate (as money).[28] The idea is simple, yet forceful, because it demonstrates that all credit may circulate within a specified domain (the money space). Even if I live in San Francisco in 2020 (and not in the fanciful goat-herding community of our earlier example), the goat IOU is still in an important sense *money* as long as the money space consists solely of me and my neighbor – I can always cash the IOU with her (a bilateral relation).[29]

We can easily conjure a slightly larger money space: say a group of twenty friends play poker regularly, but rather than exchange bank deposits or central

---

27 If we were to extend this hypothetical, we might well end up describing a community in which goats were the money of account within the community's money space. This is the final response to Ingham: the mere fact that a bilateral credit relation is denominated in something other than the already given money of account does not in and of itself prevent that credit from circulating. There are *always* multiple moneys of account. And market liquidity (what Mehrling calls "shiftability," the capacity to move one's credits from one form to another, including across moneys of account) is never a given, but rather always established by some sort of market maker.

28 Although it departs from and goes well beyond his arguments, my concept of money space was originally inspired by Ingham's claim – articulated in his summary of the state theory of money – that "monetary space is sovereign space" (Ingham 2004a: 56).

29 We could use this example to rework the empirical distinction between money and credit, as follows: if the money space consists of two parties, then we have only credit, which can be redeemed with the debtor but not transferred to a third party. Once the money space expands to three parties, then we have money, which can be transferred. On the other hand, ontologically there is no way to know in advance that the money space will not be expanded, precisely by transferring the credit to a third party. My neighbor example anticipates a point I demonstrate in the text below: inside a predetermined money space, all credit is money.

bank notes at the end of each night, they simply keep a ledger of credits and debts, occasionally reconciling the books to clear the accumulated entries against one another. In this context the Google spreadsheet listing the credits and debts would itself be the site of real money among this group. To buy five pounds of coffee from Tim, Steve could simply transfer $50 in credits held against Akim. Before the coffee sale, Akim owed Steve; after the sale, Akim owes Tim. Of course, if the spreadsheet already lists a credit/debt between Steve and Tim, then we can leave Akim out of it: the coffee sale would either reduce Tim's outstanding debt, or increase Steve's. (Or, if Tim owed Steve less than $50 to start, the sale would turn Tim's debt into credit.) In this example the money space extends to the twenty poker players (multilateral relations), because the poker players agree to allow the transfer of poker debt as payment for goods (or to cancel other debt). The credits/debts listed as assets/liabilities on the Google spreadsheet will not circulate beyond the group, but within the group they circulate just as freely as other monies would.

Both these examples depend on relatively small money spaces. Distinctly, and importantly, these are also relatively "low" forms of money[30] – that is, falling far down the hierarchy described so well by Mehrling.[31] We can formulate the point

------

[30] My examples happen to be both small (size of money space) and low (in the hierarchy of money) but there is no necessary relation between the two. That is, the size of the money space does not directly determine where the money-credit will fall on the hierarchy. Obviously there will be a general tendency for smaller-scale money spaces to produce lower forms of money, but this is not a universal law. In the text immediately below, and then again in Chapter 7, I briefly discuss IMF special drawing rights (SDR): the SDR money space is quite circumscribed, but SDR are a very high form of money-credit. Thanks to Ben Taylor for this insight.

[31] Mehrling's thesis for the "natural hierarchy of money" takes as its point of departure a tacit yet powerful rejection of the money/credit distinction. He puts the point this way at the beginning of the second lecture of his introductory course:

> Always and everywhere, monetary systems are hierarchical. One way that economists have tried to get an analytical grip on this empirical fact is to distinguish *money* (means of final settlement) from *credit* (promise to pay money, means of delaying final settlement). This is fine so far as it goes. But in one sense it doesn't go far enough because it posits only two layers of the hierarchy. And in another sense it goes too far because what counts as final settlement depends on what layer we are talking about. (Mehrling 2012: 1)

Mehrling neither proposes nor defends the thesis that all credit is money, and the "bottom" of his hierarchy is still many rungs above the locations I am exploring here, but his fundamental insight concerning the hierarchy of money already undermines any strong defense of a money/credit distinction. Mehrling's enterprise only rarely bumps up against the explicit project to develop a theory of money, but when it does, I believe Mehrling resists both any orthodox commodity theory and the state theory variant of heterodoxy. For example, see Mehrling's sharply critical review of

this way: goat IOUs and poker dollars are not very good credits, and this means they aren't very good money, but they are money nonetheless. Yes, these monies circulate in very small money spaces, but this just underscores the crucial point: all money circulates in *some* circumscribed money space. *The structural limitations that apply to the goat IOUs and the poker ledger also apply to every other form of money.* I cannot pay for my milk at Whole Foods in poker dollars, but I also cannot pay for it in rubles. And I cannot pay my friend for coffee in the special drawing rights (SDR) issued by the International Monetary Fund (IMF). Money outside its money space is always "merely" credit, yet money inside its proper money space is also nothing but credit – money-credit.[32] Once again, rather than struggle to shore up an untenable money/credit distinction, we do better with the combined claim: there is only one thing, money-credit, but not all money-credit is the same.

To complete the logic that substantiates this claim, we can now turn to the opposite end of the money spectrum and consider the highest forms of money – the first-class credits of which Innes speaks. Every attempt to defend a money/credit distinction – whether in the form of commodity, heterodox, or post-Keynesian theories of money – must ultimately assume or assert that as we move up the hierarchy we eventually *cross the line*. That is, at a certain point we leave behind mere *private credit* (bilateral relations) and shift over into the domain of genuine *public money* (multilateral relations). On these accounts we necessarily get a concept of money as that which can *always* circulate.

This is one way of expressing the notion that money is *liquid*. The basic idea holds a superficial seduction: it tells us that money is not credit because credit cannot always be exchanged for goods, while money can.[33] The existence of this "money" would indeed be reassuring, and nothing can stop us from imagining such an entity. We merely posit or define "money" as that which is "liquid" because it *always circulates*. In calling money liquid we mean that it must necessarily be accepted in exchange for our desired goods, services, or credits.

But this is a fantasy. There is no such thing as a credit of such high quality that it is guaranteed to be accepted. This is an ontic fact about any empirical example of money-credit, but as I showed above it is also an ontological truth about money as credit. *No credit can be guaranteed* because every credit is held on a debtor, and no

---

Wray's first book, which, according to Mehrling, "miss[es] the credit nature of modern money ... [and] misconstrues the nature of the modern state that issues currency" (Mehrling 2000: 401).
32 On the question of a global or universal money space, see the discussion of "world money" in Chapter 7.
33 This is another way of depicting money as that which has an existential of "guarantee of transfer." To keep the example clear, I leave out the ontological terminology.

debtor's solvency or liquidity can be permanently assured. Money can never be stable or fixed. Money itself cannot meet the criteria of our fantastical concept of *pure liquidity*; to the contrary, this phrase is a contradiction in terms, at odds with the very nature of money-credit.

We need to pause for a moment to consider a broader clutch of concepts. First, the basic idea of "liquidity" can prove useful in indicating the relative degree to which a particular money-credit or asset freely circulates or trades. A market in specific financial assets can plausibly be understood as more or less "liquid" depending on how easy or difficult it proves to buy and sell. Second, the idea of "purely liquid money" is an absurdity, because, as I have shown, no money-credit can be guaranteed to circulate. Finally, and most significantly, the concept of "money liquidity" should be grasped as one of those "deranged" concepts that manifest within capitalism.[34] If we read the phrase as suggesting *money is liquid* by definition, then it becomes nonsensical; it collapses into the second concept (purely liquid money). But if we take it as indexing the relative liquidity *of* money, as indicating the space across which various monies range in their actual and potential transferability, then the concept proves essential to any account of money under capitalism.

This book has already raised the question of liquidity in terms of the "liquidity constraint" placed on any financial entity (usually banks): Do daily incoming cash flows "line up" with outgoing cash flows (Mehrling 2011)? This usage is consistent with, but not reducible to, a standard definition of liquidity in circulation today: from the discipline of economics to money managers to ordinary language, "liquidity" is almost always taken to mean "convertibility into money." An asset is more or less liquid depending on how easy (that is, with the least delay and lowest transaction costs) it is to sell it.[35] This common usage tacitly assumes a conceptual framework in which money is liquid by definition. For modern economics and fi-

---

34 The word "deranged" comes from Hans-Georg Backhaus's reading of Marx, and his translation of Marx's term, *Verrückung*. Backhaus sees this concept as pivotal both for understanding Marx's critique of classical political economy and for grasping the objective facts of capitalism:

> Economic forms are deranged. Marx here intentionally makes use of the ambiguity of this word, an ambiguity which is innate to the German language alone. Thus, on the one hand, money is a "deranged (*verrückte*) form" in the sense that it is the "most nonsensical, most unintelligible form," that is, it is "pure madness" (*reine Verrücktheit*). On the other hand, money is a deranged form also in the other, spatial sense of "derangement" (*Verrücktheit*), as an object which is deranged (*verrücktes*), dis-placed out of its natural locus. (Backhaus 1992: 61–62, citing Marx 1973: 928)

35 Where I consistently ask whether a *bank* is liquid (can it meet daily cash demands), the standard approach asks whether a particular *asset* is liquid (can it be sold at its value).

nance, "money liquidity" is thus understood not as derangement (as I have characterized it above) but as a mere tautology. This logic subtly implies that to hold money is to hold permanent, stable value.[36] In this way the concept "liquidity" reifies a false understanding of money, as it tacitly returns us to the notion that money has value.

Crucially, Keynes offers a completely different way of understanding liquidity, defining it not as "convertibility into money" but as "stability of value." This allows Keynes to compare the relative "liquidity of money" to the liquidity of other assets and commodities. (Houses, Keynes argues, are sometimes more *liquid* than cash.) For Keynes, "liquidity of money" is a question, not a tautology. Keynes thus makes it possible to ask about "money liquidity" not as a tautological fact but as an ongoing concern: How liquid (how *shiftable* into some other asset) is this particular money-credit? In concluding, above, that "purely liquid money" is untenable, we are implicitly developing Keynes's insight. *Pure liquidity* is a synonym for permanent, stable value, and therefore a contradiction in terms because value (exchange-value) is never permanent; value is always relative, always futural. In consistently rejecting any ontological rendering of the money/credit distinction, we always face the same key question: How good is the credit? How stable is the "value" held in the commodities or represented in the credit? One type of credit, one form of money, and even one type of commodity, may be more or less *liquid* than another. For Keynes, the entire point of the concept was to compare *relative liquidities*; hence there is no such thing as *pure liquidity* (see Hicks 1962; Keynes 1930; Keynes 1936; Hayes 2018).[37]

Nonetheless, as we move up the money hierarchy, the quality of credit increases, and this tells us something significant about all credits (and hence all money). Yet as we travel this path, there simply is no point at which we "cross over" from unreliable credit to reliable money. As Mehrling puts it, "What looks like money at one level of the system looks like credit to the level above it" (Mehrling 2012: 1). In extraordinary times, even the reverse can be true, a phenomenon we witness when people no longer wish to hold money-credits (typically) located very high up the hierarchy. Perhaps better put, the rankings themselves are never fixed,

---

36 Of course, every banker and money trader knows better: credits or assets that seem "money-like" today may look very different tomorrow.

37 It is a notable irony of the history of economic thought (though, to my knowledge, one that has not been noted before) that the author responsible for coining the word "liquidity" is Hawtrey, who does so within his general defense of a radical credit theory and in the particular context of pointing out that the Bank of England faces no liquidity constraint: "The liquidity of the Bank of England is secured by its power of printing notes, and the interchangeability of its deposits with cash is absolute" (Hawtrey 1919: 83; *Oxford English Dictionary*: "liquidity").

and thus they can always be shuffled. In any case, we are always better off analyzing the actual hierarchy of money-credit, rather than positing a stable money/credit dichotomy that will never hold.[38]

In other words, we are always dealing with the same fundamental phenomenon: *money-credit*. At times credit performs adequately as money, but its facticity as credit can reveal itself at any moment. For example, in the normal course of affairs, we see US Treasury bonds as one of the highest forms of HQLA we can imagine, the finest of Innes's "first-class" credits. Nevertheless, nothing can permanently assure such status; nothing guarantees the liquid, money-like nature of these credits. Even the highest forms of money can still reveal themselves (show their nature) as mere credits.

Observers of financial markets witnessed this phenomenon in March 2020 when for a time even US Treasury bonds were no longer "liquid." To say the bonds weren't liquid means that no one was willing to "make a market" for them, literally to buy and sell them. This description of the "liquidity" of markets actually combines the standard meaning of *convertibility* (to cash) with Keynes's notion of *stability* (of value). Bonds cease to be "liquid" because "market makers," who typically always stand ready both to buy and sell (at the proper bid and ask prices), have exited the market – or better, they have refused to *make* a market at all. Hence it becomes difficult or impossible for one to *convert* bonds. And these market makers have left the scene precisely because they are worried about the *stability* of bond values. They are concerned that the volatility of the market is so severe that it is no longer "safe" to make a market, because even with a higher spread between bid and ask prices, one might end up buying or selling at utterly "wrong" prices – and in so doing lose massive amounts of financial value.[39]

At this moment in 2020, even one of the highest and most stable forms of money-credits lost liquidity; that is, US Treasury bonds ceased to be transferable and became unstable in their value. In so doing, this "money" revealed its ontological nature as mere credit; a higher form of money came to look much like lower

---

38 Ingham's position thus contains a great deal of truth when rewritten from the fixed language of ontological being into the dynamic language of historical becoming: all money is credit; not all credit *is* money; but all credit can *become* money, and all money can *degenerate* into mere credit. Importantly, these are ontic, not ontological claims. If we read Ingham as sharply distinguishing between credit that is money and credit that is not money, we might take him to be falling back into the trap that snares Macleod – namely, the idea that ultimately money and credit are different creatures. This is why I prefer to read Ingham as making only a narrower empirical argument to support the money/credit distinction.

39 The idea of market makers, so central to contemporary banking and finance, quickly and clearly pierces any hypostatization of markets as "natural." For more, see Chapter 6.

forms – a particular credit rather than general value incarnate. The "high-quality" nature of HQLA is itself *relative* to other forms of value. In a truly severe crisis, the most "liquid" form of "money" may turn out to be canned goods and toilet paper.[40] The conclusion to this line of logic will surprise no one: liquidity is itself a hierarchy. Just as there was no magic line that transported us from "credit" to "money," there are not separable domains of "liquid" and "illiquid" money-credits. Since all money is credit, any particular money can always become illiquid.

If we fix in place a specific money space, we might say that within that space certain "credits" will successfully circulate as "money," while beyond that space the very same credits will fail to circulate (and thus fail to *be* money). However, we absolutely cannot allow the concept "money space" to shore up a new version of the ontological money/credit distinction. It cannot do so because money spaces are themselves *plural, shifting*, and *unstable*. We cannot actually fix them in place: old money spaces erode, disappear, or find themselves colonized by different money spaces; new money spaces emerge, grow, and change. As money spaces alter, that which *counts* as "money" or "credit" is altered as well, and with those alterations comes another shuffling of the hierarchy of money-credits. Rather than allowing us to map a stable ontological difference between "credit" and "money," the concept "money space" underscores that money-credit is all there is. We can express the point differently by way of a productive tautology: money only circulates ... where it circulates.[41] Moreover, where money circulates it does so always and only as credit. There is nothing other than money-credit, but not all money-credits are the same.

---

40 Obviously canned goods and toilet paper are not actually *money*; they are commodities. The point of the severe-crisis example is to show that crisis can undermine the viability of all monies – of any form of credit – creating conditions under which commodities with intrinsic use-value prove more liquid (both more stable in value and, accordingly, easier to convert into other forms of value) than any variety of money. It is exactly this sense of liquidity that Keynes understood so well.

41 My line of logic in the text above extends an argument from Minsky: "Everyone can create money; the problem is to get it accepted" (Minsky 2008: 255). One can read Minsky here as supporting both Thesis 4 and Thesis 5: there is only money-credit, but not all money-credits are the same. My tautological line in the text points once more to the radical temporality of money (to the fact that all value is future value). Anyone can issue credit/debt at any time. We can say that such credit is not money until it circulates, but only if we also maintain that once it circulates, it was always already money.

4 Money and State Money

This conclusion returns us to some of the key engagements of the previous chapter, as we are now in a position to advance a number of arguments that distinguish the credit theory of money defended here from the work of post-Keynesians and other heterodox thinkers. The above framework can be used to clarify some crucial points about credit money and state money. I suggested in the previous chapter that the lineage of the credit theory was too often swallowed up by the development of state theory. Scholars writing on money today frequently fail to heed Schumpeter's warning about collapsing these two strains of analysis; they ignore the relevance of his vigorous critique of state theory. We see this consistently in the work of Wray and sometimes in that of Ingham; both tell a kind of monetary bildungsroman culminating in state money. In Wray's case this extends so far that he reads Innes as merely one element, a stepping stone perhaps, in a "tradition" that runs from Knapp through Keynes to Minsky.[42] The credit theory of money does not ignore or deny the obvious fact that state power and state money today prove central to all monetary and economic practices. But the analysis developed in this chapter gives us the tools to resist the assumption, made commonly within state theory, that state power simply establishes (declares) state money, which itself *is* money, full stop.

To start, we can take up a core tenet of state theory, one that often goes unstated, but which Ingham has formulated explicitly and concisely: "Monetary space is sovereign space" (Ingham 2004a: 56). Using the concept of money space, we affirm the following point: whatever the money space is, we can accurately attribute to that space a sort of "sovereignty." In other words, within a defined money space, a particular money has validity, authority, and thus "supreme power." In its proper money space, money is sound and credible – it is sovereign. Nevertheless, the power and validity of money – the capacity for credit to circulate as money – never *derives* strictly from or depends solely on a singular prior power, and this holds regardless of whether such putative power be social, political, legal,

---

42 Wray explicitly interprets Innes as: 1) rejecting a "pure credit" theory; 2) endorsing Ingham's thesis that not all credit is money; and 3) emphasizing the role of the state just like Knapp – "The similarities are remarkable" (Wray 2004: 238, 240, 242). My work over the course of the past two chapters already indicates decisively that I see all three claims as significant misreadings of Innes. I will not relitigate this dispute here but would like to emphasize that Innes consistently *rejects* the idea that state money is always dominant money, and never endorses a money/credit distinction: "The notion that we all have to-day that the government coin is the one and only dollar and that all other forms of money are promises to pay that dollar is no longer tenable in the face of the clear historical evidence to the contrary" (Innes 1914: 154).

or otherwise. This means that the sovereignty of money (within its limited money space) neither originates in nor can be reducible to a separate or prior sociopolitical power (community or state). This point proves essential but is frequently forgotten by those writing today within the heterodox tradition.

How then do we understand the relationship between, on the one hand, state power (and state sovereignty) and, on the other, money validity (and money sovereignty)? In a clutch of recent writings, including a short book titled *Money*, Ingham develops a powerful answer to this sort of question, an argument perhaps latent but not clearly present in his earlier work (Ingham 2020; Ingham 2021; Ingham, forthcoming). Ingham attempts to reread Knapp *through* Max Weber's own reading (of Knapp) in order to make much more of Knapp's foundational text in "state theory" than Schumpeter sees there. In these new writings Ingham formulates and reformulates the basic point many times, but a concise version reads as follows: "States cannot *directly* determine the *substantive* validity of money: that is, its purchasing power at any point in time. But they can declare and impose its *formal* validity" (Ingham 2020: 36; cf. Ingham 2021: 4; Ingham, forthcoming: 7). This argument proves well worth unpacking.

While I have consistently taken my distance from Knapp, I should like to emphasize the extent to which Knapp's work supports the core thesis of this book. Knapp insists that "we should not apply the concept 'value' to this [valid] means of payment, and therefore not to this money itself. ... [I]n the case of value we always use the current means of payment as a standard" (Knapp 1924: 30). Knapp argues for the centrality of the state in establishing the *validity* of money, not the *value* of money. As I indicated in Chapter 3, this argument failed to impress Schumpeter. However, as Ingham carefully reminds his readers, Weber sees something important here, deriving from Knapp the distinction between *"materiale Geltung"* and *"formale Geltung"* (Weber 1978: 76). Weber's translators render this in English, quite reasonably, as the difference between "substantive" and "formal" validity, yet *materiale* clearly indicates "material" (as well as "substantive") and in that context *Geltung* suggests "value" (as well as "validity"). Hence we see in Weber's German the distinction between material *value* and formal *validity*. Ingham wields these terms to draw out the difference between, on the one hand, "purchasing power" – money is not a commodity and therefore has only substantive validity, not material value – and, on the other, "valuableness" (Ingham 2021: 4; Ingham, forthcoming: 7). In other words, states can declare what counts as legal tender – Knapp calls this "validity by proclamation" – but they cannot establish "substantive validity" or "substantive value" by decree (Ingham 2021: 4; Ingham 2020:

35).[43] Ingham always rightly insists that the latter only gets sorted out in the concrete economic "struggle between issuers, users, debtors, and creditors" (Ingham, forthcoming: 7).

How, then, do we understand the state's role in these definite struggles? We can schematize as follows: the state's powers to tax, to police, and to define legal tender give it the capacity to partially determine *a money space*.[44] Further, the state may constrain, spur, or control to some degree the power and validity of various forms of money-credit (up and down the hierarchy). We can quickly enumerate examples:

1) Through currency and bank regulation, counterfeit and money-laundering laws, the state can reduce or eliminate monies that circulate in small, local money spaces.

2) By establishing what counts as legal tender[45] – i.e., that which extinguishes a court-adjudicated debt – the state can significantly and directly influence the

---

43 As I make clear with the citations, Ingham himself moves back and forth across the possible translations of Weber's *materiale Geltung* that I suggest – that is, from validity to value.

44 The state can determine *a* money space because it has twin powers: to issue its own debt, and to *indebt* its citizens by taxing them. However, the state cannot determine *the* money space because money spaces are always plural. Undoubtedly the state can try to police various money spaces, but it can never fully control them.

45 As pointed out previously (Chapter 4, Footnote 20), there is a broader debate within (and against) state theory about the status and importance of legal tender. Wray emphasizes that the fundamental claim of state theory – "Money is a creature of the state" – should not be reduced to the power of the state to declare legal tender (Wray 1998: 18). Rather, state power is much greater than this. In particular, the power to tax, and to determine the money of account in which taxes are paid, proves far more significant (Wray 1998: 55). In response, a few brief points. First, Wray's defense of state theory on this count fails to address Schumpeter's critique (discussed in Chapter 4), which targets not legal-tender laws but the entire complex of powers by which the state regulates the "institution" of money. Second, we can view this debate as a minor variation on a larger theme – namely, the money/credit distinction. Having rejected that distinction, our own account here need not worry much about legal-tender laws. Our question is always the same: "How good are these credits?" If the answer is "quite good," then we will care very little whether they are legal tender (a point Wray accepts), or even whether they are acceptable for tax payments (a point he does not consider). Chinese citizens hold massive amounts of US Treasury bonds because they think such bonds are good credits, despite the fact that USD-denominated debt cannot be used as legal tender or to pay taxes in China. It is only as we move down the hierarchy of money (and the quality of credits gets weaker) that legal-tender laws, taxation laws, and other regulations, customs, and norms come into play. If I have to choose between two equally solvent debtors, but one will owe me in a money of account with which I can pay my taxes and legally extinguish my own debts – then that's a bonus.

money hierarchy. Other things being equal, legal-tender credits will be preferred to non-legal-tender credits.[46]

3) By taxing its citizens and requiring payment in the form of specific monies, the state can quickly establish state money as exactly that credit capable of extinguishing citizens' tax debt.[47]

4) State money will usually, but not always, dictate that a state money space roughly coincides with the geographical borders of the nation-state itself. The tax power gives the state both incentive and means to establish and maintain a state-issued money as one of the highest forms of money within the country.

5) States can establish central banks as the bankers' bank, giving states enormous potential influence over commercial banking and the economic conditions of a country.

Cumulatively, these powers all press toward a consolidation of three elements: nation-state geographic sovereignty, state money, and national money space. In other words, the phenomenon that we typically take as natural or given[48] – that nation-

---

46 Even this point proves more complicated than it might at first seem because most of us, most of the time, are paying one another in *non-legal-tender* monies. Confining myself to the US context, both federal statute and Supreme Court precedent establish the coins and notes of the Federal Reserve banking system as legal tender. Indeed, US law makes the "coins and currency" of all *national banks* legal tender. See 31 U.S.C § 5103 (1983). National banks are established by federal charter, and are separate from state banks under the US "dual banking system" (OCC 2003). But this leads to a curious result in practice. First, legal-tender law allows a long list of banks to issue their own notes and coins as legal tender, but of course today none of them do so. Second, a number of very significant banks by size are not national banks at all. Finally, even for those properly designated as national banks, the law does not, to the best of my knowledge, establish that payments of deposit accounts (checks, ACH transfer, digital transfer) count as legal tender. My deep gratitude to Emily Zackin for research help on this important topic.

47 This power extends far beyond the influence on money itself, as we know from numerous colonial examples. By taxing a local population in the colonizer's money of account, the colonial power can coerce the people of the colonized country to work for wages paid in the colonizer's money of account. In numerous examples, such money is first made available when the colonizer pays its occupying soldiers in state money (i.e., tokens of state debt). However, soldiers are only able to *spend* this money if and when the state imposes a *tax burden* on the local population. Such a burden creates "demand" for this new money. That is, it forces local merchants to accept the money as payment, and it requires many other members of the colonized community to seek waged work.

48 However, anyone can see that such a tendency must not be confused with a natural law because many sovereign nation-states – from France to El Salvador – lack a sovereign money of account. Money space and sovereign territory do not always line up, and even when they appear to

states have their own "sovereign currencies" – must be understood as a complicated balance of dynamic forces. And these forces have knock-on effects that reinforce the primary tendency. UK citizens want to hold their credits in GBP for all the reasons listed above: because local money has been outlawed; because GBP is legal tender;[49] and especially because GBP is the money in which such citizens must pay their taxes. But as a US citizen, none of the above are reasons for me to hold credits in GBP. Nonetheless, when I fly to London for a conference, I wish to hold some credits in the form of GBP for the basic reason that in the UK money space, GBP is the dominant money of account, and only credit/debt denominated in GBP will be useful for me there. Put differently, the money space for USD (where I currently hold most of my credits) does not incorporate pubs and shops in London.[50]

Nonetheless, and to reiterate, the above phenomena must not be conflated with the distinct and overly simplistic idea that money is itself a "creature of the state," that which is declared as such by a sovereign power (Lerner 1947: 313; cited in Wray 1998: 36; also cited in Wray 2000: 58). Weber himself grasped this point well. Perhaps the subtlety of Weber's position has been missed by some state theorists (though surely not by Ingham), for while Weber makes much positive use of Knapp, he also takes his distance, describing Knapp's theory as "incomplete for substantive monetary problems" (Weber 1978: 78). Weber sustains the fundamental distinction (in Knapp) between formal validity (valuableness) and substantive value, but he rejects the idea that the state itself retains full control over formal validity. Weber writes:

> It does not, however, seem reasonable to confine the concept [of validity] to regulations by the state and not to include cases where acceptance is made compulsory by convention or by some agreement. There seems, furthermore, to be no reason why actual minting by the state or under the control of the political authorities should be a decisive criterion. ... As

---

do so, the spaces are not clearly circumscribed. Indeed, money spaces cut across sovereign spaces in multiple dimensions.

49 Here my formulation echoes standard discourse today, in which GBP, "pounds," comes to appear as "money." Technically, however, my statement in the text is false, for as I discussed in Section 2 of this chapter, GBP is not a thing. GBP cannot be "legal tender" because "GBP" is not money but merely the denomination (the money of account) for any particular and concrete money-credit. The difference matters, because some credits denominated in GBP may well be legal tender, but certainly not all are. The general logic I articulate in the text still holds: UK citizens will prefer money-credits denominated in GBP because GBP is a common money of account, and those money-credits that are legal tender in the UK are also denominated in GBP.

50 Although, it does extend in complicated ways to London City financial institutions. But that's another story, partially told in Chapter 7.

Knapp would agree, it is only the existence of norms regulating the monetary form which is decisive. (Weber 1978: 79)

In the following chapter I suggest that the norms to which Weber refers here may well manifest in the precepts and practices of today's money markets. For now, I draw a more circumscribed conclusion: while the formal validity/substantive value distinction proves quite helpful in illuminating the scope of state power vis-à-vis money, we must resist any tendency to assume that the state *determines* even the formal validity of money.

On the one hand, we can readily accept that because nation-states have the power to regulate banking and money practices and establish legal-tender laws, along with the higher powers of taxation and policing, credit/debt denominated in state moneys of account will therefore usually circulate freely within the borders of the nation-state. On the other hand, here as elsewhere, when it comes to money, there are no guarantees, and there are always limits. First, those state monies will usually be unable to circulate outside state borders, yet money does not stop at the border but rather crosses it all the time. Second, there is absolutely no assurance that nation-state money will always circulate within its borders – see Russia in the late 1990s or Venezuela in 2019.[51]

In the previous chapter I mentioned Innes's account of tally sticks. Wray and Ingham both refer to this history as well, and in each case they see it mainly as part and parcel of the story of state money. But it's not at all that simple. Tally sticks were not state money. Rather, they were private monies circulating in relatively small money spaces that only later became acceptable payment for taxes – a move that dramatically increased the money space in which they could circulate. To say the state does not have the power merely to declare and determine money is not at all to deny that the state does have the power to dramatically *affect* money. If the US government announced tomorrow that citizens could pay their taxes in bitcoin, this would surely have an impact on the circulation of bitcoin, or at

---

51 Adam Tooze paints a vivid picture of the US-dollar money space invading the post-Soviet Russian-ruble money space, thereby creating conditions in which Russian political sovereignty was helpless to prevent the undermining of ruble sovereignty:

As the new millennium began, dollars made up 87 percent of the value of all currency in circulation in Russia. Outside the United States, Russia was the largest dollar economy in the world. International investors in Russia were required to pay their local taxes in American currency. Russia became the ultimate experiment in dollarization, a nuclear-armed, former superpower with a currency supplied from Washington. (Tooze 2018: 120)

least on its value as measured in USD.[52] Put in more colloquial terms, we might say that the state cannot create and determine and control money by declarative fiat, but surely the state can sometimes co-opt non-state money.

Above I noted that the state frequently holds the power to regulate private monies into near-extinction. Here we see an alternative option that also betokens state power: the state can legitimate a money already circulating in smaller money spaces, and in so doing both enlarge the viable money space and in some sense render that private money a "state money" – this is roughly what happened with tally sticks. Thus I have unpacked the genuine potency of state power vis-à-vis money, but crucially, I have also called into question a narrow understanding of *state money* as a concept, by showing that state money must be understood as a "creature of the state" not in the sense that the state brings it into being sui generis but only in the sense that an already existent money can be transformed into, can take the form of, state money. In the end, the state is neither the ultimate originator nor the supreme controller of money.[53]

This conclusion has obvious and massive consequences for how we think about practical money questions today. Speaking more broadly, this new theory of money, which affirms all five theses, provides a novel framework for grappling with what we might call today's most pressing "money problems." To carry out that work, however, requires much more detailed engagement with today's markets in money.

---

52 This would not turn bitcoin into money any more than allowing citizens to pay taxes in barrels of oil would make oil money. See Chapter 7 for extended engagement with bitcoin.

53 As I allude in a number of places, my argument here could be read as a fuller development of Schumpeter's early critique of state theory for its flawed logic in positing money as an institution of the state (Schumpeter 1956: 160–61; cf. Schumpeter 1954: 1056–57). As a final note, heterodox theorists never fail to mention that money is created "endogenously" when banks make loans, but I have now shown that the basic principle of money as credit/debt goes much further than this. *Any* two parties can "create money" by issuing credit, and there is no logical reason (though there are surely many practical reasons) why such credits cannot come to circulate more widely. Therefore the argument for "endogenous" money, while valid, cannot be claimed only by state theories of money; indeed, state theory tends to misconstrue the argument – to turn money creation into a state power, not so much "endogenous" as "sovereign."

Chapter Six
Money Markets

1 Money Problems

The previous chapter filled in the final elements of the new theory of money developed over the course of this book, and crystalized that theory by defending the five theses. While these moves highlight the distinctiveness of the theory, it is certainly not completely *new*; it draws from, at the same time that it partially reconstructs, the previous history of theories of money. First, building from the primary insights of Innes, and the broader claim theory as described by Schumpeter, it consistently maintains that all money, in its nature, is credit. Second, reading Ingham supportively, it defends the empirical claim that we can observe a difference between money tokens that circulate and credit instruments that do not. However, third, taking some critical distance from Ingham, it advances the more radical claim that ontologically, in its very being, all credit has the capacity to be transferred. This primary position leads directly to a more portentous fourth thesis – that at an ontological level all credit "is" money because ultimately there is nothing other than money-credit.

Such a claim need not prove as controversial as it may sound to some ears because it must always be heard in conjunction with the fifth and final thesis: all money-credit forms a hierarchy, so affirming the ontological sameness of money and credit does not negate empirical differences among various instances of money-credit. There is never money but always *monies*. The requisite hierarchy of money means that while there is only ever money-credit, money is not all the same precisely because some money-credits are better than others.

Most importantly, Chapter 5's arguments must be sited within the wider context of the money array. Though we need to analyze the money token in great depth and detail, we must also follow where it points: toward the concrete creditors who hold this token, and the definite debtors on which the token makes a claim of denominated debt. In the methodological remarks that opened Chapter 1, I emphasized that to develop a theory of money is not in itself to *explain* the entire history of money. Nor is it, I would now add, to solve all the concrete money problems we face today. Understanding money does not "fix" money, nor does it deductively determine monetary policy. But to say that is not to suggest that the theory developed here be understood as purely abstract, nor that it be taken as a formal model designed to operate according to its own internal principles. On the contrary, as I have stressed from the beginning, a theory of money is a way of seeing

https://doi.org/10.1515/9783110760774-010

money, of grasping it conceptually in its particular manifestations. Developing such a theory therefore does not lead to remainder-less solutions to all the problems that money poses to societies today, but it should equip us with better tools for understanding those problems such that we can construct better responses.

To start to prove this point, we can begin at the meta-level by indicating how our theory of money improves upon the two pure types – orthodoxy and heterodoxy. First, we can now append to the long list of weaknesses that plague the orthodox, commodity theory of money (A1x on our matrix) the fact that rather than equipping us to solve contemporary money problems, it positively encourages us to evade them. With this assertion, I have in mind everyone today who advocates some version of "sound money": this includes so-called gold bugs who explicitly call for a return to a gold standard; implicit and explicit defenders of deflation and deflationary polices; and anyone else lured by the promise that if only we could force money to have an essential, intrinsic value, then value itself might somehow be fixed, preserved, and protected.

From Milton Friedman's monetarism in the 1960s to President Donald Trump's 2019 nomination of Judy Shelton[1] to the Federal Reserve Board, the hope remains the same: as a natural, market-regulated entity (i.e., a commodity), money will take care of itself. The idea appears to be that we only face money *problems* when state interference – from the issuing of "fiat currency," to running government deficits, to central bank intervention – creates such problems. Therefore, the "solution" is always to deny that there are any "naturally" occurring problems, eliminate all regulations, and deal with money only through a fixed set of technocratic rules. Monetarism originally suggested controlling the "money supply" and allowing it to increase gradually, but all attempts to do so were spectacular failures. The reason for such failure is plain: money is not a commodity, so there is no *supply of* or *demand for* it.[2] However, rather than coming to the obvious conclusion, and rejecting the overall approach, monetarism's mission to control the supposed supply of money morphed into the strategy of "inflation targeting" based on the so-called Non-Accelerating Inflation Rate of Unemployment (NAIRU). This hypo-

---

1 Shelton's nomination stalled in the US Senate and was eventually withdrawn by President Biden. At the time Trump nominated her, Shelton strongly advocated a return to a gold standard and a 0 % inflation target for the Fed. She had previously argued for a repeal of the US Federal deposit insurance fund (Wikipedia, s.v. "Judy Shelton").

2 We must distinguish between human desire, on the one hand, and the "demand schedule" as drawn by neoclassical economics, on the other. Obviously people *want* money, but we cannot translate this desire into a demand curve. This is not to deny the existence of attempts by modern economics to draw "the demand curve for money," but to suggest that the necessary presuppositions of such a project prove untenable.

statization serves only to naturalize a relation that has always been political (that between capital and labor). The details matter less than the basic point: monetarist theories only ever deal with money problems by blaming them on "politics."

The pure type of heterodox theory (B2y) clearly proves superior to the orthodox ideal as both a theory of money and as a framework for grappling with today's money problems. Yet in many of its most popular versions, it winds up yet again *inverting* the commodity theory. I developed this claim in Chapter 4, by showing that where a pure metallist theory describes money strictly in terms of naturalized economic relations (the unfettered free market, including a market in money), the heterodox theory in its chartalist form tends to transform money into a pure state function, and thus to project or presuppose an untenable degree of state control – untenable not just relative to political capacity but in terms of the nature of money.

We witness this phenomenon clearly in the simplified version of MMT that circulates today (especially, it must be admitted, on social media), which so often boils down to the this claim: "deficits don't matter." Worse than the slogan itself (which does a good deal to correct falsehoods generated by both orthodox money theories and by neoclassical economics) may be the core of the argument in support of it – namely, the idea that because state money is "sovereign money," the state can always issue as much of it as it likes. On this account the state is always ultimately in control of "its" money. As a recent, glowing review of Stephanie Kelton's recent book puts it, the government "cannot run out of money any more than a score keeper of a football game can run out of points" (Despain 2020). The reviewer colorfully draws out the "points" metaphor, but its source lies in Kelton's own text (Kelton 2020: 442) – and it's a very poor metaphor for money.

Perhaps describing money as points could be helpful in highlighting the difference between a commodity theory's commitment to intrinsic value and the Keynesian emphasis on the importance of money of account. Like points, money of account concerns abstract denomination and a measure of quantifiable differentiation. But the usefulness of the simile ends there: when the scorekeeper or referee awards points, they are not creating credits that they then owe to the player or team to whom they are issued. Points are abstract and nominalist, but once you have them they are yours; they do not measure a relation of credit/debt to another party but rather represent a quantity of positive, singular value. Moreover, points can only be created/granted by the (sovereign) scorekeeper, whereas money-credit can be issued by anyone at all, and in practical terms most of it is issued not by governments directly but by banks and other financial institutions. Kelton claims that when the government taxes you, it is like the scorekeeper subtracting points: the government/scorekeeper doesn't actually get anything (Kelton 2020: 442). But the metaphor again breaks down: the scorekeeper has a magical ability to create "points" out of nothing. But when the government "creates money," it only does so by becoming a debtor to whomever holds those credits (whether they be bonds, central bank reserves, or central bank coins and notes[3]). And this means that when the government brings in tax revenue and thereby destroys money, it does in fact "get something" – namely, a reduction in its outstanding debt.

It is of course quite true that a government can always issue new debt to cover current and future spending, but issuing new debt is not the same as awarding more points precisely because the government is a debtor and the scorekeeper is not. The government has to face solvency questions that do not affect the referee. Any team will be happy to be issued new points, but not all creditors will always want to continue holding the debt of a particular government. Working through this extended example helps us to see the "inversion" described in Chapter 4: MMT and other post-Keynesian approaches run the risk of suggesting that all money problems can be solved in the exact same way – namely, the government will just issue/create "more money." And if money were like points in a sporting match, then the problem would be solved just that easily. But once again, money is just not that simple.

If we want to deal with our current money problems in a thoughtful and rigorous way, we first need to start with a more sophisticated theory of money and then recognize our need to grapple with these problems in a manner that proves much more complicated (including technically complex) and messy (including politically fraught). This book has developed such a theory, and in this chapter I begin to conclude the work by carrying out some of the groundwork necessary for eventually addressing our money problems.[4]

2 Money Creation, Part 1; or, What Is a Loan?

One of the challenges in dealing with contemporary issues around money lies in the vast size and enormous complexity of today's money markets. For example, in 2019 the average daily turnover in the foreign exchange (forex) markets was $6.6 trillion. These are enormous markets, and *they are markets in money.* As I de-

---

3 Here I again simplify by referring to central bank notes ("currency") and central bank reserves as government debt, when in most cases they are technically debts of a central bank whose balance sheet is distinct from that of the national treasury. The general point holds because these central bank obligations ultimately prove to be obligations of the national government.

4 The point of these engagements is to round out the theory of money defended in the previous chapters, and to give a sense of how it might approach a subset of the many questions we face today regarding the economics, politics, and culture of money. This is not a policy text, and thus these are not policy recommendations or definitive accounts of any of these issues.

tailed in Chapter 3, by reimagining economic exchange as the swapping of a commodity for a credit, we simultaneously bring to light the importance of a distinct phenomenon we can call *financial exchange* – the swapping of one credit for another, or the exchange of IOUs.

In one sense financial exchange proves simpler than economic exchange, because the former swaps entities of the same *kind* (money-credits), while the latter mutually substitutes entities of two different kinds (money-credits and commodities). However, looked at from another angle, even the most basic example of financial exchange proves complex, if not mysterious. To see this angle we must bring out the ambiguity or ambivalence of the words "loan" (noun and verb) and "borrow" (verb) as they apply to our two different entities – money-credits and commodities. If my neighbor asks to *borrow* my hammer and I agree to *loan* it to them, we can plainly see that there is only one entity (the hammer), and it remains my property both before and after the loan. My neighbor takes temporary possession of the hammer, but they owe me precisely because it is mine and they must give it back in the future. It sounds trivial to spell this out, but I do so to contrast it with the other uses of *loan* and *borrow.*

Loaning money bears almost no relation to loaning a hammer. The two actions prove so very much distinct that, on logical grounds, they shouldn't even be given the same name (though we know that language use has never followed the dictates of logic). It goes without saying that I can only loan my neighbor a hammer if I already have a hammer; similarly, my neighbor cannot create a new hammer by borrowing it. When we turn to the case of money, those conditions no longer hold.

To loan or borrow money is to create money, to literally bring into existence the money that is loaned or borrowed. There is no money before the loan (though of course there could have been some other money). Unlike the hammer, with a money loan I do not retain ownership over a single entity. The hammer my neighbor borrowed was always mine; they could use it, but they had to give it back. Hence there was always just one asset (the hammer). While the money my neighbor borrows is their asset (they can spend it), in loaning to them I create a second asset, a new claim on them as the borrower, i.e., the loan, which is my asset. This might seem more confusing than it needs to be, but it is standard practice among banks, whose typical operations prove far more complex than we are usually willing to admit. To clarify our understanding of money, we need to analyze the most elemental of those practices.

"The essence of banking," says Mehrling, "is a swap of IOUs" because "when a bank makes a loan, it adds to its balance sheet both an asset (the loan) and a liability (a deposit in the name of the borrower)" (Mehrling 2011: 65). Mehrling thus describes banking according to the exact terms we have used to define financial exchange: the swapping of money-credits. Moreover, his account points to the essential role of the banker as the creator of money-credit, which can be illustrated simply by looking at the balance sheets of the banker and the borrower.

Bank A		Borrower B	
Assets	*Liabilities*	*Assets*	*Liabilities*
loan to B	deposit from B	deposit at A	loan from A

The above does not show an example of financial exchange but merely the issuing of a loan, and thus the creation of money-credit.[5] The balance sheet demonstrates

---

5 Failure to grasp that money only emerges through the creation of both an asset and a liability and thereby involves two distinct parties (bank and borrower) – failure, that is, to *picture* the balance sheets – can lead even the most brilliant and astute students of money into ambiguity or confusion. Here, for example, is Ingham's recent presentation: "Modern banks lend by creating a deposit of *new money* for the borrower with taps on the computer keyboard. ... [M]odern bank money is *socially* created by the borrower's legally enforceable *promise* to repay the debt. The deposit is a *private debt* owed to the bank which becomes *public money* when it is spent by the borrower" (Ingham 2020: 63). The first sentence isn't exactly wrong, but it proves obtuse because it attempts to describe money creation as a *one-step process*. Yes, the deposit is, in fact, new money, but it cannot come into being without the corresponding loan. And this leads Ingham into a definite error when he calls the "deposit" a debt *owed to the bank*. No, deposit accounts are the liabilities of banks; they are what banks owe their customers. *Of course Ingham knows this* (he says as much three sentences later), but because he has not separated the deposit account (the credits of the customer) from the loan (the debt of the customer), he does not fully arm himself to deal with the complexities of what happens when the customer spends. We see this in Ingham's conclusion, where he argues that spending makes the private debt "public," i.e., the party who receives the money as payment takes its origin as private bank money to be "utterly irrelevant" (Ingham 2020: 63). Ingham's logic goes from the single origin of credit (private bank money) to its singular circulation, where it becomes public money. But that's not what actually happens. A bank can never issue credit; it can only ever issue debt – debt that functions as credit for its holder. But when that holder "spends" the credit, *they transfer the debt.* Let's say I take out a home-equity loan from my bank (step 1), and then I swipe my bank debit card at Home Depot (the home-improvement store) (step 2). Swiping my card reduces my deposit account at my bank, but it simultaneously increases the deposit account at Home Depot's bank. To complete this transaction, my bank will send Fed reserves to Home Depot's bank. However, no new Fed reserves are created in this process, and the money in Home Depot's bank account is no different in kind from the money in my bank account: both are commercial bank deposits. Where, then, does the putatively "public" money come from? If it is created at all, then that creation occurs at the site of the original loan and the swap of IOUs. Money creation cannot rightly be understood as the issuance of purely private credit (Ingham's "deposit of *new money*") that then gets circulated (thereby becoming "public money"). The initial swap of IOUs creates bank money that can circulate, but as it does it will continue to be bank money. The money is just as much "private" and/or "public" every step of the way.

plainly what I argued above: loaning money to my neighbor creates two assets. Some readers might protest: I am not a bank and therefore cannot create a new deposit account for my neighbor; I can only hand over money I already have – say, a $100 bill – just as with the hammer. In reply I only ask that we look at the household balance sheets, both before and after the loan.

BEFORE

Me		My Neighbor	
Assets	Liabilities	Assets	Liabilities
$100 bill			

AFTER

Me		My Neighbor	
Assets	Liabilities	Assets	Liabilities
$100 loan to neighbor		$100 bill	$100 loan from me

My overall balance sheet remains the same, though I now hold a claim on my neighbor rather than on the Fed. But my neighbor's balance sheet has expanded. By adding across the two balance sheets, we find total assets have increased from $100 to $200.

This is money creation. The capacity for capitalist systems and monetary societies to expand and contract money-credit proves essential to their being; individuals living within such societies need money-credits in order to feed, clothe, and shelter themselves. As Mehrling emphasizes, the money hierarchy is dynamic: "At every time scale we see expansion and contraction." It is also, I would add, unpredictable and beyond the control of any single agent or group of agents (including governments). Moreover, during an expansion everything looks like money, while during contractions "the hierarchy reasserts itself" (Mehrling 2016: 10). Here we mark one of the most important differences between our theory of the money array and any effort to conceptualize money without a debtor. Money creation occurs neither through mining, nor any other form of commodity production, nor through the edicts of states. Only a theory of money as credit/debt can properly account for the incessant expansion and contraction of money-credits that is the heart of capitalist societies (and as with human beings, also the organ most likely to fail us).

The power of the balance-sheet approach does not stop with its capacity to illuminate the nature of money loans or to clarify the process of money creation.

Activity in the money markets usually involves financial institutions on both sides of the transaction, and in this context balance sheets become almost required tools – without them we may not even understand what is going on. Balance sheets help us follow the money, to track the movement of the IOUs that bankers are constantly swapping.

To demonstrate, we can look at perhaps the paramount money market in operation today, the so-called "repo" market, in which we observe roughly $2 to $4 trillion in daily transactions (Cheng and Wesell 2020). "Repo" stands for "repurchase agreement," which is itself an oblique name for a particular type of secured loan. Secured loans require collateral, which typically takes the form of some asset that the borrower agrees to forfeit upon default on the loan (for example, for almost all residential mortgages, the title to the house serves as collateral to secure the loan). Repo loans entail a distinct, complex, and very strict security agreement: rather than pledge to forfeit specific assets *if* he should default, the borrower in a repo agreement actually hands over the asset (usually a security such as a government bond[6]) at the inception of the loan.

Concretely, the borrower sells the bond to the lender (at less than its market value) and simultaneously agrees to buy it back from the lender at a specified date[7] for a predetermined price (higher than the initial sale price, but lower than the market value). The difference between the sale price and the buyback price of the bond constitutes the interest rate on the repo loan – the *repo rate.* The difference between the initial loan amount (the sale price) and the bond's market value is known as the *haircut* – the amount the borrower will lose if he fails to come up with the cash to buy back the bond. Gary Gorton and Andrew Metrick provide a clear and helpful example: "If an asset has a market value of $100 and a bank sells it for $80 with an agreement to repurchase it for $88, then we would say that the repo rate is 10 percent (= 88 – 80 / 80), and the haircut is 20 percent ([=] 100 – 80 / 100)" (Gorton and Metrick 2009: 3). Repo is a contractual agreement between borrower and lender, not an open market purchase of a security conducted between a market maker and an investor. Accordingly, the repo contract does not *establish* the market price; rather, market price is an exogenous *given* – a variable plugged into the repo contract. In other words, when drawing up the repo contract, the "market price" is just whatever price the security happens to be trading for at that moment. To reiterate, the contract will typically set both the pur-

---

6 It is possible to repo many other securities as well (corporate bonds, mortgage-backed securities, etc.), but the majority of the market is in government bonds, and keeping our focus here simplifies the explication.

7 Most repo loans have a term of less than three months, and a large percentage are overnight loans, but they can also have terms of up to a year.

chase and repurchase prices *below* that market price: the difference between purchase price and repurchase price determines the interest rate; the difference between purchase price and market price determines the haircut, itself a reflection of how much collateral the borrower is offering.

All the above describes repo from the perspective of a borrower who is "doing repo" by borrowing (where borrowing involves selling the bond first and buying it back later), but the entire transaction can be looked at from the side of the lender who is "doing reverse repo" by loaning money (which takes the form of buying the bond today while agreeing to sell it back at a higher price in the future).

Repo sounds confusing *because it is confusing,* both terminologically and in the financial and contractual complexity of the loan.[8] While most explanations of repo jump directly to the mechanics of the market itself, we must pause to emphasize the real purpose of the sophisticated engineering. Unsecured loans are a simpler form of money-credit than secured loans because they are nothing other than relations of credit/debt between two parties. But the lack of security can also lead to a lack of trust, which translates directly into a lack of liquidity in the money markets.[9] Secured loans, by contrast, necessarily require a more complex legal structure, sometimes involve commodity markets, and often become entangled with stubborn material realities. The obvious example is foreclosure. If a bank decides a homeowner has defaulted on their mortgage, at least three things stand in the way of the bank's efforts to claim the collateral on the loan: 1) a whole series of legal protections designed to shield homeowners from losing their house; 2) the fact of physical possession, which may require police power to evict homeowners; and 3) even if the bank obtains title (through the courts) to an empty house (through the cops), they still have to sell the house on the market in order to get to the end goal – money.

---

8 The language I use above to describe *repo* and *reverse repo* captures the most common usage of the terms in the United States, because it describes the repo market from the perspective of securities dealers, who are the dominant players and market makers here. However, when the Federal Reserve engages in the repo market, the language is transposed: when a securities dealer does repo, they are borrowing, but when the Fed does repo, they are loaning (and vice versa for reverse repo).

9 Calling a *market* illiquid is shorthand to indicate lack of liquidity in the *assets* traded in such markets. To say, as Matt Levine frequently does, that "people are worried about bond market liquidity" means people are worried about the liquidity of bonds. As I discussed in Chapter 5, we can understand the *liquidity* of bonds as an index of their "shiftability" into other money-credits. Note that usually, but not always, when someone says a market lacks liquidity, they really mean there are not enough *buyers.* (A market is also illiquid if no one is selling, but rarely does this lead to the same panic as a lack of buyers does.)

In this context we can make sense of the complicated technology of the repurchase agreement. Oversimplifying, we might say that repo solves the problem of unsecured lending without the attendant baggage of (typical) secured lending. Repo is unique both contractually and legally. The contractual nature of repo means that neither party needs to trust the other to comply with the agreement, nor do they need the explicit intervention or backing of outside authorities (such as courts or deposit insurance).[10] If the borrower fails to repay, the creditor already has the security and can sell it (thereby realizing the haircut as profit). If the lender cannot return the security (say they go bankrupt overnight) then the repo loan turns into a sale without repurchase, forcing the borrower/seller to take the haircut.[11] The distinctive nature of the repo contract means that the defaulting party has no standing in bankruptcy court: the non-defaulting party simply keeps the cash or security (Gorton and Metrick 2009: 9). Borrowing in the repo market is like getting a mortgage in which you sell your house to the bank (which now owns the title outright) for the same price as the amount of your home loan, agree to buy the house back at the cost of your total mortgage payments, and also waive your right to occupy the house and any legal protections for homeowners (until such time as you have fully paid off – that is, bought back – the house).

As long as we remind ourselves that markets are never pure and never exist in nature (they are always *made* by dealers), then we might call repo a "purer" form of money market. Just as money is the circulation of exchange-value untethered from the physical body of commodities, so repo markets allow for the swapping of money-credits with far fewer entanglements with commodity markets or legal infrastructure. It is therefore no accident that repo plays such an outsized role in today's money markets. Of course, at its core, the repo market is just like any other market in money: it involves the swapping of money-credits for other money-credits, all of which can be clearly tracked on the balance sheets of finan-

---

10 Obviously all markets, but particularly money markets, depend ultimately on relations of authority within the overall social order. One cannot do repo in a state of nature. The point is that the social technology of a repo agreement isolates the parties to it from other outside legal and political forces.

11 In the text above I use the stylized example from Gorton and Metrick to explain the basic elements of repo. Their case uses large, round numbers, in order to simplify the math needed to calculate the interest rate and haircut rate. The actual differences between market, sale, and repurchase prices usually prove much smaller (e. g., $100, $99.50, and $99.90, respectively). Indeed, in practice, dealers will frequently do repo with a zero haircut (sale price equal to market price), because they are repo-ing securities for a client as more of a service than a money-maker (BIS 2022a). Note also that for the typical short term of repo loans, it is highly unlikely that the institution making the loan will go bankrupt overnight. Thanks to Tim Schere for helpful discussion on this point.

cial institutions. The clearest example of repo involves three agents, which we can stylize as follows:

1) a money market mutual fund that holds excess cash and would like to earn interest on it
2) a bank that wants to hold as little cash as possible but often needs short-term funding of its assets
3) a securities dealer that makes a market in cash and securities by standing between parties 1 and 2

By their remit, money market funds (MMF) invest in short-term, very liquid assets. They therefore have a lot of cash, and while they do invest some in direct bank instruments, such as certificates of deposit, they have far too much to place in unsecured bank savings accounts (for individuals such accounts are *insured* by the Federal Deposit Insurance Corporation (FDIC) up to $250,000, but they are not *secured* by collateral). They therefore approach a securities dealer who will "do repo" with them; this means the dealer borrows the cash by agreeing to sell government bonds to, and then repurchase them from, the MMF. The repo loan is booked as a liability on the balance sheet of the dealer and as an asset on the balance sheet of the MMF. At the same time, large banks need to borrow to meet their daily and overnight funding needs. These banks have significant holdings of US Treasury bonds as assets on their balance sheets, and they can literally fund those assets in the repo market. That is, they repo their bonds with the securities dealer precisely so as to fund ownership of those bonds.[12] From the perspective of the securities dealer, this second transaction is a reverse repo: they are loaning money to the bank. Just like any bank or dealer, the securities dealer makes money on the spread: they loan money in the repo market (to the bank) for more than they borrow in that market (from the MMF). We can chart all of this by looking at the balance sheets of all three agents, and by adding in clarification about the *movement* of the security (the bond) and the cash being borrowed.

Bank		Securities Dealer		Money Market Fund	
Assets	*Liabilities*	*Assets*	*Liabilities*	*Assets*	*Liabilities*
	reverse repo	reverse repo	repo loan	repo loan	

━━▷ bond moves in this direction ━━▷
◁━━ cash moves in this direction ◁━━

---

12 In other words, the bank wants to hold bonds on their balance sheets, and they raise the money to do this by repo-ing those very bonds overnight. This sounds paradoxical, but it is a standard practice of many large commercial banks today.

Note that the balance sheets above contain entries only for the repo and reverse repo loans, and they exclude all the other assets and liabilities that these three institutions also hold. This is the view of repo from the perspective of the securities dealer, who never holds the cash or the security.

In his online course "Economics of Money and Banking," Mehrling explains the repo market by drawing a chalkboard diagram much like the above (Mehrling 2015).[13] My own explication of the repo market as a quintessential example of a money market does not deviate from Mehrling's account, but it does place it strikingly into context – both in the general terms of our broader theory of money, and in the particular articulation of financial exchange. Therefore we need to emphasize something almost always left out of most summaries of repo: the two entities moving in opposite directions here, bonds and "cash," *are both money-credits*. Commentators on the money market typically refer to "cash" quite casually, but we should never forget that financial institutions do not pay one another with coins or notes; nor do they pay each other with bank deposits. Individuals pay each other with bank deposits; banks pay each other with *central bank reserves*. Thus the "cash" moving from the MMF, through the securities dealer, and to the bank is actually Fed reserve funds. The bond moving the other direction is explicitly government debt, and just as obviously a money-credit.[14]

---

13 A Google Images search for "repo market explained" results in many copies of said diagram.
14 I have found over the years of presenting this work that a small minority of readers react quite negatively to the idea of bonds as money. Perhaps this stems from a tendency to limit the concept "money" to whatever a particular individual understands as "cash." In any case, one can offer a number of replies. First, bonds might well be taken as money-credit par excellence as they starkly fulfill the conditions of the money array: they are tokens of credit/debt denominated in moneys of account. Second, I am not breaking new ground by seeing bonds as money. Macleod not only defended that theoretical position in 1889 but also backed it up empirically by citing British case law showing that not just bonds, but indeed *foreign bonds* could serve as "currency," which for Macleod was the most significant name for *money* (Macleod 1889: 95, 97–101, citing Gorgier v. Mieville [3 B. & C.]; cf. Schumpeter 1954: 1043).

In this context I propose a corollary to Mehrling's hierarchy-of-money thesis. Mehrling's thesis: there is a hierarchy of money-credits. As one moves up or down the hierarchy, what looks like money (or credit) changes – in general everything above your current position looks like money, while below you looks like credit. My corollary: what functions as "cash" similarly depends on both one's location along the hierarchy, and distinctly, what type of institution "you" are. For the average citizen, bank deposits are cash; but individuals are not even allowed to hold, much less spend, central bank reserves. In contrast, from the perspective of a commercial bank, what individuals think of as "cash" is nothing of the sort (it's a liability). For commercial banks, central bank reserves are "cash." Meanwhile, if you are the Central Bank of the Argentine Republic, "cash" becomes your dollar-deposit account at a large New York or London bank; or if you are the European Central Bank, "cash" may be your access to the Fed's swap lines.

Despite its complexities – or better, in some ways because of them – the repo market is a market in money, and it illustrates the basic principle of financial exchange as the swapping of money-credit for money-credit. As the balance sheets make clear, we cannot understand these money-market practices under the terms of the neoclassical model of economic exchange (the exchange of real goods), nor even under our theory's reconceptualization of economic exchange (the swapping of a commodity for money-credit). Markets in money are based on what we have called financial exchange: the swapping of money-credits for money-credits. We therefore locate an entire realm dominated by market actors who, it would seem, could not care less about economic exchange precisely because they do not exchange goods and services (commodities) but only credits (money).

These economic actors look nothing like the *homo economicus* imagined by neoclassical economics. The latter uses money to acquire commodities, which he then consumes, either directly (in order to live) or indirectly through productive consumption (i. e., consumes so as to initiate or sustain a production process). But as their name implies, money-market agents deal in money, not commodities. In one respect, then, money-market dealers simply ignore economic exchange and focus entirely on financial exchange. In financial exchange the goal is not commodities but rather money itself. The primary and direct aim of money markets is nothing more or less than making money, manufacturing a profit (M→M'). But in order to make money from money, actors in money markets must also concern themselves fundamentally with two other concerns: hedging risk and maintaining liquidity – with the latter including both the standard sense of access to cash and

---

Hence we should not confuse *cash* with money (the theory of which I have been developing throughout this book). Cash is a limited and relative concept: it's the type of money that a particular actor – situated in a particular location – can use most easily to settle debts or buy goods and services *directly* (i. e., without first changing the money form). Cash will almost never be located far down the hierarchy, yet at the same time, for most actors cash is not in fact located at the very top of the hierarchy. US Treasuries are clearly near the top of the money hierarchy, but they are not cash for most agents. Of course, in a strange and important way, US Treasuries are cash from the perspective of the Fed. When the Fed wants to "spend," they do so by selling Treasuries to commercial banks; the Fed hands over the bonds and takes back its own reserves.

Finally, the entire point of the repo market can be grasped as an alchemical transfiguration of bonds into "cash" (Fed reserves) and back again. And while the technical configuration of repo is of recent vintage, over 150 years ago Marx observed the phenomenon of "public bonds, easily negotiable, which go on functioning in their hands [the creditors'] just as so much hard cash would" (Marx 1990: 918; also quoted in Ingham 2020: 67, though Ingham misattributes the cite to Volume III rather than Volume I of *Capital*).

Keynes's sense of preservation of long-term value. Participants in the money market always have these three goals in mind: return, hedging, and liquidity.

Crucially, and as demonstrated in Chapter 3, this process of financial exchange does not operate in a vacuum; rather, it remains intimately linked to economic exchange. Put directly, liquid markets in goods (economic exchange) depend on these liquid markets in money (financial exchange). This is a different formulation of Mehrling's primary thesis concerning what I would call the dialectical relationship between money markets and commodity markets.[15] Financial exchange in the money markets is the first source of liquidity, and this liquidity is the very blood of the capitalist system of circulation. What finance theory calls the "allocation of capital" – the supply of funding that capitalist firms require in order to engage in economic exchange – therefore cannot be untethered from financial exchange. Capitalism cannot exist without banking and the money markets.

This constitutive relationship stands out in a crisis. In a financial crisis (a crisis of financial exchange) overnight funding seizes – liquidity disappears. Painting a picture of crisis reveals the second dimension of the dialectic: the money markets are not sealed off from the rest of capitalist society. Financial exchange depends on economic exchange, because the *collateral* from capital markets supports the existence of money markets. That is, "capital," in the form of stocks and bonds, is one of the primary assets on balance sheets of financial institutions. If those capitalist firms fail, the asset markdowns will directly affect the money markets. At the extreme, those markdowns can make financial institutions insolvent; they will then become illiquid (no one will lend to them), and then they will fail. This is why every capitalist crisis *includes* a financial crisis, even though not all begin with a financial crisis. Neither financial exchange nor economic exchange can be said to come first; each presupposes the other. In tracing this dialectic we also identify the feedback loops that drive both bubbles and contractions.

A basic understanding of money markets both deepens our understanding of the nature of money and helps us to formulate and map some of the most pressing money problems today. From the start we need to be very clear about not only what we learn from an analysis of money markets, but also the limitations and constraints of the market metaphor. In particular, I address in turn first the issue of the "price" of money, and then the specificity of the logic of the derivative.

---

15 Mehrling usually refers to this phenomenon as the "practical intertwining of money markets and capital markets" (Mehrling 2011: 98). Using the standard terms in finance discourse, Mehrling insists that short-term funding ("money markets") is translated into long-term funding ("capital markets") (Mehrling 2011: 29). I am using "money markets" in a more capacious sense to include everything within my theory's category of financial exchange.

3 The "Price" of Money

The theory of money propounded in this book circumscribes – or perhaps better, deflates – Keynes's privileging of money of account as itself serving as the concept of money. As we have shown, denomination is but one aspect of the broader money array. Nevertheless, on one key point almost everyone – from neoclassical economists to Keynesians to value-form Marxists – can agree: money as denomination serves as *measure of value*. This aspect of money leads to a basic definition of price: price is an expression of the value of an entity, conveyed in money terms. Price provides an answer to the question of worth, an answer formulated specifically in the money form.

Based on this logic we might reasonably argue that while a commodity "has" a price (we can formulate its value as measured in money), money itself "is" price (it *is* the mode of expressing that value). Therefore, money itself cannot have a price for just the reason that money is measure. We can observe a direct analogy with weight: the kilogram is a *measure* of weight, but it does not *have* weight. Various objects are more or less heavy, and this can be expressed through kilograms, but kilograms are not themselves heavy.[16] Returning to the language of money, we might draw a preliminary conclusion: money has no price.

We cannot measure the value of money in price terms (i.e., in terms of money): first, because as we have argued throughout, money has no value; but second, because such an expression would be nonsensical.[17] What is the price of $4? Would we really want to answer, "$4"? The equation $4 = $4 does not express the

---

16 Working with the parallel analogy of length, Christopher Arthur suggests that it is "not too absurd" to say that the "standard" meter "measures one metre itself" but that with money the situation proves more extreme "because money is in effect *measure as such*" (Arthur 2004: 100). I take Arthur's point, which is that money constitutes "the value dimension" itself, but I'm not sure it's any less absurd to say a meter measures a meter since the "standard meter" is itself the measure of the standard meter – i.e., the meter is *measure as such* (of length in meters) just as much as the dollar (of value in dollars).

17 Marx states explicitly that "money has no price" and he argues in various ways that £1 = £1 is nonsensical (Marx 1990: 189; Marx 1977: 75; Marx 1973: 72, 138). I read him as repeatedly affirming that money *as money* has no value. That is, the uptake of the passages in which Marx explicitly states that "money has no price" is to uphold the idea that money has no value. Marx's framework assumes that price, expressed in terms of money (denomination), serves as *measure of value*. Price is value expressed in money. Money can serve in this role only so long as it continues to be excluded from the set of commodities that are themselves being measured (i.e., that "have" value). In this context, to say that "money has no price" is to indicate clearly that money cannot be measured in value terms – because it has no value. In other words, Marx is making a point not about the nature of price vis-à-vis money but rather concerning the nature of value vis-à-vis money (see Chambers n.d.).

price of money; it is merely a senseless tautology. In the writings from his notebooks, wherein Marx grappled most deeply with a theory of money (a project he effectively abandoned), he brought this line of thinking to a parsimonious conclusion: "Exchanging money for money makes no sense" (Marx 1973: 138).

But Marx himself failed to push his investigation to the next level: it may, at one level of analysis, seem nonsense to exchange money for money, *yet we do it all the time.* Exchanging money for money is the definition of financial exchange and the center of activity in the money markets. We cannot just dismiss exchanging money for money as nonsense; we have to explain (make sense of?) the nonsense, because financial exchange is not merely something that capitalist social orders do, but something fundamental to their very functioning.

One way of unraveling this paradox is to start by observing that the so-called tautology of $4 = $4 actually contains a sleight of hand. After all, in the money markets, it's quite true that no one ever exchanges $4 for $4; actors in the money markets would readily agree that to engage in such exchange would hold no purpose or meaning.

To demonstrate the extent to which money *does* have a price, we must skip over the equation $4 = $4, which is only a distraction, and point instead toward a very different equation, what we might call an "impossible equation." I borrow this phrase from an early work of Jacques Rancière, who draws from Marx to argue that the classical equation of economic exchange – that is, the exchange of commodity for commodity in some proportion, $xA = yB$ – must be seen for what it really is: an impossible equation, an "identity of opposites" (Rancière 1989: 106).[18] The equation of economic exchange *posits as equal* two entities that are utterly heterogenous insofar as each has a completely distinct use-value.[19] One way to understand capitalism is to grasp it as "that system which makes such an impossible equation possible" (Chambers 2022: 91). In any case, traditional economic exchange – and therefore also our updated version of economic exchange[20] – is based upon this impossible equation, $xA = yB$.

---

18 Rancière goes on to show that the difference between Marx and the classical political economists is that the latter fail to see that the equation is impossible: they simultaneously naturalize both the existence of commodities and their relative equality with one another. In contrast, Marx first identifies the equation as "impossible" and then goes on "to theorize the possibility of this impossible equation" (Rancière 1989: 107).

19 For more on use and use-value, see Chapter 7, Footnote 25.

20 Chapter 3's reinterpretation of economic exchange, as the swapping of a commodity for a credit, inherits and radicalizes the underlying paradox of traditional economic exchange. Rather than positing the equality of two distinct use-values (two commodities fixed in given proportions), our equation posits the equality of two utterly different types – a commodity and a money-credit. Here again, any explanation for what makes the impossible possible must lie with the capitalist social

What, then, is the impossible equation that expresses the nature of *financial exchange?* We have already indicated that the equation to express the swapping of a credit for a credit cannot be $x = $x (e. g., $4 = $4). $4 = $4 is a silly equation, but not an impossible one.[21] The impossible equation of financial exchange is better expressed as a more direct variant on the equation of economic exchange – that is, $x = $y. Here we have one measure/amount of a particular denomination of money-credit posited as equal to a different measure/amount. To return to our favored example, the equation would look something like this: $4 = $4.07. This equation clearly seems impossible.

How do we theorize its possibility? As a start, we can turn to the concrete practices of dealers in the money market. This allows us first to uphold the assertion "money has no price," at least in the more limited sense that money does not have *a* price. At the same time, and in a different sense, we must reject the notion that money has no price because, like every other asset, money has *multiple prices*. $4 = $4 is a trivial or frivolous equation because no dealer would ever offer to sell $4 for $4. But we must emphasize that dealers are *never just offering to sell (or to buy)*.

Rather, dealers always offer both to buy and to sell money at *different* prices. Hence the "price" of $4 will prove multiple, not singular, because it will always depend on whether a dealer is buying or selling. For example, a forex dealer might buy $4 for the price of €3.30, but they would sell $4 for the price of €3.36. This means the dealer is exchanging dollars for euros at a rate of 1.212 when they buy dollars, but at a rate of 1.190 when they sell dollars. The impossible equation of financial exchange lies hidden, just barely below the surface, in the fact of these different buy and sell prices (which express different exchange rates). The math is simple. If we take the dealer buy rate of 1.212 and apply it to calculate the value of €3.36 – the price the dealer receives when selling $4 – the result is $4.07. In other words, if the dealer sells $4 and then buys it back, they end up with $4.07. Hence $4 = $4.07.[22] This impossible equation is a daily reality for money-market dealers.

---

order as a whole: capitalism is a system that constantly exchanges money-credit for commodities. The details of that explanation (see Chambers 2022) go beyond the scope of our narrower treatment in this book of the theory of money.

21 The general formula for the impossible equation consists in positing as equal two things that are not even of the same kind. $4 = $4 is, in fact, a valid relation of equality (thus not impossible), but as a tautology it is meaningless (which is Marx's point).

22 This conclusion does not directly refute Marx's point, because no dealer will offer to sell dollars priced in dollars. $4 = $4.07 can only be *derived* as the impossible equation by going *through* other currencies. Money can only "have a price" in a different money, so the price of money depends on the multiplicity of monies.

The forex example proves the most straightforward, but other money-market practices, despite operating at dazzling and bewildering levels of complexity, rest on the same underlying logic (see Mehrling 2016). For example, if a dealer borrows money through the repo market at rate x, they will loan money through reverse repo at rate y (where y > x). The term structure, required collateral, and other details of these transactions may prove incredibly sophisticated, but underlying it all is the fundamental fact that, after all the math has been done, rate y is greater than rate x (at least according to the dealer's own calculations). Interest rate swaps and credit default swaps can become even more intricate and esoteric, but the basic logic of the swap of IOUs does not change.

We can tie these threads together as follows. Money has no value, and thus to the extent that "price" is itself "measure of value," it makes no sense to assert a singular price for money. But if we take "price" in the nominal sense as nothing more than the rate at which two assets exchange, then obviously money can have a price because money has an exchange-value. Mehrling in fact insists that we understand an exchange rate not as the value of assets in terms of assets (the metallist view), nor as the claim value of goods in terms of goods (the chartalist view), but as merely the price of money in terms of (other) money (obviously the money view).[23] Understood in this circumscribed sense as exchange rates, the "price of money" proves to be a terribly important phenomenon because the money markets are in fact driven by the differential and changing prices for different forms of money.

To insist on the importance of the money markets, as we do here, and to affirm this nominal notion of the price of money, does not weaken our prior and fundamental claim that money has no value.[24] Money exchanges for money at dif-

---

23 Mehrling translates the chartalist view into the relative price of goods by way of the argument for purchasing power parity. But the basic idea is simple: if money is nothing more than a ticket claim, then economics is still the circulation of goods for goods (with money as claim), not the exchange of goods for credits (Mehrling 2016).

24 The discussion in this section intentionally sidesteps the neoclassical paradigm's blunt answer to this question. For decades, introductory economics textbooks have told students that "the interest rate is the price of money," and such a notion is also implicitly built into certain Keynesian models. Fortunately, today even mainstream economics seems to be moving away from this shibboleth. Without taking up the complicated topic of interest, we can say a few things concisely. First, there is no such thing as *the* interest rate; there are always multiple rates. And this is because, second, interest is not a purely "monetary" or even "economic" phenomenon; at its core it is a relation of power. As Marx acutely observes, the possession of money-credits (valid claims on valid debtors) gives one "the *power* to demand an *interest*" from those desperately in need of such money-credits (Marx 2015: 445). Power differentials thus give rise to different interest rates. In the broadest sense,

fering rates, and the fact of these differing prices, operating along the hierarchy of money, makes it possible for the money markets to provide liquidity. In this sense, the *prices* (plural) of money prove crucial to contemporary capitalism. But the rhetorical line "money has no price" also indicates something significant: the claim immediately calls into question the entire classical and neoclassical view of money as a commodity with a supply and demand. To say money has no price is to assert that the thing which *measures* value does not itself *possess* value. The valid empirical fact that monies are exchanged for one another (at prices) should not be denied, but it also should not be allowed to confuse us – to trick us into believing either that money is a commodity or that it has value. The prices of money are like, but also very much unlike, the prices of commodities. To explore these similarities and contrasts requires closer scrutiny of money markets.

4 The Logic of the Derivative

In developing his illuminating "money view," Mehrling focuses tightly on the money markets themselves. I have already expanded his conception above by weaving it into our previously developed conception of economic exchange (as the swapping of money-credit for commodity) and financial exchange (as the swapping of money-credit for money-credit). Using that framework, I now pose a question that is excluded necessarily from the neoclassical paradigm, and simply not broached by Mehrling: How does the logic of the dealer function and the money markets *reflect back* on economic exchange? In other words, what happens when we treat commodities as if they were money?

The core idea can be formulated parsimoniously: the logic of the money market – that is, buying and selling in order to profit, or buying and selling in order to change risk exposures and maintain liquidity – can be, and frequently is, applied to other markets.[25] This means that many markets that are not literally markets in money operate the "same" way money markets do. To put this point in our earlier

---

we can say that "*interest is like rent – it is the fee you pay for the use of something you do not own*" (Chambers 2022: 138).

25 As should be clear from the approach described in Chapter 1, I refuse any and all naturalization of markets. Thus the many references to "markets" that follow in this section of the text all consistently presume a massive background of social, political, legal, and cultural work that makes a "market" possible in the first place. Goods and credits do not circulate in nature; they circulate in, and only in, society, always according to terms dictated and constrained by the social/legal/political/cultural arrangements of those societies. And finally, we can never forget that markets only exist if and when dealers *make* such markets.

language, the suggestion is that individual market actors may choose to engage in economic exchange but do so for the *purposes* of financial exchange. Better still, we might say that such actors *appear* to be engaging in economic exchange, but in reality they are engaging in a deranged form of financial exchange – a form of financial exchange that somehow includes entities that are not obviously money-credits.

To unpack this idea we can start with an abstract/ideal understanding of economic exchange.[26] Market actors would engage in economic exchange for one of two broad reasons: because they find themselves in possession of commodities (either recently produced, or old inventories) whose value they seek to realize in money terms, or because they have immediate need of commodities (either for direct consumption or as inputs to a production process). The raison d'être of economic exchange involves swapping money, which is the necessary form of capitalist value, with commodities, which are twofold entities existing both as exchange-value and as use-value.

But what happens when we render that ideal type impure by addressing a case in which actors take a money-market approach to commodity markets? A dealer would thus buy commodities not to consume them or use them for production; they would acquire commodities strictly for their exchange-values. This is another way of describing merchant capitalism (Banaji 2020). The dealer is therefore treating the commodity as if it were not actually a commodity (with both use-value and exchange-value); they are treating the commodity like money. At this juncture it is worth specifying that like a commodity, money has an exchange-value; indeed, in a certain sense money-credits *are* exchange-value untethered from the physical body of commodities. Money is therefore utterly unlike a commodity because it is a form of independent and somehow autochthonous exchange-value (Marx 1973: 153). Therefore, when our market actor treats a commodity like money,[27] they

---

26 That is, financial exchange as conceived in this book, not as understood by classical political economy or neoclassical economics.

27 The discussion in the text completely brackets a crucial issue: in order to *treat* a commodity *like* money, it almost always proves necessary to *refashion* the commodity so that it truly is *more like* money. As we know, each *unit* in a money of account is completely indistinguishable from every other unit. This truth about money emanates from its nature as an abstract measure of denomination. This is but a corollary derived from Innes's oft-quoted line that "the eye has never seen nor the hand touched a dollar": precisely because we cannot see or touch dollars, we can make each unit the same. In stark contrast, each commodity is a unique product of a human production process. If we inspect a group of commodities we will always find variation. For this reason, it is only possible to make a money market in *standardized* commodities. Importantly, dealers don't actually trade in "bushels of wheat" but, for example, as Donald MacKenzie puts it, in "bushels of Chicago No. 2 white winter wheat" (MacKenzie 2006: 13; see also Cronon 1991). The latter is a standardized

are simply focusing on the exchange-value of the commodity to the utter exclusion of its physical form (and attendant use-value).

For example, speculators in oil do not have any interest in using the oil as fuel; they just want the price to go up. More precisely, speculators taking a long position want the price to go up, while those taking a short position want it to go down.[28] But the primary point holds: neither plans to heat their house for winter or start up a manufacturing process. This can lead to real problems at the limit, where the fundamental differences between, for example, a bond (money-credit) and oil (commodity) become manifest. I return to this thorny issue below. For now I merely want to reiterate the basic point: once the logic of financial exchange extends to

category of commodity such that any bushel of Chicago No. 2 white winter wheat is meant/said/assumed to be the same as every other. Therefore, prior to making money markets in commodities, the "standard commodity" must be defined (practically, legally, contractually) and then brought into being through standardized production and inspection processes. Note that in the world of traders, there can be some conceptual slippage and confusion surrounding the word "commodity" since some traders apply this term only to what we will call a *standardized* commodity. A custom leather handbag is still an economic commodity, but it cannot be traded on a commodities exchange, nor be used as the underlying asset to create a derivative.

28 A "long" position is one in which the actor profits if the value of the asset goes up; vice versa for a "short" position. In this context one should also emphasize the ideal-type distinction between *speculating* and *hedging*. Any position, short or long, can be chosen *either* as an outright bet on the movement of the asset, *or* as a hedge against a position already taken. We can imagine money-market dealers who are "matched book" dealers – this means they hedge every long position with a short position (and vice versa), thereby earning money only on their fees or bid–ask spreads. In practice, of course, there is no such thing as a dealer who has a completely matched book, but we can apply the same distinction at the level of each dealer – that is, by separating their balance sheets into a "matched book" portion and a "speculative" section (see Mehrling 2011). A sense of the significance of hedging reveals as misguided the sometimes popular sentiment that the "problem" with money markets is the short sellers. In particular, short positions provide hedges to long positions (often enabling those positions to be taken in the first place), and in general, shorting provides liquidity for markets. Derivatives prove particularly important for short positions, because it is almost always harder to take a short position in a market. (For example, to take a long position in a stock, all one has to do is buy it and hold it until the price rises. But to short a stock requires: *borrowing* the stock on loan, with interest; immediately selling the stock for cash; waiting for the price of the stock to drop; then buying the stock and returning it to repay the loan. Note that if the price of the stock goes up, not down, the potential losses to the short seller are infinite.) Sometimes the only way to short an asset is through derivatives, a point illustrated famously in the run-up to the GFC: many market actors noticed the apparent bubble in residential house prices, but had no way to short the housing market. The creation of a particular derivative, the credit default swap (CDS) on mortgage-backed securities (MBS), solved this problem. Even here, however, there is no way to take a short position without a counterparty taking a long position. Sellers of CDS on MBS took in millions of dollars in premiums (from CDS buyers) prior to the period when they lost billions of dollars.

or overdetermines the markets in commodities, we witness within a capitalist social order the manifestation of a type of "money market" in entities that are not actually money. *Oil is not money*, but most of the time nothing stops the oil speculator from treating oil as a speculative trade in exactly the same way she might treat German euro bonds or US dollars.

This extension of money-market logic leads to the creation of an entire array of financial constructs,[29] most of which can be accurately understood as money-credits but many of which include some sort of linkage to commodity markets or the broader realm of economic exchange. This abstract description uses the language we have developed in the preceding chapters in order to give expression and form to what is usually called a derivative.

The textbook definition of a derivative is straightforward, but without context it usually does not seem to say very much. A *derivative* is a specific type of *contract* between two parties; most significantly, the contract is tradable (i. e., transferable to another party). The price of the contract (the derivative) depends on – and therefore changes according to changes in – the price of a separate "underlying" asset that is specified in the contract. By creating a derivative, market actors gain the ability to take a position (short or long) in an asset without actually purchasing that asset.

Futures contracts are often cited as the most basic form of derivative. The example can helpfully crystalize our discussion by linking the concept of a derivative to the earlier (rather crude) example of a speculative market in oil. The mainspring of the futures contract is an agreement that one party will sell to a counterparty a preset amount of a standard commodity, for a set price, on a specific date in the future. At the first level, the contract itself merely fixes the terms of the sale. Many online "explainers" on futures therefore like to imagine what we might call a "natural" contract between an oil producer who wants to sell oil and a manufacturer who needs to buy it. They sign the futures contract as an essential element of economic exchange, but with a slight variation: rather than swapping commodities for money-credits today, they commit themselves today to swap

---

29 These can always be created anew, and we know that the brightest minds on Wall Street often devote themselves to fabulous forms of fabrication. Nonetheless, as I show in the next chapter with the important example of the bill of exchange, there is nothing *new* about the process itself. If we define so-called financialization in the strict terms laid out here – namely, as the *extension* of the logic of financial exchange – then we must also affirm that financialization has been an ongoing process since the earliest stages of merchant capitalism. For just this reason, I reject the thesis that today we live in a new *stage* of capitalism called "financialized capitalism" (implying that previous capitalist periods were somehow *unfinancialized*). Shoshana Zuboff offers a prominent and problematic example of this tendency (Zuboff 2019).

commodities for money-credits in the future – at a set price, determined today. Because these contracts are tradable, this relatively simple form of economic exchange gives rise to the possibility of financial exchange. It makes possible the creation of a derivative market that exchanges not the underlying assets, but these contracts.

This sort of explanation schematizes some basic elements of derivatives, but at some cost to a more penetrating understanding of markets in commodities and money. The problem with the standard example is that it presumes a direct contract between two parties in such a way as to reify the idea of a natural market in the underlying asset. This type of account privileges economic exchange as primary (the contract is between producers and users of oil) and makes the derivative market seem, indeed, derivative – merely a secondary phenomenon. In reality, however, money markets in derivatives function quite differently.

Above all, futures contracts are not agreed between producers and consumers; they are bought and sold by market makers. All futures contracts are transacted between one market actor and the dealer who makes the market. And this makes the derivative much more than a contract in that term's general or legal sense. To highlight the differences we can consider a simple *forward contract* in which party A contracts to buy a commodity for an agreed price at an agreed time, and party B agrees to deliver the commodity for that price. This constitutes a legal commitment to engage in economic exchange (the swapping of money-credits for commodities) at a date in the future, but it is not an example of what we are calling financial exchange. The basic forward contract is merely a legally binding private agreement between two parties; it is not a *futures contract*, and most importantly, it is not a tradable money-credit.[30]

In contrast, futures contracts are sold by dealers, who make a market in them the same as any dealer ever does: by setting the bid and ask prices at which they stand ready to buy or sell such contracts. Regardless of whether I choose to buy from or sell to the dealer, once I take a position with that dealer through a futures contract, I have created a claim – this is the futures contract itself, the derivative. If the price moves in my favor (up, if I have bought; down, if I have sold), then my

---

30 Forward contracts play a not insignificant role in contemporary capitalist practices because large companies (and their banks as counterparties) use them to hedge foreign currency and interest rate risk. And forward contracts can be settled in cash, rather than in the commodity itself – if the price exceeds the contract price, the seller pays the buyer the difference, and vice versa – making them true derivatives in the sense that they allow one to take monetary positions on the underlying commodity without directly trading the commodity. But I confine my analysis here to derivatives that take the form of money-credit as they help to elaborate my conception of financial exchange and develop the overall logic of the derivative.

stake in the contract (my ownership of the derivative) becomes an asset. This is the case because I now own the right (through the futures contract) to buy the commodity at a price lower than its current market value (or sell it at a higher price than its current market value). Hypothetically, this means I could wait until the delivery date, pay the contract price, take ownership of the commodity, and then sell at market price for a profit. Practically, it means that the value of the derivative itself is positive, and I can close out my position with the dealer by having him pay me. If the price moves against me, all of the above logic is reversed, and in holding the derivative I hold a liability to the dealer.

Notice the key elements that emerge in this nuts-and-bolts description of the futures contract:
1) The contract is a form of credit/debt – one party owes the other.
2) The credit/debt is denominated in a money of account.
3) The credit/debt is transferable.[31]

The conclusion here seems inescapable: *derivatives are money-credit.*[32] In turn, markets in derivatives are markets in money. As we have shown, the key aspect of the derivative is not the contract per se. After all, millions of legally binding agreements between parties are signed and executed every day, but most contracts are not derivatives. A derivative is distinct because entering into the contract creates a transferable relation of denominated credit/debt. The elements that mark the derivative as a singular type of contract are precisely the conditions that make it money.

This leads us to a second, practical observation about our previously discussed oil futures market: the largest oil producers are also the biggest players on the fu-

---

31 To reiterate the conceptual clarification from the preceding chapter, "transfer*able*" means it has the potential to be transferred, but no guarantee that it finds a willing party to accept the transfer.

32 Throughout my discussion I focus mainly on derivatives on non-money entities (e.g., oil futures) because they provide a powerful illustration of how a money market can be constructed from a commodity market – how the logic of financial exchange can overdetermine the logic of economic exchange. In the text above I state emphatically that "oil is not money," but now we need an addendum: derivatives on oil (oil futures) are money-credits. Moreover, in addition to derivatives on non-money, we can create derivatives on money (e.g., currency futures) and even derivatives on derivatives (e.g., CDO-squared). Aside from the futures contract that I work through here, the other example often used to explain derivatives is the options contract, which encodes a right to buy (a call option) or sell (a put option) something (typically a stock) for a specific price at a specific date. Options contracts are initially bought or sold, and as the price of the stock moves, the contract can itself be bought or sold (or closed out). Options are therefore money-credits.

tures market. They sell the majority of their oil not on the "spot" market, and not through private forward contracts but through the sale of futures contracts to dealers. Indeed, if we want to understand the market for oil in some broader sense, we cannot narrow our analysis to a commodity market for oil as determined by spot prices. The market for oil must also constitutively include the derivative market.

To see what I mean by this last claim, google "price of oil." All the top hits will point to a chart showing the price for the current month's *futures contract*. Of course, one can refine the search and google "oil spot price," but the results will not be *current* market prices. Rather, the search will return results that provide a historical record of previous delivery prices – that is, a post-hoc reconstruction of the market in oil. And this reconstruction, these historical prices, cannot be understood to exist independently of the derivative market. For example, the spot price data for WTI Crude Oil shows a price on 20 April 2020 of –$36.98. But we know that no one who actually already had oil in their possession on 20 April 2020 was willing to pay someone else $37 to take it from them. Rather, the ones willing to pay $37 were the futures traders who had buy-contracts they needed to roll over – precisely so that they could *avoid* taking possession of any actual oil.[33]

To clarify, logically one *could* conceive of a scenario in which someone with oil storage facilities sold oil today for –$36/barrel (meaning they paid someone else $36/barrel to haul away oil). But this could only possibly occur because today's seller knew (or predicted/gambled) that they could use their freed-up storage space to buy oil for delivery tomorrow at –$37/barrel (someone paying them to take the oil).[34] This means that we can only make sense of what's happening in the "spot market" by considering movements in the futures market. The only reason to sell oil "on the spot" today for –$36 is because the derivative market has made it possible to buy at –$37 tomorrow.[35]

---

33 As the price dropped, dealers demanded that traders either provide more cash for their margin account or close out their position (further pushing down the price) and many traders chose the latter option. For more on margin trading, see Chapter 7, Section 3.
34 Sincere thanks to Alex Andre for extended discussion of the futures market and futures trading, and for helpful engagement on this specific example.
35 To tie up the logic here, we could imagine a world with no futures contracts on oil at all. If there were no oil derivatives, would it still be possible to conduct spot trades in oil for negative value? I can come up with no viable scenarios to answer in the affirmative. While we can conceive of spot transactions for negative value, they are only possible within a world that also contains derivatives on oil. It is tempting to think of *spot* prices as the *present market* prices of the *actual* commodity, the *underlying* asset. However, while there surely is the fact of actual cash paid for actual oil in the world, the concept of a "spot price" as the present-moment market price is itself something of a conceptual construct – not the reality of "what people pay in the moment" but a

For these reasons, the derivative market cannot be understood as parasitical or dependent on the primary market in oil (or on the primary contracts between producers and buyers). Indeed, in a certain sense (and only in a certain sense) *the market in oil is the derivative market in oil futures.* And there can be no doubt that the oil futures market – as a market of money-credits, a movement of prices – functions more like the ideal conception of "the market" in both classical and neo-classical conceptions. Yet if we try to get directly at some sort of "natural oil market," we will find the task impossible: there is no way to understand how the entity constructed and understood as the "oil commodity" is bought and sold without involving the intermediation of the market in oil futures contracts.

This is neither to say that there is no market in the standardized commodity "oil" (the underlying asset) nor to suggest that the overall oil market is *only* the derivative market. The claim is rather that one can never separate the underlying market from the derivative market. One can never find a distinct commodity market with spot prices operating independently of the derivative market. Rather, "the market in oil," broadly conceived, entwines the derivative market in oil futures with the concrete trading of standardized barrels of oil.

Ultimately, only through its operation as a market in money does the market in the commodity function fully.[36] We can unpack this claim by starting with the fact that a market in derivatives operates like other money markets. Even the briefest conversation with a money-market trader reveals that, from their perspective (i. e., from the structural perspective of the dealer function, see Treynor 1987), it matters not at all what's being traded. That is to say, *as money-credits* (and only as money-credits[37]), euros, credit default swaps, and T-bills are all the same. They are money-

---

reflection of the abstract marginalist idea of a "market in equilibrium." Spot prices may be better understood not literally as present market rates available "on the spot" but as "past futures prices." They are a historical reconstruction of market prices, one very much influenced by the derivative market. There is undoubtedly a concrete reality – practices in which barrels of oil are delivered for money-credit – but that reality does not exist separately from or independently of the reality of the derivative market. Indeed, the possibility for a market in oil depends on the existence of the derivative. The derivative might not be *first*, but it is surely not *second.*

36 And the logic of the derivative sometimes makes it possible to separate those markets in a way that privileges not the "underlying" but the derivative. This is one way to understand the otherwise literally incredible story of the nickel market in early 2022 (Levine, 30 November 2022).

37 The other side of this coin cannot be neglected: traders care very much about the difference between the *market* in T-bills and the *market* in euros. Indeed, the differences in cultures between the traders and dealers who work in one sort of market versus another can prove vast. For example, Alex Andre deftly shows that, as a general rule, stock and futures traders have an utterly different relation to risk than options traders (Andre 2021: 60). Nonetheless, at the ontological level, the derivatives themselves look the same because they look like money-credit. And the investors whose money is being used to trade these financial assets are not themselves all that concerned

credits with a market value that may go up or down, which may serve as a better or worse hedge, and which may be more or less liquid.

The logic of the derivative therefore proves absolutely central to the process whereby commodity and other markets are treated as if they were money markets – the process that mediates between financial exchange and economic exchange. The derivative plays this role for the straightforward reason that while a commodity seems necessarily to belong to the realm of economic exchange, the derivative on that commodity necessarily belongs to the domain of financial exchange. The derivative is a form of money-credit, but one necessarily linked (even if sometimes weakly) to commodities. Money markets and commodity markets are thus inextricably and necessarily entangled by the existence and circulation of derivatives.

Nonetheless, at the next level of analysis, derivative markets are not exactly like money markets, precisely because of the former's distinctive relationship to the underlying asset. All markets are ultimately and indirectly connected in one way or another (because of global capital flows), but a derivative's link to the market in its underlying asset is unique. A historic frost in Florida that destroys orange crops may have all sorts of knock-on effects for the Florida economy, especially for orange-growing companies and their employees. But in addition and related to those possible effects, it will have an immediate and dramatic impact on the orange futures market. To grasp the relation between a derivative market and the market in its underlying asset, we need to pay heed to two principles. First, the price of the underlying asset is not established or maintained independently of the price of the derivative, and thus the market in the underlying asset is not foundational or determinative of the derivative market. As we have already seen above, derivative prices can at times *drive* the price of the underlying asset.[38] But second,

---

about the differences between and among markets; once again, what matters to them is the holy trinity – return, hedging, and liquidity.

38 The 2000s housing bubble would not have been possible without the market in what we might call "housing derivatives" – namely MBS (literally a bond constructed through the amalgamation of individual mortgages, so not technically a derivative) and collateralized debt obligations (CDO). A CDO on MBS is a derivative on housing-market bonds. All of the (now-infamous) loose and fraudulent lending practices were enabled and encouraged by the market in MBS and CDO: mortgage originators had no reason to worry whether their customer could repay a mortgage because originators planned to sell the mortgage on to firms that would then package the mortgages together to create MBS. Indeed, individual homeowners themselves came to think of the housing market like a money market, to think of their house like money-credit; thus, many sought "leverage" in the market by buying the most expensive house (or multiple houses) they could with the least amount of money down (i.e., collateral). In the height of the bubble, mortgage brokers would advise high-credit, high-income customers to take out interest-only mortgages and avoid the standard 20% down payment by taking out a second loan for that 20% (so-called 80/20 loans). The putative

there is nonetheless a concrete reality to the market in the underlying asset that can impinge more directly on a derivative market (in that asset) than it would generically on some other money market. The derivative market is always subject to major disruption or reshaping by changes in particular practices that affect the market in the underlying asset.

This clarification does not alter the core argument here: the relation between financial exchange and economic exchange (between money markets and commodity markets) can only be grasped through the logic of the derivative, because a derivative effectively creates a money market in the very same space as the commodity market.

* * *

I asserted early on in this book that no theory of money could be considered robust if it did not speak to and account for the massive money markets that lie at the interstitial center of global capitalism today. This chapter aims to make good on that claim by utilizing the book's wider theory of the money array (including the particular ontological argument for money-credit) in order to illuminate some of the basic structures of money markets (including markets in derivatives).

Capitalist economics centers on and runs through money. This is why, early on in the book, I used a radical reading of Innes to make the case for rethinking economic exchange. Rejecting both classical and neoclassical accounts of exchange as the swapping of commodities, we have redefined exchange as the swapping of commodities for money-credits. This chapter has explored some of the payoff of that approach.

That analysis allows us to see starkly that "financialization" and "financial capitalism" are not new historical events or types of capitalism. Money has always been the lifeblood of capitalism, and capitalist exchange has always been "finan-

---

goal in this trade is to maximize a home buyer's overall market investment, by putting their cash in other investments, such as stocks and bonds. In other words, for a brief time in the early 2000s, the housing market in the US became a money market. While similar phenomena emerged across much of Europe and parts of Asia, the US proved special, partially because of its distinctive laws concerning mortgage default: in most countries borrowers are obligated for the full amount of their mortgage; in the US, under most circumstances, only the house itself stands as collateral. As a concrete example, this means that one could have borrowed $500,000 in 2004 to buy a $500,000 home and then taken out a second mortgage for $100,000 (withdrawing cash) in 2007 when the house was valued at $650,000. Then in 2009, when the house's value had dropped to $400,000, the owner could simply stop paying the mortgage, give up ownership of the house, and move out – keeping the money that was cashed out in 2007.

cial."[39] Money markets surely play a larger role today than they did a century ago, but they are not new, they are not somehow external to capitalism (as if we could just get rid of the "financial" part of capitalism and return to the goods-producing parts), and their part in the drama is not necessarily *that* much bigger. To give just one key example: late nineteenth-century global capitalism centered on the City of London and fundamentally depended on both the financial instrument called the "bill of exchange" and the institutionalized practice of banks "discounting" bills. But most importantly, as we see in the next chapter, the bill of exchange is nothing more or less than a derivative. Having a fundamental grasp on money markets and the logic of the derivative thereby gives us a clearer view of the recent capitalist history of money, and it offers us purchase to critically consider the biggest issues in money today.

---

39 The primary "financialization" thesis presupposes a traditional model of economic exchange, i.e., one that excludes money. Only from that basis would one be surprised, or see as new, the rise of trading in money. If one reconceives of economic exchange as the swapping of commodities for money-credits, then money becomes fundamental to society. Historically, we know that swapping money-credits has been with us since the beginnings of capitalism, if not earlier.

Chapter Seven
Money Today

1 Is It Money?

As we have seen, most thinking about political economy has been dominated by historically incorrect or, at best, impoverished theories of money. This basic reality often makes it difficult to figure out if something is or is not money. The legacy of functionalism continues to enfeeble not only explicit theories of money but also even the best work on money markets and contemporary money practices. The former fail to push past the frontline empirical questions in order to explore more deeply the complicated nature of money. The latter frequently limit their contributions by resting comfortably with standard definitions of money as given in economics textbooks, or by simply assuming that all things traded like money must be money (or more generally, that all things *traded* the same must *be* the same). Here we can get a sense of the deep importance not just of the practical use of derivatives but, as explored in the previous chapter, *the logic of the derivative.* That logic makes possible the creation of money markets out of entities that are not money.

This practice is crucial to contemporary capitalism, but that fact must not lead us astray – as it can do if we allow ourselves to naturalize the derivative and its logic. In other words, just because we treat an entity like money does not make it money. We make markets in all sorts of things that are not money: oil, gold, and pork bellies are all traded in the same manner as USD and GBP bank deposits, but this fact is not evidence that pork bellies are money. The essence of money is not to be found in the fact that money-credits are traded, even if money markets prove to be one of the most important monetary phenomena in contemporary capitalism. Put differently, the being of money is not "to be traded," despite the fact that the trading of money always accompanies capitalism.

In specific terms this means that, having developed a working analysis of money markets in the previous chapter, we now need to draw back from them and place some markers down that help us attain a perspicacious view on the nature of money. We want to avoid the myopia of those who lose their way in the fog of the money markets. This is one way of describing what happened in April 2020 to derivatives traders who thought that buying oil futures at a price of less than $1.00/barrel was a riskless opportunity for profit. Because they tacitly conceived of the derivate on oil as a pure form of money, like "cash," they assumed its price could not go negative and that there were no downsides to holding this

https://doi.org/10.1515/9783110760774-011

form of money. As described in the previous chapter, derivatives contracts are a form of money-credit, but they are a complicated and impure form. Unlike cash, the contract in oil futures retains a direct relation to the commodity: the purchaser of the contract does not just buy something with a denominated value; they also *contract* to take delivery of barrels of oil at the agreed price. And because storing oil itself involves real economic costs, the value of an oil futures contract can go negative – as owners of those contracts rush to sell them in order to avoid having to take delivery of oil. *Oil is not money*, a fact we forget at our peril. Even if oil futures are a form of money-credit, they are not the same as other forms. In the real world, those differences matter – sometimes a lot. In this final chapter we return to the core tenets of our developed theory of money and use its logic and concepts to cast light on some of the more perplexing contemporary money phenomena – to answer the question, "Is it money?"

Early in the previous chapter, I made passing mention of "gold bugs," whose fundamental precept is that gold, in its very nature, is money. The theory of money developed in this book shows such a claim to be nonsense, but more than this, our theory helps to show *why* it's nonsense: ontologically, money (as credit) differs fundamentally from a commodity (as a useful good with exchange-value). But as we have seen, to develop such an argument requires a rather sophisticated level of ontological thinking: to see why gold is not money, we have to grasp the difference between commodity-gold and money-gold.[1] In itself, gold is a commodity and not money, yet we can take the commodity and use it as a source for the creation of tokens of money-credit. In doing so we create coined money made out of gold, and when one stops to think about it (which we have done over the course of this book), this is a fantastic creature: in becoming money-gold it ceases to exist as commodity-gold. And finally, the moment such coins are hoarded for their intrinsic value, they revert to commodity-gold, ceasing to be money (i.e., money-gold).[2]

---

1 I recur to this distinction throughout the book, but perhaps no one puts the point better (surely no more succinctly) than Cencini: "Even commodity-money is not a commodity" (Cencini 1988: 17).
2 If we combine this fundamental argument, first mentioned in the Preface, about the difference between money-gold and commodity-gold, with our discussions of secured loans and derivatives from the previous chapter, we can build a much clearer picture of silver and gold coins. Take a US silver dollar. Contrary to a dogmatic version of chartalism (which would ignore the material basis for the token), we must account for the potential being of the silver dollar as commodity-silver. The money-silver is a token of debt, but because the token takes the form of commodity-silver, we have, in effect, a *collateralized* loan. Your deposit account is a loan to the bank: if the bank issues you paper banknotes, that loan is unsecured; if they issue you silver coins then the loan is partially secured by the silver as collateral. This may matter in two very different scenarios. First, if your bank goes bust, your money (in the form of money-silver) disappears, but you will

2 World Money

This core logic of our theory of money allows us to unravel an important paradox – namely, that during the height of the "gold standard" gold was not itself money. The pinnacle of the world monetary system putatively based on the gold standard extended across the nineteenth and into the twentieth century. But the global money of account during this period was, first, the British pound sterling and then, later, the US dollar. International payments were made almost exclusively in credits denominated in GBP and USD, respectively. It is of course true that for large stretches of this time, the Bank of England and US Federal Reserve promised to exchange GBP or USD for a particular weight of gold at a fixed rate. However, almost no individuals took them up on that offer. Why not? Because *such individuals did not want gold bars; they wanted money.* Finally, when the stability of the money of account came under pressure such that it appeared as if many actors might, in fact, want to exchange GBP or USD for gold – at just that moment the guarantee of "redeemability" was suspended.[3]

This raises a much larger and important problem of how and what we understand "world money" to be. Here again our new theory of money can serve as a useful tool to cut through a great deal of confusion and render the topic much less opaque. In this case the key is to return to our concept "money space," that "domain" (noncontiguous and permeable) in which particular money-credits are

---

be left with the commodity-silver collateral, which you can sell to recoup some of your loss. Second, if the silver market skyrockets, your loan may become overcollateralized, tempting you to abandon the money-silver token and seize the commodity-silver collateral (i. e., by melting down the coins). To do so will almost certainly be illegal: your debtor has not defaulted on their loan, and thus you have no legal right to steal their collateral. This case reveals the coin as having what Colin Drumm, following Mehrling, calls both an "inside" option (token of denominated debt) and an "outside" option (international silver market) (Drumm 2021; Mehrling 2012). I would emphasize that the "outside" choice – seizing the commodity collateral for the money loan – is not really a *money* option, but this is not at all atypical: the "outside" of money is often some non-money assets, as one can easily see by looking at the asset side of central bank balance sheets – and the fact still proves important for understanding the strange twofold being of the silver coin. Finally, we can consider a related edge case. Coin collectors speculate in a particular segment of the commodity-silver market. If they buy non-legal tender coins, and the silver market craters, the value of their coin could drop as low as the market will go. Instead, if they buy legal-tender coins, in the event of a silver-market collapse they will hold the option to treat the coin as money-silver, effectively setting a price floor of $1 on the commodity-silver purchase. That is, when the coin dealer sells a 2023 American Eagle silver dollar for $90, he also delivers a put option (with the US Treasury as counterparty) to sell the coin for $1 at any time. Thanks to Henry Scott for valuable discussion of these issues.
3 No recent text better illuminates this point than Zachary D. Carter's biography of Keynes (Carter 2020).

in fact routinely and reliably transferred. Using that concept, we understand "world money" as the name for money whose money space (putatively) reaches all the way across the globe, traversing numerous local-private and national-public money spaces. This is not the place to explore the many complex economic and crucial political issues raised by world money, but the conceptual structure elaborated in this book allows us to frame those issues concisely.

Logically, by understanding all credit as money and all money as circumscribed by its money space,[4] we see that there will always be a problem when two agents who occupy different money spaces need to engage in economic exchange.[5] The first solution would be to abandon money for such a transaction and actually settle accounts by making payments in commodities. This has surely occurred historically (though it has never been all that frequent or common); under this heading we would place actual payment in gold, which, when it is transferred by weight between countries, is commodity-gold. Gold has never served as *world money* but rather as the *standard commodity* reverted to world over in the *absence* of world money.

In other words, during the relatively brief period of a functional international "gold standard," the actual world money was first GBP and then USD,[6] and the overwhelming majority of international transactions were covered not by shipping bars of gold but through alternative solutions, which I discuss immediately below. When gold was shipped between countries, it was in the form of commodity-gold – the standard commodity used to "back" money under the gold standard.[7]

A second response to the lack of a common money space would be to introduce a "higher" form of money, one that intersects in some way with the relevant actors' respective money spaces. Examples might include the period in which the euro existed as money of account while euro nations still retained their own currencies (1999–2002) or the limited use of IMF special drawing rights (SDR). If both agents can access this higher money space, they can conduct economic exchange

---

4 This is another way of formulating the point that money-credit is all there is. Within the proper money space, all credits *are* money, but outside that space they are *only* credit.

5 In the case of financial exchange, this problem is solved not by having individuals directly barter money-credits, but through dealers who straddle and traverse various geopolitical and money spaces in order to make a market in money (by standing ready to buy or sell various money-credits).

6 "GBP and USD" is shorthand here for "credits/debts denominated in GBP and USD." To paraphrase Innes, a pound is not a thing; credit (denominated in pounds, and usually in the form of bank money) is the only thing there is.

7 Here we should emphasize Ingham's point: such payment would not amount to barter, but to payment in kind denominated in the standard money of account (Ingham 2020: 107).

despite the fact that their standard money spaces (e. g., national moneys of account) do not overlap.[8]

The third option proves critical because it demonstrates the interpenetrating and noncontiguous nature of money space. For this solution, agent A (in country X) can access the money of account of agent B (in country Y) by becoming the client of a local bank in country X, which bank itself holds deposit accounts at a bank in country Y. This abstractly describes the eurodollar market – US dollar–denominated deposit accounts held in US banks by European banks. This crucial example offers a view of the dollar-denominated money space extending well beyond US government territory.

However, to call the US dollar *world money* does not mean that everyone can use US dollars everywhere and for all transactions. When I visit my friend in England and we go to his local pub, I cannot pay for our pints with a $20 bill. In practical terms, I find myself in the money space of the pound sterling, and I need access to credits/debts denominated in GBP in order to buy the round. This everyday example might tempt us to conclude that each country has its own distinctly separated money space. But such a conclusion would prove hasty because international markets in money and commodities cross borders each and every day. I might elbow my way up to the bar next to a wealthy investor. Regardless of whether he is British, American, or Japanese, he is almost certain to have millions of money-credit in dollar-denominated assets (stocks, bonds, eurodollar deposit accounts, etc.). Like me with my $20 bill, the investor cannot use these credits to buy a pint, but he doesn't want dollar-denominated credits to buy beer: he wants to hold his credits in dollars for the usual reasons: return, liquidity, and hedging.

In this sense my friend's local English pub is both inside and outside the US-dollar money space – it intersects with that money space in some complicated form of non-Euclidean geometry. Because capital flows globally, US dollars (and to a lesser extent the other "major" currencies[9]) flow everywhere. Neither the in-

---

8 The IMF offers a short online explainer on SDRs, wherein they explicitly pose the question "Is it money?" and answer decisively in the negative. The logic of the IMF answer depends on first equating "money" with national "currencies" and thereby denying SDRs money status. They say SDRs are not money "in the classic sense because they can't be used to buy things." That's bad logic that leads to a bad answer; it's like saying Fed reserves are not money because I cannot buy groceries with them. But I can buy groceries with bank money, and my bank will then pay the grocery store's bank in Fed reserves. Similarly, country A can exchange SDRs with country B and receive foreign currency in return, which they then use to buy COVID-19 vaccines.

9 There is no formal definition or assigned status of "major" currencies, but both forex traders and the Bank for International Settlements often refer to the most-traded currency pairs as "majors." The top four pairs are commonly listed as the US dollar paired with, respectively: Japanese yen, euro, UK pound, and Swiss franc. However, this traditional account does not square with cur-

vestor nor I can use dollars to buy our pints. However, if we happen to be in one of the many British pubs owned by international conglomerates, the investor could effectively use US dollars to buy the entire pub itself. In sum, the existence of euro-dollar bank accounts solves the problem of international economic exchange while also making it possible for a domestic money of account to serve as world money in an important sense.

Finally, perhaps surprisingly, and certainly most importantly, the problem of distinct money spaces can be solved not by moving to a common space "outside" the separate, native money spaces (option 2), nor by accessing the world money space directly (option 3), but rather through the creative production of an outside space that is actually internal to economic and financial exchange. This outside that is really inside can be produced through the logic of the swap. A swap is a money-market derivative. It is best understood as a swap of IOUs on each of the balance sheets of two (or more) agents (Mehrling 2011: 65). Each agent makes a loan to the other in the lender's domestic currency, thereby giving each borrower access to a foreign-currency deposit account.[10] Mehrling explains the origins of currency swaps under the Bretton Woods system as a technical device of banking that made it possible to evade capital controls, which explicitly prohibited trading currencies directly. The parallel loan structure means that "no money ever travels across national borders." In our language, the money-credits remain *inside* their respective domestic money spaces: "But although there are no *net* flows, any reasonable person would agree that the deal involves quite substantial notional *gross* flows" (Mehrling 2011: 65). The swap therefore makes it possible to reach outside the money space while putatively adhering to the law that requires money to stay inside the domestic money space.

Crucially, the swap uses the logic of the derivative to solve the problem of separate money spaces without the need for an alternative space. As Mehrling insightfully recounts, the logic of the swap was later expanded to interest rate swaps and credit default swaps. We cannot therefore make sense of the dizzying array of derivative products that dominate the money markets today without placing their

---

rent practice. First, the US dollar completely dominates: in April 2022, for example, "it was on one side of 88% of all trades" (BIS 2022b). Second, the US dollar trades with more frequency against the yuan, Canadian dollar, Australian dollar, and New Zealand dollar than it does against the franc.
10 To be clear, our economic agents (e.g., capitalist firms) almost certainly cannot do this deal directly: they need a bank to create the swap for them, and the bank only does so by creating a bid–ask spread that generates a profit. Note also that the swap is a derivative because the value of the swap contract (which is how banks today actually book swaps on their balance sheets) will move based on the value of the "underlying asset," which is the loan itself (and its value can change as exchange and interest rates shift).

history in the context of trying to solve the basic problem of exchange across money spaces.

But this phenomenon is itself not really new. Since the days of merchant capitalism, derivatives have structured the global flow of goods. From at least the fourteenth up through the nineteenth century, the bill of exchange was the dominant financial instrument structuring global trade. We can draw from Mehrling's account of the swap and link it to my earlier discussion of the derivative so as to provide a succinct explanation. As a derivative, the swap makes it possible to construct world money out of standard domestic currencies. Yet the fourteenth-century bill of exchange was itself a derivative money-credit that could traverse multiple money spaces, facilitating economic exchange across multiple countries. In its basic form, the bill of exchange was a forward contract. Mehrling describes the late nineteenth-century bill of exchange in Britain as follows:

> Firms issued bills in order to buy inputs for their own production processes, and they accepted bills as payment for their own outputs. The bill of exchange was a promise to pay at a specific future date, perhaps in ninety days. For a fee, banks would "accept" bills, which meant guaranteeing payment. For another fee, banks would "discount" bills, which meant buying them for less than face value, the difference amounting to a rate of interest to be earned over the term to maturity. As payment for the bills, banks would offer either currency or a deposit account credit. Either way, the proceeds of the discount were most typically not held as idle balances but rather spent in payment of other maturing bills. In this way, the discount mechanism was crucial for British firms' management of their daily cash flow, in and out. (Mehrling 2011: 22–23)

Notice that the bill functions as a derivative in two senses. First, we can look at it from the perspective of the bank that discounts or accepts bills from those merchants who hold them; the bank is valuing the contract at a different price than its literal text. This is just the circulation of a forward contract (a simpler form of a futures contract). Second, we can take the perspective of the merchant who sells the bill to the bank: that merchant is substituting a credit default exposure to the firm on which he wrote the bill for a credit default exposure to the bank that discounts it. Thus the transaction functions something like a credit default swap. (In essence, any time one switches debtors – e.g., moves money from one bank to another – one is swapping credit-default exposure.)

The early modern European bill of exchange proved to be an even more complex financial instrument than the British bill described above by Mehrling; the early modern bill combined the credit swap with a foreign exchange swap.[11]

---

11 A bill is like a check because it is a token of credit/debt, written or filled out by the creditor, "drawing on" a debtor. However, a check draws directly on a bank, whereas a bill is *sold* to an ex-

Bills of exchange *circulated* precisely where national currencies could not. Therefore for both the twentieth-century swap and the earlier bill of exchange, world money takes the form of the derivative.

3 Money Creation, Part 2

Many overviews of the theory and history of money give pride of place in their accounts to the debate over "endogenous money" versus "exogenous money," sometimes even suggesting that this axis has been the primary site of contention in the history of money theories (see Sieroń 2019). This book has taken a very different tack. In Chapter 2's presentation of the money matrix, we followed Schumpeter in depreciating this argument – for two important reasons. First, one's position on exogenous versus endogenous money creation will follow directly from one's position on commodity versus claim theory. Any claim theory must affirm that money-credits are brought into being at the moment new loans are issued (and destroyed when those loans are paid off). In simple terms, this makes the money-creation question ancillary to the claim-versus-commodity question. Second, the argument for exogenous money creation – that money first comes into being outside the social and economic order, only then to be introduced into that order at a subsequent stage – simply does not hold up to the historical record. Certainly many classical and neoclassical economists have affirmed a commodity theory of money that therefore saw money creation as exogenous (money comes from mining), but absolutely no one familiar with banking practices has done so. As we briefly explored in Section 2 of the previous chapter, the fundamental act of banking – the swap of IOUs – creates money, and any serious treatment of the history of commercial banking demonstrates this point decisively. We cannot forget that banks are capitalist firms in the business of making loans to make

---

change banker, but *draws on* a private party. The party being drawn on is the one who *owes* for delivered goods (or rendered services), and is thereby being *billed* by the party who delivered the goods (or rendered the services). Drumm provides the clearest, most helpful explanation of medieval bills that I have read, so I will borrow his example of a London merchant, Albert, who exports wool to an Antwerp merchant, Bernard. Albert then writes out the bill (drawing on the debt Bernard owes him, specifying both the due date and amount) and then *sells* that bill (for London money) to a local London exchange banker. The exchange banker, part of a larger banking network, *remits* the bill to a colleague in Antwerp, who then *delivers* the bill to Bernard. If Bernard *accepts* the bill, he commits to *pay* it (in Antwerp money) by the due date. (Bernard could also *protest* the bill, and turn to litigation.) For much more, see Drumm, 2022.

money.[12] Further, any study of the more recent history of central banking practices shows that the overwhelming majority of money creation still comes from commercial banking. Indeed, the important primers released by the Bank of England after the 2008 crisis go out of their way to underscore this point (McLeay et al. 2014a, 2014b). The growing role of central bank policy and interventions has not minimized the role of commercial bank money creation, but rather leveraged it for central banks' own policy ends.

All of this means that the theoretical chapters of the book had no need to explore money creation in depth. However, this late juncture provides the perfect opportunity to speak to the importance of endogenous money creation in today's money markets. Standard accounts of money creation focus on the local banker issuing a loan: whether it be to a capitalist firm starting up production, or to a family planning to remodel their home, money comes into being the moment the bank puts the loan (as asset) and the borrower's deposit account (as liability) on the bank's balance sheet.

Yet the money markets do more than trade money; they create it. A significant portion of brokerage accounts are "margin accounts": these are effectively secured loans from the broker to the customer, using customer cash and portfolio holdings as collateral. In practice this means that a customer can deposit, for example, $100,000 in cash into their account, and then immediately buy $150,000 worth of securities. Alternatively, they could deposit $100,000 in cash; buy $100,000 in US Treasury bonds; and then *withdraw* $50,000 in cash. In both cases the extra $50,000 is endogenous money creation (and in both cases the brokerage customer will be paying interest). The amounts involved are not trivial: in the United States alone at the end of 2021, there was over $900 billion in margin debt held at (i.e.,

---

12 In refuting the standard neoclassical argument that banks act as "intermediaries" between savers and borrowers, and thus only loan out money that has previously been deposited, Minsky famously argues that banks create money "out of thin air" through the swap of IOUs process I described in the previous chapter. Critics have protested against this phrase from two very different directions. Some, such as Paul Krugman, have defended the standard account – in which banks "lend out" deposits (Krugman 2012, quoted in Wray 2015). Others, such as Ingham, have tried to clarify that the issuance of a loan is not like fairy dust that creates ex nihilo. Rather, the money created by the bank loan exists because a "legally enforceable *promise* to repay the debt" also exists (Ingham 2020: 62). Minsky's metaphor is obviously constructed as a sharp critique of the old model of banks as intermediaries, and therefore I read Ingham as offering not a critique of Minsky but merely a clarification of the limits of the metaphor when taken out of context. See Minsky (1960) and the lucid discussion of this material by Wray (2015), including a powerful challenge to the standard Keynesian approach.

owed to) brokerages. Endogenous money creation (and destruction[13]) goes on constantly in the money markets precisely because in trading money it proves so simple to create new loans merely by creating offsetting assets and liabilities. The logic of the swap is the fulcrum for money-market practices, and this logic makes money creation possible. The basic margin account is only the tip of the iceberg.

To offer just one more example, we can see that short selling also acts as functional money creation. Take a stylized example in which a short seller "shorts" 100 shares of a stock valued at $10/share.[14] This act involves three parties, and their balance sheets start out this way:

Short Seller		Dealer		Stock Buyer	
Assets	*Liabilities*	*Assets*	*Liabilities*	*Assets*	*Liabilities*
		100 shares		$1,000.00	

Then the seller "shorts" 100 shares of the stock, which means the seller simultaneously borrows the stock from the dealer and sells it to the buyer. The balance sheets now look like this:

Short Seller		Dealer		Stock Buyer	
Assets	*Liabilities*	*Assets*	*Liabilities*	*Assets*	*Liabilities*
$1,000.00	loan from dealer (−100 shares)	loan to SS (+100 shares)		100 shares	

Again we observe the phenomenon of balance-sheet expansion. In this case it all occurs on the balance sheet of the short seller. Both the dealer and the stock buyer have merely changed the form in which they hold their assets (still valued at $1,000), but the short seller started with no assets or liabilities and now holds $1,000 worth of each. The ultimate difference between assets and liabilities has not changed (it remains 100 shares and $1,000), but both the assets and liabilities have increased by 100 shares of stock. In other words, the "long" position in the stock has increased from +100 to +200, while a new short position exists, −100. This expansion of credit – in this case in the form of stock – is the very definition of money creation. And note that the process can continue in sequence because the buyer in our scenario above could then decide to loan their stock to another short seller.

---

13 By June 2022 over $200 billion in money had been destroyed as margin account balances declined to less than $700 billion total.

14 This example assumes away margin rates (interest charged for borrowing stock), movement of stock prices, or any other complications. The simplifications make the fundamental structure of money creation easier to identify.

Some readers may encounter the example of stock shorting as money creation and feel an urge to raise this objection: If the difference between assets and liabilities (+$1,000) has not changed, then how can there be "more money"? Here it can be helpful to remember two things. First, in the ur-example of money creation as the issuance of a loan, the banker creates an asset (the loan) and a corresponding liability (deposits), thereby expanding the balance sheet but not altering the overall difference between assets and liabilities. Second, if all loans were repaid, there would then no longer be any money in circulation. Money is nothing other than circulating debt: *more money always means more debt, and less debt always equals less money.* Put otherwise, with money-credit, one agent's assets are always another's liabilities. The key to any monetary system lies in how money-credit assets and liabilities are distributed across the social order – how they are arranged so as to form the hierarchy of money.

This point allows us to address succinctly another of today's hot topics in money: so-called central bank digital currencies (CBDC). The basic idea is neither technically complex nor conceptually complicated. As we know, central banks issue their own bank money, which currently takes two forms: 1) physical coins and notes that circulate widely and can be held by both individuals and commercial banks; 2) central bank reserves, digital deposit accounts available only to commercial banks. Individuals pay each other in bank money, but then their banks pay each other in central bank reserves. The creation of a CBDC would allow all citizens of a particular country to hold central bank reserves directly (in digital form, through a website or smartphone app), just like commercial banks. Advocates of CBDC typically make three arguments in its favor: increased access, reduced "friction," and overall stability.[15] Anyone can open an account, pay for anything with a tap, and never have to worry about losing their money (or its value).

The first argument is valid, laudable, and politically significant. Speaking narrowly to the US context, the problem of access to banking proves dire indeed, and conceptually, at least, a CBDC would solve this problem by giving "unbanked" US

---

15 Ironically, these are the same three arguments often made by advocates of crypto stablecoins. In the case of the CBDC, the idea is a "digital coin" in the sense of a *direct* claim on the central bank; in the case of stablecoins, the idea is a digital coin *without* banks. Of course, as I indicated in the Preface, while the initial promise of proof-of-work tokens was to eliminate banks (third parties), the rise of stablecoins actually depended on a major departure from the intended path – because the need for a "trusted third party" was brought back in. And thus we find ourselves in a strange situation: all the large and viable stablecoins are merely digital tokens issued by shadow banks. In that reality, the difference between tether and a CBDC comes down to this: holding your digital deposits on the central bank; or holding them on a very small, almost utterly unregulated, and severely undercapitalized shadow bank.

citizens direct access to a Fed bank account. Nevertheless, this very real problem could be solved without any need for the revolution in money and banking practices that a CBDC portends, and there is nothing inherent to a two-level system of commercial and central banks that leads to the acutely American problem of lack of access to banking. Other countries have commercial banking systems that do not exclude millions of their citizens from access, and the problem in America could be solved more simply and directly with regulatory changes. The second argument for CBDC, reduced friction in transactions, is trivial. *Digital money already exists.* Most money in circulation today is commercial bank money, and it can already be transmitted electronically using credit cards, smartphones, and computers.[16] The first two arguments on behalf of CBDC therefore have nothing inherently to do with CBDC.

Everything hinges on the third argument, *stability.* This argument necessarily, even if tacitly, invokes the recurring dream of money: if only we could have a money that was *sound* – a money with stable value. It is easy to see how the idea of a CBDC would emerge out of the vision of money offered by state theorists: If money is a creature of the state, then why not just have the state issue all money straight to (all) citizens? If the value of the dollar is determined by the Fed, doesn't it make sense to get my dollars directly from them? The allure of this argument feels almost palpable, as it seems as though we would solve all the problems of money in one fell swoop. But if we look carefully, we should also see warning signs flashing. One can spot at least two major problems with the proposed creation of a CBDC.

First, the very idea of a CBDC rests on an untenable theory of money. The CBDC imagines a world in which everyone gains the right to use the same money – central bank money – rather than having to navigate a hierarchy in which some institutions can access central bank reserves and some cannot – in which some institutions get bailed out by the government and some do not, etc. Eliminating the hierarchy of money sounds and feels radically democratic. But the hierarchy of money is not a product of bad (anti-democratic) politics; rather, the hierarchy proves inherent to money as money-credit. Because money is always a claim of credit on a debtor, there will always be better and worse forms of money – because there will always be better and worse debtors. In a certain sense, by envisioning a world with only one form of money – with no money hierarchy – the proposal for a CBDC imagines the end of money as we know it. As a thought ex-

---

16 To be clear, to say that digital money already exists does not mean that everything a CBDC promises is already reality. Today individuals can hold money digitally, but only as commercial bank money. Offering digital central bank reserves to individuals *would* in fact constitute a dramatic transformation of the money system – as I detail below.

periment, one might try to conceptualize such an elimination of the money hierarchy by starting with a deeply egalitarian social order (where everyone is equal). The problem here is that from these beginnings, it becomes quite difficult to see how money would emerge in such a society – much less what money practices would look like. We wind up where we started: money without the money hierarchy makes no sense. The problem lies not with the goal of a more equal society, but in the misconstrual of the very nature of money.

Money relations themselves encode relations of hierarchy. Because the creditor holds a claim on the debtor, the money relation is always already a power relation. A democratic society can justly implement laws and regulations that seek to prevent the money relation from being leveraged into a relation of political domination, but that does not alter the basic fact of the money array as structured by power. Money is simply incompatible with the wish for a domain or order outside of (thereby somehow protected from) power. Indeed, at a certain level of abstraction, we can say that *money is always anti-democratic.* If a society could hold a referendum on money relations, with the choice being (1) *maintain* current credit/debt relations or (2) *erase* them all, the vote would always be to eliminate all debt, because debtors always significantly outnumber creditors.[17]

And this brings us to the second, very much practical, problem with the proposed CBDC. We can see immediately that the CBDC would collapse the hierarchy of money by effectively eliminating the viability of commercial banks and commercial banking practices. Faced with the simple choice of holding deposits on a commercial bank or holding them at the Fed, only serious regulatory contrivances could slant the choice in favor of a commercial bank. And given the current regulatory regime, commercial banks need a certain amount of deposits; if those go away, banks are no longer viable as banks. By giving all individuals direct access to one of the highest forms of money-credit, central bank reserves, the CBDC

---

17 Indeed, something similar has happened throughout history in the form of debt jubilees, as Graeber ably shows (Graeber 2011). We must underscore that the type of wide-scale debt cancellation that Graeber discusses was really only viable, or even technically possible, in pre-capitalist societies in which inequality remained deeply encoded into the social order in ways far exceeding money relations. If I am a lord with land, arms, good relations with the king, and serfs to work my land, then I can allow the erasure of debt without significantly altering my overall standing in the social order. The debt jubilee reduces inequality, but it surely does not eliminate it. In capitalist societies, however, things look quite different: the overwhelming bulk of our inequalities are *monetary inequalities.* If Jeff Bezos and I both had all of our money assets eliminated tomorrow, he would surely still have more than I in the form of yachts and houses and cars. But the bare fact of these possessions would hardly matter if he no longer had access to the money-credits needed to buy diesel fuel for his yacht, or pay the property taxes and upkeep on his houses – not to mention the need to buy food.

would so shake the current hierarchy of money that it is hard to see what the results would be.

Money is created and destroyed by commercial banks. In capitalist societies today, money is (commercial) bank money. Implementation of a CBDC could create an existential crisis for commercial banks. Surely many advocates of the CBDC understand this implication and take it as a point *in favor* of the proposal for a CBDC – stick it to the banks. I am not sure it's that simple. In creating a CBDC, the central bank would be eliminating the very mechanism through which almost all central bank monetary policy gets implemented. Capitalist economics depends on the expansion and contraction of money-credits, and this ventilation system is run by and through commercial banks. Unless so circumscribed in its implementation as to be nothing other than a public-relations move, a real CBDC would threaten the viability of this system. Would it lead to post-capitalist utopia, or to our "common ruin"?

4 Bitcoin: Digital Metallism

With the question of utopia, we come to the final, and most significant, money topic today – cryptocurrency. In this context, our question from Section 1 of this chapter has been asked and answered thousands of times over the past few years: *Is bitcoin money?*[18] A November 2021 Google search on that question produced just shy of 87,000 hits and included a Google "snippet" – the Google algorithm's best guess as to the "correct answer" – citing a 2015 article to the effect that "bitcoin is not money because it functions poorly as a medium of exchange, unit of account, and store of value" (Hazlett and Luther 2020, citing Yermack 2015). David Yermack invokes the spirit of Francis Walker when he states succinctly that economists define money as that which "functions as a medium of exchange, a unit of account, and a store of value" (Yermack 2015: 32). From here it is an elementary exercise to show that bitcoin: can barely be used as medium of exchange;[19] provides a horrible store of value; and simply does not serve as a

---

18 Of course, this question presupposes some sort of response to the prior question, "What is bitcoin?" I provide a concise answer just below in the text, but I point those readers interested in more of the technical details to two key sources: Levine (2022) and Mariz (2023). For arguably the sharpest concise critique of what he rightly calls "cryptoassets," see Diehl (2021).
19 On the rare occasions when bitcoin is used to buy things, its extreme price volatility (as measured in a major money of account) coupled with the lack of a fast and cheap payments network, makes such usage extremely limited and compromised. This explains why the use of bitcoin as a medium of exchange is almost always a public-relations stunt.

unit of account. Yermack therefore provides a scholarly version of an argument one will find repeated in hundreds of news stories and blog entries: bitcoin fails to be money because it fails to *function* as money – and money is that money does.[20]

It's true that bitcoin is not money, but the functionalist argument here, as always, proves poor because it fails to explain why. Indeed, we could imagine a scenario in which people started to use bitcoin wallets in limited fashion to pay for goods and services, and at some point the minimal criteria for the functionalist definition might be met. As I show below, even in this hypothetical case, bitcoin would still not be money. *Bitcoin can never be money.*

To prove this point, let us begin at the beginning: the publication of the original white paper by the pseudonymous Satoshi Nakamoto. The opening paragraph

---

20 Ironically, clicking the Google Search snippet link takes the user to the Hazlett and Luther article abstract, which argues the opposite of Yermack: "We maintain that the standard approach classifies an item as money if and only if it functions as a commonly accepted medium of exchange. Then, we show that the demand for bitcoin is comparable to the demand for many government-issued monies." Hence "bitcoin is money" (Hazlett and Luther 2020). Hazlett and Luther stake out an unconventional position on bitcoin but do so by relying on utterly conventional thinking. They quibble with Yermack's tripartite functional account of money, countering with a definition of money "as a commonly (or, generally) accepted medium of exchange" (Hazlett and Luther 202: 145). From here their logic takes some tortured turns:
1) Equating "accepted as medium of exchange" with "demand for money" (145).
2) Measuring demand for money with the formula: market capitalization as total "money supply" multiplied by the "price" of money, i.e., its exchange rate with some other currency.
3) Calculating these market caps and comparing bitcoin with all world currencies, where its market cap ranks seventh at the time of their writing.
4) Recognizing the weak logic of step 1 and thus distinguishing between "speculative demand" as measured in market-cap data and "transactions demand" as that which must be demonstrated to prove that bitcoin is money.
5) Offering this proof for transactions demand: "Bitcoin serves no non-monetary purpose. Its only usefulness, if it has any use at all, is in functioning as a medium of exchange. Hence, *speculation must ultimately be concerned with the extent to which bitcoin will function as a medium of exchange*" (148, emphasis added).
6) Bitcoin is money. QED.

There is no need for a point-by-point engagement with this astonishing piece, but I will highlight step 5 in the argument, a move which is like assuming the tulip bubble was driven by believers in the future use-value of tulips. Put differently, their logic rests on the rigid assumption that market prices for a derivative must ultimately be founded on the value of the underlying asset. In our earlier discussion of the logic of the derivative, we already proved this assumption false, but both the history and present of market prices in derivatives shows it just as false, and does so on a daily basis. The fact that people speculate on bitcoin today simply cannot be translated into future "demand" for the *use* of bitcoin as a medium of exchange.

maps the problem that bitcoin and blockchain seek to solve: third-party trust. The goal of bitcoin and a proof-of-work blockchain[21] is to make it possible for party A to pay party B "without the need for a trusted third party" such as a financial or governmental institution (i.e., a bank of some sort) (Nakamoto 2008: 1). Put differently, bitcoin aims to eliminate the need for bank money – and thereby, perhaps, to eliminate banks.

To achieve this lofty goal, bitcoin grounds its new vision of money on the very old idea of a coin, newly reimagined: "We define an electronic coin as a chain of digital signatures. Each owner transfers the coin to the next by digitally signing" (Nakamoto 2008: 2). Bitcoin is a computer program that establishes a peer-to-peer consensus protocol to maintain a decentralized database, using cryptography to create, specify the ownership of, and allow for the transfer of these "electronic coins." The bitcoin blockchain makes it possible to authenticate the *transfer* of coins from one user to another, and to create new coins through the verification/mining process. The coin itself is a singular entity, not a relation between parties – that is, the coin is nothing more or less than a long, unique string of alphanumeric characters.

Although the white paper makes no such suggestion, early enthusiasm around possible utopian bitcoin futures led some to contemplate the idea of bitcoin becoming a new money of account.[22] Of course, bitcoin has failed here too. Indeed, bit-

---

21 My analysis of bitcoin should apply in a general sense to any proof-of-work blockchain, but it does not apply to proof-of-stake blockchains or to most stablecoins. In the former case, proof of stake, despite selling itself as an advancement over energy-burning proof of work, actually fails entirely to implement a decentralized ledger (see Mariz 2023). In the latter case, the large and dominant stablecoins hardly even pretend to be decentralized. While the tokens exist on the blockchain, they are very much tokens of debt issued by institutions, and token holders become not owners of coins but mere depositors at stablecoin shadow banks.

22 Using Keynes's twofold terminology, we might see bitcoin as promising to become not just a new form of money-credit *instrument* (money proper) but a de novo alternative money of account. This would be a money of account wherein the ledger was held not by banks and other financial authorities, not by central banks and governments, but *distributed* across all users/owners of the money itself. This radical idea that bitcoin might literally replace dollars and euros as the dominant money of account has contributed mightily to much of the confusion around bitcoin. To state the problem in general terms: to aim to establish a new money of account simultaneously sets the bar too high and too low. Too high because the emergence of a money of account – that is, the *name of money* – happens historically for a series of complicated social and political reasons. For example, the euro became a money of account because of the political project of the European Union. So the idea that we would start measuring value in terms of bitcoin – that bitcoin would become *denomination* – is not something that could occur solely due to the technical feats achieved by the blockchain. Too low because we can always create a new money of account simply by creating a new credit that we denominate in that money of account. In our hypothetical example from

coin's putative "success" – understood in terms of its increasing value as a speculative asset – attests to this fact. Dollars, euros, and other major moneys of account all serve to measure bitcoin's "value." No one prices things in BTC, even those rare entities that purport to take payment in BTC, and no one measures their household balance sheets in bitcoin. This issue remains tangential to the question "Is bitcoin money?" because "serving as money of account" would just be another functionalist category. At the level of our broader theory, for bitcoin to be money we must see examples of bitcoin-denominated money-credits, held by specific creditors on particular debtors. "Is it money of account?" is the wrong question.[23] At the particular level, and as always, functionalism will not work here: US Treasury bills are not money of account (dollars are), but US Treasury bills *are money-credits* (while the abstract "dollar" is not).

Hence we need to ignore the heavenly hopes of the bitcoin believers, and focus more modestly on the question of bitcoin as money-credit. Every functionalist approach confines its analysis to the empirical register and therefore limits our capacity to explore the being of bitcoin. But this is exactly what we need to analyze – the ontology of bitcoin. Moreover, once we shift to this register, the analysis itself proves straightforward. This book has shown that the being of money is credit; bitcoin fails utterly to be money because it fails to be credit/debt. The raison d'être of bitcoin – to establish transferable digital coins without reliance on a trusted third party – is antithetical to the nature of money. In the white paper's rhetoric around money, in the computer architecture it proposes, and in the implementation of the code for the first proof-of-work blockchain, bitcoin consistently and quite explicitly rejects credit/debt.

In a colloquial but illuminating sense, this book argues throughout that *money is bank money.* To have money we must have the money array: creditor, denominat-

---

Chapter 5, "goats" become a money of account, and logically there is no reason why they could not do so. More to the point, the fact of being the name of money does not tell us anything at all about that which answers to that name – that is, in Keynes's terms, "money proper." To put this point starkly: dollars are not money in the sense of the money stuff. Dollars are money of account, the name we give to the denomination of actual money-credits (money stuff). In almost all respects the theoretical vision of the bitcoin white paper is dominated by the metallist view – money as a commodity of intrinsic value and limited supply. Yet in this one respect we might read the early enthusiasm as also trapped by the Keynesian misstep that I diagnosed in Chapter 1: the belief that "money of account" somehow is, *simpliciter,* the full and proper concept of money, and consequently that the game is to *become* money of account.

23 Anything can *function* as money of account in the limited sense that we can express the value of one asset in terms of some other asset. Nothing stops me from saying my house is worth 8 bitcoins, but I can just as easily say my house is worth 2,000 barrels of oil. Such statements will turn neither bitcoin nor oil into money.

ed token, and debtor. When I look at the asset column of my household balance sheet, I find both money and non-money assets. To tell the difference I need only ask: Which of my assets are *listed on someone else's balance sheet as a liability?* My bank deposits are liabilities for my bank, and the $20 bill in my wallet is a liability for the Fed – these are money assets.

Bitcoin is not money, not because it *fails* to function as money, but because its purpose is to be something other than money. Despite what its advocates might say, when we look at the code itself, bitcoin *aims to be not-money*. As we know, for many believers the broader goal of bitcoin is to rid the world of banks. This is not mere rhetoric: vis-à-vis a basic money array (creditor, denominated token, and debtor), the blockchain code eliminates the debtor and turns the creditor into a simple owner. Bitcoin cannot be money because the ontology of bitcoin precludes money-credit. Put differently, the being of a bitcoin proves quite unlike the being of a £1 coin. The latter is a credit on the Bank of England, for which it represents a debt (measured in 1 pound sterling). The former also has a quantity and denomination (1 bitcoin), but it lacks a debtor – and does so by design.

Bitcoin could only hope to be money if the orthodox theory of commodity money were true. Indeed, bitcoin thoroughly replicates the false ontology of coinage that anchors all metallist theories – namely, the idea that coins have positive, intrinsic value. But we know this idea has never held: historically all coinage has in fact been token money – a symbol of credit for the holder and of debt for the issuer. To repeat just one key line from our initial arguments in Chapter 3: money (as credit) cannot be singular; it *always* involves a relation to an outside party (debtor). I hold money when I hold a credit against someone else. The quarter in my pocket is a debt token of the US Treasury.

In contrast, the bitcoin in my digital wallet is singular. By design, bitcoin is never credit – thus never money. My money-credits are always and only claims on my debtors. What Nakamoto calls "an electronic coin" turns out to be much more like a fixed weight of "virtual gold" than an actual denominated money coin. The blockchain serves to verify that the coin truly belongs to me, that I have neither stolen nor counterfeited it. If I hold a bitcoin, no one owes me. It may be an asset, but it is an asset like a commodity. It is not debt, and thus not a liability for anyone. This means that the blockchain ledger is not a bank ledger of assets and liabilities, but only a database listing ownership of digital coins – a property register.

We reach the same simple end point as functionalist and other accounts – bitcoin is not money – but our conclusion is much richer because we can see that the being of bitcoin as "not money" is much more than an accident or the result of a particular historical development. Rather, *bitcoin is purposively not money; it is expressly designed to have a nature other than money, and this means bitcoin can never become money.* The problem that Nakamoto set out to solve, the third-party problem, is not a problem (and thus not in need of a solution) but is rather inherent to the being of money.[24] By designing bitcoin to circumvent this structural feature of money, bitcoin's creators guaranteed that bitcoin was not, nor could ever be, money-credit.

5 The Ontology of Bitcoin

We can therefore answer our initial question in the negative – *bitcoin is not money* – without worrying overly much about the specific historical details of bitcoin's development and current use. Yet we should not ignore the phenomenology of bitcoin, because we should not rest with the initial question. If bitcoin is not money, *what is it?* Interestingly, while the primary question has been posed repeatedly, most commentary stops there. Our theory can do more.

In particular, we can write a richer ontology of bitcoin itself. Nakamoto says that the digital coin created by the blockchain is intended to function like "digital cash"; hence bitcoin tries to replicate the being "cash." Of course, as discussed above, a bitcoin is not really like a $20 bill; it's like the metallist theory's mythical coins of intrinsic value. A bitcoin is like Jevons's "standard coin" or Menger's "most saleable commodity." If that sounds like the projection of nineteenth-century orthodox theories of money on to Nakamoto's twenty-first-century technological innovation, we should note that Nakamoto himself explicitly offers the metaphor of

---

24 Perhaps the most forceful response, not only to my argument here about bitcoin, but also to the entire theory of money developed in this book, would be a kind of outright rejection based on the possibility of a future money radically different from past forms. This would mean accepting the historical record showing that no concrete money practices have ever met the criteria for a metallist theory of money, but then refusing to allow this past to determine the potential future being of money. In other words, though gold was never money, what if bitcoin could be? What if bitcoin (or some other future technology) establishes fungible intrinsic value? What if we obviate the need for money as bank money because we learn how to use easily tradable digital assets as our medium of exchange, means of payment, store of value, and money of account? Answers to these questions surely fall beyond the scope of this book, but I would indicate two possible lines of response for those interested in this hypothetical. First, money as money-credit should not be taken as a mere historical contingency, because capitalist societies absolutely depend on the endogenous expansion and contraction of money-credits as part of the production, circulation, and realization of value that functions as the economic engine of such societies (Mehrling 2012; Marx 2015). The metallist theory is incompatible with the actual functioning of capitalism. Second, as I noted in the Preface, the concrete historical development of cryptocurrencies serves as further evidence that the dream of tradable intrinsic value proves illusory. Crypto set out explicitly to eliminate bank money – and wound up reinventing bank money.

"gold miners expending resources to add gold to circulation" (Nakamoto 2008: 4). Combine this with the rule limiting total supply of bitcoin, and we see that despite all the rhetoric about money, bitcoin always modeled itself on the commodity. The white paper details a system to transfer "money" wherein money is understood in just the sense of the commodity theory.

Bitcoin thereby aims to construct a unique, perverse form of commodity. In a way, the question so frequently posed to bitcoin – Is it money? – has always been the wrong one. We should ask instead: Is bitcoin a commodity? A proper reply requires a few words on the ontology of the commodity. As Marx shows, commodities are strange creatures because their nature is twofold (Marx 1977: 6). A commodity is, at one and the same time, both a use-value and an exchange-value. As a use-value[25] it has an immediate, technical, and material *use* to which it can

---

25 "Use-value" is an apparently obvious but actually somewhat technical concept developed within classical political economy; its meaning has been obscured or eclipsed by the common sense of the neoclassical paradigm. That is to say, one of the many ways in which the "marginalist revolution" effected a paradigm shift was in its replacement of use-value with the new concept of *utility* (including marginal utility). The two terms are absolutely not synonyms. "Utility" is the name for a relative property of a commodity, its "usefulness." The idea of utility is strictly *subjective:* it indexes whether (and to what extent) something is *useful to the individual actor.* While utility is always social and psychological, use-value is "immediate[ly] physical"; it names the material nature of a commodity (Marx 1977: 6). This means that use-value is not a "property" of a commodity; it is the very being of a commodity. The commodity *is* a use-value. To sharpen these contrasts, let us take an example – say, a shovel. Neoclassical economists would consider the *utility* of the shovel only by asking "Is the shovel useful to me?" If I have no need for digging, either in the present moment or in my expectations about the future, then the shovel has no utility ("utility to me" is simply redundant). The classical economist, however, would argue that the shovel is a tool that digs, and as such, it *is* a use-value. It is and remains a use-value, whether or not it eventually gets used. The shovel's existence as a use-value remains a fact about it, independent of its owner's needs or wants. Just as not being used does not negate the being of a commodity as a use-value, so the fact of general use cannot establish the use-value of a thing. Money is "used" and money is "useful," but money is not a commodity and it is not a use-value. This is just the other way of formulating our essential point about money-credit as always pointing outside itself to the debtor. In and of itself – positively or intrinsically – money is nothing at all. Money only exists as part of social relations of credit and debt. I can surely "use" money, and it can be "useful," but my use of it depends on those social relations. Using money is therefore utterly unlike using a shovel. An entity such as money can thus be a part of larger social practices that we may deem important or "useful," yet still not *be a use-value.* For Marx, the twofold ontological nature of commodities – their being as both use-value and exchange-value – proves so important because the being of a commodity as exchange-value is purely social (the price depends on the market, on needs, wants, and desires of society), while the being of a commodity as use-value is material and "technical." This does not make the concept of use-value essentialist or transhistorical: in a society that utterly lacked either the concept or practice of digging, the shovel would not *be* a use-value. Within our society, however, we can look at the shovel before us and understand it as a tool that *can dig,*

be directly put; as an exchange-value it has a market price. Use-value is *value in use:* a hammer is valuable in or for pounding nails. Exchange-value is the (potential) realization of value in money terms: a hammer sells for $10.

Bitcoin is not a commodity because it clearly fails to meet these basic conditions: while it is surely an exchange-value as measured in a money of account such as dollars or euros, bitcoin is not a use-value. A bitcoin itself (a "digital coin") – perhaps unlike the blockchain technology on which it is based – cannot manifest as a use-value. There is nothing one can do with the coin other than buy or sell it. Let me emphasize that buying and selling (or buying and holding) are not themselves "uses" in the sense of commodity use-value. The use-value of oil is not that people speculate on it in oil markets but that it is, among other things, a source of fuel. To illustrate this crucial point, we can compare bitcoin to the sort of actual gold coin that it appears to be mimicking. In 1820s Britain the "sovereign" was a gold coin worth one "pound sterling," i.e., £1 GBP. As we know, as money-credit this coin is a symbol of debt of the British government and circulates as such; it is no different from a £1 note, which is also money-credit. As money-gold the sovereign (like the guinea before it) is not itself a commodity. Nonetheless, the underlying token is constructed out of gold, and gold is a commodity. The gold metal is a use-value: it can fill cavities or serve as a conductor of electricity. If the holder of the sovereign melts it down, then they have transformed money-gold into commodity-gold. They might even choose to sell the commodity-gold for its exchange-value as a commodity, which could at times be greater than its denomination in money (£1).[26] Gold is a commodity because it is not only an exchange-value but also a use-value.

Bitcoin is not a use-value and thus cannot meet the criteria for being a commodity. We are vexed in our efforts to grasp the nature of bitcoin precisely by the fact that it is neither money (because it is not credit) nor a commodity (because it lacks a use-value, and is therefore not twofold in its being), yet it seemingly attempts at every turn to look like commodity money – to take on the form of digital gold.

The first component of our positive response to the question "What is bitcoin?" must be that bitcoin is a mimetic technology. *Bitcoin mimics the commodity form* (and falsely purports to be money on the basis of this mimesis).[27] The rule of a

---

even if we have no need of digging at the moment. It can *be* a use-value without that use-value being *realized* through current use. As I show in this text: bitcoin fails this test; it is not a use-value.

26 This seems to have been the case around 1819, when the primary supply for France's coinage was itself melted-down British guineas (Clancy 1999).

27 Put differently, the bitcoin "play" is dual: first it passes itself off as a commodity, and then it consequently purports to be money (conceived in metallist terms).

"limited supply" of coins, and the attendant requirement that creating the coins requires the "work" (including massive energy expenditure) of "mining" them, are both designed to give bitcoin a commodity-like appearance. The digital coins are meant to have some intrinsic value (as commodities do in the form of their use-values), and this is the guiding reason why individuals would want to hold and transfer such coins, as well as why they would then increase in value. Indeed, during the price run-up in 2021 (when bitcoin experienced a fivefold increase in market value), bitcoin was often depicted through comparisons to gold: both bitcoin and gold were purported, based on the fact of their limited supplies, to serve as hedges against inflation.[28] This leads us to a preliminary conclusion: *bitcoin is a faux commodity – fake gold.*[29]

I showed above that holding a bitcoin, verified by the blockchain, is nothing at all like holding money-credit. Now we see, rather, that holding bitcoin is like holding an asset, for which the blockchain verifies ownership. Holding bitcoins is *like* owning land or oil or any other commodity. Of course we are still operating within the terms of the simile: it is "like" holding land or oil because bitcoin operates according to a mimetic logic. But like all mimesis, the bitcoin mimicry of the com-

---

28 In the face of actual inflation in 2022 and the attendant collapse of bitcoin prices, this narrative quickly disappeared.

29 As this manuscript was going into production, Matt Levine published "The Crypto Story," a major effort to write the definitive account of crypto – an intention signaled in the piece's alternate title, "The Only Crypto Story You Need." In some ways Levine eschews the oft-posed question of whether bitcoin is money; his concern lies with the practical realities of crypto's emergence as part of the landscape of contemporary finance. Nevertheless, at the end of a long footnote, Levine distinguishes bitcoin from financial assets such as stocks, bonds, and derivatives, a distinction that dovetails neatly with those I am drawing here. Having defined a financial asset as a contractual claim on cash flows, he writes:

A lot of crypto is consciously not like [a financial asset]. Bitcoin is "digital gold." It's specifically not a financial asset; owning a Bitcoin doesn't represent a claim on anyone else. A Bitcoin exists as an independent thing that you can own, not a contractual relationship between parties like stock or a bond. In the text I use "financial asset" in the extremely loose sense of, like, "a thing with a fluctuating price that you can see on your computer screen and that hedge funds can trade." But cryptocurrencies aren't technically financial assets, or not always anyway. (Levine 2022)

With this last phrase Levine keeps open the possibility that some crypto-firm tokens could act like stock in the company, *not* that bitcoin could become money. Later Levine drives the point home more forcefully: "Bitcoin are *not debt*. They're just Bitcoin. They exist in themselves, on the blockchain, rather than being liabilities of banks" (Levine 2022).

modity never reaches the real, and therefore ultimately holding bitcoin is incommensurable with holding a commodity. Commodities are tangible and material (even if digital), and they are use-values. I can burn oil for fuel, build a house on land for shelter, or use a spreadsheet computer application to balance my household books – but I can do nothing of the sort with bitcoin.[30] Indeed, with bitcoin my only options are those we find for financial assets as expressed in standard stock recommendations: buy, sell, or hold. It is not difficult to spot the difference between bitcoin as a kind of faux commodity, and actual commodities (including digital ones) in the real world. Commodities are entities with specific, concrete use-values, while at the same time they are also tradable (transferable) entities with exchange-value. Bitcoin can of course be traded just like any other commodity, yet bitcoin has no use-value.

We can unpack terms as follows, starting with money and commodities: a commodity is twofold in its very nature as it *is* both a use-value and an exchange-value; the essence of money-credit is to be exchange-value (measure of value) untethered from the physical body of a commodity and thus disconnected from use-value. Bitcoin is a faux commodity precisely because it *has the illusion of use-value but no actual use-value*. It can, of course, have an exchange-value because it has a market price that someone is willing to pay for it. Nonetheless, that exchange-value, unlike with real commodities, has nothing to do with its physical use-value because bitcoin has none. And the price at which bitcoin trades, unlike money-credit (unlike all forms of credit), has nothing to do with the validity of the credit (the strength of the debtor) because bitcoin is not a credit against another party.[31]

---

30 Note that bitcoin's failure to be a use-value has nothing directly to do with its digital nature, which is beside the point. Computer software and online services are both digital and very much real commodities with practical use-values. Bitcoin has no such use-value.
31 At the end of Chapter 5, and in the context of a very different discussion, I raised the hypothetical of the US government deciding to accept bitcoin in payment of taxes. We can now say again that such an action would not make bitcoin money. It would simply mean that as a legal means of payment for taxes owed, the US government agrees to accept a specified payment in kind. That is, they would take payment in the form of a designated commodity – in this case, a faux commodity. This would be odd, but certainly not unique. After all, if they wanted to do so, the government could accept barrels of oil or any other standard commodity as means of payment.

6 Crypto Markets

This leads to the most significant question of all: If bitcoin is neither money nor a commodity, then why is there such a massive market in it – a market that looks and appears to function just like a money market? This question rarely gets asked directly, but it underlies the basic sense that bitcoin is important and that bitcoin might be money after all – or, if not money, at least a revolutionary new technology. If trillions of dollars have been moved into the crypto universe, then something must be going on there.[32] Perhaps the strongest evidence in support of bitcoin being money or money-like appears on price-list pages of crypto websites: these read just like the listings for stocks, bonds, derivatives, and national currencies. Crypto markets appear to be money markets. But are they? Our work in the last chapter on money markets (and thus on financial exchange) makes it possible to answer this question.

As of my writing in late 2022, the total value of all "minted" bitcoins is just over $400 billion, having gone as high as $600 billion in June 2021. Ethereum comes next at a total value just over $200 billion, followed by three stablecoins totaling approximately $150 billion. The list itself expresses the intuitive appeal of an argument like that of Hazlett and Luther, who conclude almost solely on the basis of its "market cap"[33] that bitcoin must be money.[34] Their implicit logic appears to be: if it is

---

[32] That's a big "if." While it proved common during both the 2021 crypto run-up and the 2022 "crypto winter" to describe the crypto universe as valued at $1–$3 trillion, the actual amount of money moved into crypto (as opposed to bogus mark-to-market valuations of issued tokens) proves drastically smaller than that. For more details on market cap, see Footnote 33.

[33] It has become standard practice to refer to the "market cap" of a cryptocurrency or stablecoin, but this is a misleading use of that terminology. "Market capitalization" names the total value of all floating shares (or total shares) of a corporation's stock, and therefore serves as an indicator of the total value of the company: if you bought all the shares of stock available, it would cost you this amount, and you would then "own the company" in the sense of owning all its stock. But bitcoin is not a company – it does not make a product, does not earn profit, and it is not for sale – so referring to its market cap only serves as a sleight of hand, by suggesting that bitcoin is like the Walt Disney Corporation (as of my writing, the Disney market cap is just a bit less than the total value of all bitcoins). As I show, when used to refer to stablecoins, "market cap" is even more misleading. For the definitive explanation and critique of crypto market cap, see White (2022).

[34] Hazlett and Luther's article uses data from 2018, estimating bitcoin's market cap at $129 billion. Both their number and mine are indeed very large numbers, but we have to ask: *Compared to what?* Hazlett and Luther compare the "market cap" of national currencies (against which the bitcoin number ranks highly), but we have already shown that this comparison is meaningless because bitcoin is neither "currency" (in this sense of money of account) nor money-credit. And bitcoin's so-called market cap number does not seem so impressive if we take other markets as our

traded like money, it must be money (money is that money trades). Of course, Chapter 6's development of the logic of the derivative reveals the weakness in such reasoning. Lots of things are traded like money that are not in fact money.

Nevertheless, the size and scope of the bitcoin market offer a clue to bitcoin's nature that can lead us to a better simile: perhaps *bitcoin is not-money like oil is not-money.* We know that the market in oil looks like a money market because derivatives are money-credits, and thus the market in oil futures is a money market. The fact that a derivative on oil exists makes possible a money market in "oil" (i. e., oil futures). This line of analysis would suggest that if we want to explain the market in bitcoin, we need to locate/discern the bitcoin derivative.

Unfortunately, this is no mean feat for the obvious reason: the bitcoin market itself is not a futures or options market. Bitcoins are not derivatives on some underlying asset; bitcoins are the assets. When traders buy and sell bitcoins, they are not swapping futures contracts for bitcoins, as they are for oil. Rather, we want to say they are buying *actual* coins – faux commodities but "actual" digital coins – not a derivative on these coins. How do we explain the bitcoin market as something that looks like a money market but manages to do so apart from a dominant derivative market?[35] This question cuts to the core of the peculiar nature of bitcoin.

---

comparison: gold ($10 trillion); total outstanding credit default swaps ($1.5 trillion); *daily* turnover of the forex market ($6.6 trillion) (BIS 2019).

35 It should come as absolutely no surprise that derivatives on bitcoins – futures contracts (and even options on futures contracts, i. e., second derivatives) – have in fact been created by dealers and do trade on exchanges. However, the mere existence of derivatives on bitcoins does not solve the mystery of the nature of bitcoin, and this for a few reasons. First, as a derivative on a faux commodity with no use-value, bitcoin futures exist only as a kind of degenerate form of derivative. They cannot simply be assumed from the outset to be the same kind of entity as a derivative on an actual commodity. That is, the price of oil is related to, yet distinct from, the price of oil futures, and the former maintains a link to concrete reality (the production, distribution, and *consumption* of oil) – and this matters when we try to make sense of the derivative market in oil. Second, the bitcoin derivative market is extremely small as a ratio of the overall market in the faux commodity itself. Derivative markets are typically much larger than the market in the underlying asset; this is true for both commodity-market derivatives and money-market derivatives (see BIS 2023). This relationship is inverted for bitcoin. For example, where oil futures are roughly eight times larger than the oil market, the bitcoin futures market is only one fifth the size of the bitcoin market. Clearly the derivative market is not the same driving force for the bitcoin faux commodity as it is for other commodity markets. Third and finally, even if the derivative market for bitcoin looked similar to other derivative markets, and even if we wished to ignore the radical difference between a faux commodity and a real commodity, we would still be left to explain how the bitcoin market itself functions like a money market – in a way that does not occur for other commodity markets. Here we recall Chapter 6's discussion of futures markets, where we showed that spot prices in commodities are not an actual daily market price but simply a record of past purchases and sales that cannot be disentangled from the derivative markets. The "money market" in bitcoin ex-

The bitcoin market resembles a derivative market, despite the fact that bitcoin is not money-credit and despite the fact that what is being traded are not derivatives on bitcoins but actual bitcoins. How is this possible?

The answer lies in the unique nature of bitcoin as a faux commodity, as digital gold. To unfold this claim we start with the logic of the derivative: the derivative makes it possible to create a money-credit entity out of a commodity or commodity-like entity. A derivative is a form of money-credit for two reasons: the derivative contract establishes a relation of credit/debt between two parties, and as a strictly financial entity, the derivative (partially) disconnects the exchange-value of the underlying asset from any use-value it might have (if that asset is a commodity).

As a technology that mimics commodity-gold, bitcoin is *immediately* derivative-like because it is immediately untethered from use-value. Bitcoin is neither money (because it is not a form of credit/debt) nor a derivative (because the price of bitcoin is not derived from the price of some underlying asset). Nevertheless, in its technological mimicry of a commodity, in its capacity to create faux gold, bitcoin establishes one of the key aspects of both a derivative and money: it is a pure, independent form of exchange-value. Bitcoin has accomplished what a derivative on a real commodity aims for: the creation of a homogenous tradable asset. The difference lies here: a normal derivative establishes its price on the basis of, and in distinction to, the underlying asset's value, whereas the faux commodity (bitcoin) has one, and only one, price. There is no spot price for bitcoin as there is for oil.

Crucially, given the fact that bitcoin is neither money nor a derivative, a market in bitcoin cannot form "naturally" or on its own. The mimetic technology that constructs the faux commodity of "digital cash" is insufficient to create a money market in bitcoin, so we must be wary of concluding that the trade in bitcoin emerges directly from the original white paper and the first implementation of the bitcoin network – or of thinking that any faux commodity would necessarily circulate organically in money markets.

To see why, we underscore a pivotal fact about the bitcoin network: *one cannot trade bitcoins on the blockchain.* The blockchain makes it possible for the owner of a bitcoin to *transfer* it to another network user (who then becomes the new owner of the faux commodity), but financial exchange (or economic exchange) cannot be carried out on the network. Financial *exchange* requires swapping money-credit for money-credit, but there is no way to accomplish such a swap *within* the block-

---

isted well before the first bitcoin derivative was created, and even today still seems to function much more independently of the futures markets than is typically the case.

chain – as that technology cannot circulate credit/debt but only change ownership of pre-existing assets.[36]

The crypto money markets would never have emerged were it not for the emergence of *exchanges*. These internet sites (or smartphone apps) construct a space (a market) where users *can swap faux commodities for real money.* The bitcoin code and bitcoin network create neither money nor even a space for financial exchange. They merely construct the faux commodity itself – mine the digital gold – which can then be exchanged only *outside* of the bitcoin network. Both the early (sometimes inefficient, sometimes legally grey) exchanges, and today's more established (yet still sometimes legally grey) exchanges make a market in the faux commodity possible by facilitating the transfer of bitcoin from user to user *on the blockchain* by literally moving money-credits (bank money) from person to person *outside the blockchain.*

Returning to our earlier discussion, we can now conclude that the exchanges make the market in bitcoin possible because the exchanges act like banks (see Levine 2022) – and their existence performs a derivative-like function.[37] That is, the

---

36 Arguably one could use the blockchain to accomplish a rudimentary form of economic exchange: you give me a commodity (directly, in the physical world), and I transfer bitcoin to you. Notice, however, that this is not truly economic exchange as we have defined it because rather than swapping commodity for money-credit, we would be exchanging a real commodity for a faux commodity. In other words, consistent with its Mengerian vision of money, bitcoin creates the possibility not for electronic exchange, but merely (one-sided) electronic barter.

37 Crypto markets also look a lot like stock markets, and not just because people are trading both crypto and stock on their Robinhood app. Despite their ubiquity, stocks are also somewhat bizarre entities: they are a bit like, but also unlike, many other things. A stock is a share of ownership in a capitalist firm; stocks are known as *equities* because each share of stock denotes a percentage ownership in the firm. The stockholder therefore owns some portion of a capitalist firm, but the stock is not a commodity because it has no direct use-value. Owning stock conveys certain rights – for example, to liquidation value, or to vote on certain company decisions. Yet the stock does not give any formal rights to future profits (dividends). Stocks do not produce direct rents the way ownership of other properties does. Stocks are classed with bonds as "securities" because both are claims on a company. But whereas a bond is clearly a money-credit (a loan to the company), the nature of a stock's "claim" proves much more amorphous. The stock is not a specifically denominated money claim (the company does not *owe* the stockholder a specified debt). We can see two moments in a company's history when a stock turns into a money claim: first, if the company is sold; second, if the company goes bankrupt. In the first instance stockholders themselves will be bought out at an agreed share price; in the second case, stockholders will hold a claim against the company's assets, though those claims have secondary status compared to bond holders.

Stocks get grouped with bonds under the classical definition of a "financial asset" as "a contractual claim on the cash flows of some person or entity" (Levine 2022), but here again their inclusion seems odd because the actual *contractual claim* proves vague or nebulous in the case of a stock. The bond I hold on Apple Inc. specifies exactly how much they owe me, and when; my shares

exchanges allow bitcoin, a faux commodity, to circulate the same way a derivative on a real commodity would do. Summing up, we can identify two necessary (but insufficient) conditions for a bitcoin money market to come into being:

1) The creation of the mimetic technology itself, the construction of a *faux commodity*, which, by definition, will be a singular entity (not a relation of credit/debt) posited as having intrinsic value, and capable of being assigned an exchange-value. The digital gold mimics real gold, but has no use-value.

2) The emergence of a space where the faux commodity can be traded for money. Such a space makes possible a unique form of exchange: the swapping of real money-credits for faux commodities. Only on these exchanges does money exist and circulate.[38] Money circulates through the exchange, while the blockchain network updates and verifies the transfer of ownership of the digital coin.

---

of Apple stock indicate no such thing. Despite all this, a market in stocks exists because dealers make such a market by offering to buy or sell these partial ownership claims – *shares* – at specified prices.

As with the bitcoin exchanges, the creation of a stock exchange performs a derivative-like function: it transforms a non-money entity (a legal title to partial ownership) into a money-like entity (a tradable share with a market price). The stock exchange makes stocks appear even more like bonds: both are claims on a company, where such claims can be priced, bought, and sold, and companies can fund their operations either by issuing stocks or bonds. As with bitcoin, stocks are not a derivative on an underlying commodity because the price of the stock is not tied to some other asset (the stock *is* the asset). Of course, the comparison to bitcoin hits a hard limit in the fact that to own stock is to hold legal title over an actual firm that makes and sells products, generates revenue, and may turn a profit (or might go bankrupt). The stock always points toward the firm and its real-world practices. To own bitcoin is to be verified on the blockchain as the valid owner of a unique alphanumeric string. The bitcoin points nowhere else.

In case I have failed to make stocks seem weird, I will conclude with a note about how the "ownership" above actually works today:

Nobody owns stock. What you own is an entitlement to stock held for you by your broker. But your broker doesn't own the stock either. What your broker owns is an entitlement to stock held for it by Cede & Co., which is a nominee of the Depository Trust Company, which is a company that is in the business of owning everyone's stock for them. This system sounds convoluted but actually makes it easy to keep track of things: If I sell stock to you, I don't have to courier over a paper share certificate, or call up the company and have it change its shareholder register. Our brokers just change some electronic entries at their DTC accounts and everything is cool. (Levine, 14 July 2015)

38 And when the exchanges blow up, the money disappears. The bankruptcy of FTX, with the loss of billions of dollars of customer funds (real money, sent to the exchange through bank transfer), provides the most prominent example.

The faux commodity functions like a derivative if and only if there is an exchange on which it can circulate. Combining the bitcoin/blockchain technology with the exchanges for trading bitcoin gives rise to the unique bitcoin market.[39]

Such a market does not quite fit either of our models for exchange. The market in bitcoin is not exactly like the market in blue jeans (economic exchange) because bitcoins have no use-value. Yet it is also not quite like the forex market (financial exchange) because bitcoins are not a form of money-credit. We might say the bitcoin market is a deranged form of economic exchange, one in which faux commodities circulate in exchange for real money. Or we might say that the bitcoin market most closely resembles a futures commodity market. Bitcoin trades like derivatives on real commodities trade. But even here the analogy is incomplete because bitcoin itself *is* the "underlying" asset. There is no need for the derivative because, as a faux commodity, bitcoin already functions like a derivative.[40] Bitcoins are like oil futures without spot prices.

----

39 To address decentralized finance (DeFi) properly would require another entire chapter, and much of the DeFi space is dominated by Ponzi schemes and rug pulls. There may be at least one exception: the "decentralized stablecoin" DAI. DAI is the only example I know that meets the criteria of "crypto money," where, by "crypto," I mean truly decentralized and fully maintained on the blockchain (thus excluding all the major stablecoins), and by "money," I mean money as money-credit (thus excluding all the proof-of-work coins which are not credit/debt). DAI is issued only when a user takes out a corresponding loan, called a "collateralized debt position" (CDP). It is a swap of IOUs on the blockchain: DAI is the user's deposit money, and CDP is the loan. The CDP loan is secured by locking up 150 % of the value of the loan in ether (ETH) that the user already holds. If the price of either ETH or DAI moves in such a way as to put pressure on the securitization of the CDP loan, the smart contract can automatically liquidate the collateral and sell it to cover the repayment of the CDP loan. DAI therefore functions similarly to both margin trading (using crypto collateral to take out loans to buy more crypto) and repo (the smart contract functions like a repo dealer, automatically taking ownership of the collateral for the loan, if need be). DAI therefore makes possible a tiny amount of money creation within the crypto universe. Here again, Levine's recent argument echoes my account: "DeFi is good at lending crypto secured by crypto. The collateral lives on the blockchain; the loan lives on the blockchain; they're connected by smart contracts on the blockchain. It's all pretty neat. But this sort of lending crypto against crypto doesn't *do* much" (Levine 2022). The italicization of that penultimate word means a lot, for as Levine explains, all DeFi can really do is create margin for trading crypto, whereas "a mortgage lets you buy a house" (Levine 2022).

40 One might try to interpret bitcoin as a derivative based on the value not of the coin itself (with intrinsic value) but on the blockchain technology, with the latter serving as the "underlying asset." This will not work for two reasons: 1) buying a bitcoin entails *use* of the blockchain, but the owner of bitcoin receives no legal ownership over the blockchain technology; 2) in general "technology" does not have an asset price because it is not itself a commodity with specifiable exchange-value. Undoubtedly, the raison d'être of patent and intellectual property law is to transform technology and ideas into legal commodities, but the blockchain is not and cannot

7 Money and Capitalism

It tells us something important – about money and money markets, about capitalism today – that in late 2022 bitcoin is trading at over $20,000/coin (having gone as high as $68,000/coin), yet no one seems to really know what bitcoin is. My point in making the extended argument for bitcoin as a faux commodity, and for the bitcoin market as a derivative-like market, is not simply to get bitcoin "right" for its own sake but rather to expand our theory of money and indicate some of its suppleness and extensibility – to demonstrate one of the many ways it can link up with and contribute to a much wider body of work in political economy, political theory, and public policy. To reprise the opening line of the book, money is both the starting presupposition and the logical telos of a capitalist social order. We live in societies structured not only *by* but also *for* money. This means that any theory of society, any theory of culture, and any theory of politics proves incomplete, perhaps even unviable, if it cannot account for money and money practices.

Earlier in this chapter I noted the common move to invoke a definition of money through a tacit reference to the neoclassical paradigm's normal science – that is, by referring to how "economists define money." But it does not matter how economists define money if they are wrong. And, lest there be any confusion, they are completely wrong. Money is not a commodity, and money has no value. Money is more than the money stuff; it is the entire array that includes denominated token, creditor, and debtor, all realized within a viable money space. But even at the level of the money stuff, the money token is always credit/debt, and all credit/debt, ontologically, proves to be of the same nature – to be money-credit. Capitalist social orders can thus be redefined as societies organized on the basis of available money-credit, which they use to organize production to generate more money-credit. Reformulated within the language of our theory of money, capitalism sounds strange indeed. This, I submit, proves to be one of the great merits of our theory. Only by denaturalizing capitalism can we ever expect to understand it – and only by understanding it could we ever hope to change it.

---

be commodified in this way. Much of the blockchain code is open source, but more importantly, the whole point of a decentralized database is that it's held *publicly*. The core tenet of blockchain is the idea that no one can *own it.*

Bibliography

ACLU. 2018. *A Pound of Flesh: The Criminalization of Private Debt*. Report accessed 26 January 2023 at https://www.aclu.org/report/pound-flesh-criminalization-private-debt.

Adkins, Lisa, Melinda Cooper, and Martijn Konings. 2020. *The Asset Economy: Property Ownership and the New Logic of Inequality*. Cambridge, UK: Polity.

Aglietta, Michel, and André Orléan, eds. 1998. *La Monnaie Souveraine*. Paris: Éditions Odile Jacob.

Aglietta, Michel. 2018. *Money: 5,000 Years of Debt and Power*. Translated by David Broder, Pepita Ould Ahmed, and Jean-François Ponsot. New York: Verso.

Anderson, Benjamin M., Jr. 1917. *The Value of Money*. New York: Macmillan.

Andre, Alex. 2021. "The Concealed Gift." *Anthropological Theory* 21, no. 1: 50 – 81; https://doi.org/10.1177/1463499620912964.

Arthur, Christopher J. 2004. *The New Dialectic and Marx's* Capital. Leiden: Brill.

Backhaus, Hans-Georg. 1992. "Between Philosophy and Science: Marxian Social Economy as Critical Theory." In *Dialectics and History*. Vol. 1 of *Open Marxism*. Edited by Werner Bonefeld, Richard Gunn, and Kosmas Psychopedis. London: Pluto; 54 – 92.

Bagehot, Walter. 1873. *Lombard Street: A Description of the Money Market*. London: Henry S. King.

Bal, Aleksandra. 2015. "How to Tax Bitcoin?" In *Handbook of Digital Currency: Bitcoin, Innovation, Financial Instruments, and Big Data*. Edited by David Lee Kuo Chuen. New York: Academic Press; 267 – 282.

Banaji, Jairus. 2010. *Theory as History: Essays on Modes of Production and Exploitation*. Leiden: Brill.

Banaji, Jairus. 2020. *A Brief History of Commercial Capitalism*. Chicago, Illinois: Haymarket.

Bell, Stephanie. 1998. "The Hierarchy of Money." Levy Economics Institute of Bard College Working Paper no. 231.

Benes, Jaromir, and Michael Kumhof. 2012. "The Chicago Plan Revisited." IMF Working Paper 12/02. Accessed 26 January 2023 at https://www.imf.org/external/pubs/ft/wp/2012/wp12202.pdf.

Bhaskar, Nirupama Devi, and David Lee Kuo Chuen. 2015. "Bitcoin Exchanges." In *Handbook of Digital Currency: Bitcoin, Innovation, Financial Instruments, and Big Data*. Edited by David Lee Kuo Chuen. New York: Academic Press; 559 – 573.

BIS (Bank for International Settlements), Monetary and Economic Department. 2019. *Global Foreign Exchange Market Turnover in 2019*. Triennial Central Bank Survey. Accessed 26 January 2023 at https://www.bis.org/statistics/rpfx19_fx_annex.pdf.

BIS. 2022a. "What Drives Repo Haircuts? Evidence from the UK Market." BIS Working Papers no. 1027. Accessed 29 January 2023 at https://www.bis.org/publ/work1027.pdf.

BIS. 2022b. "Triennial Central Bank Survey: OTC Foreign Exchange Turnover in April 2022." Accessed 23 March 2023 at https://www.bis.org/statistics/rpfx22_fx.pdf

BIS. 2023. "Global OTC Derivative Market." Accessed 29 January 2023 at https://stats.bis.org/statx/srs/table/d5.1.

Breen, T. H. 2001. *Tobacco Culture: The Mentality of the Great Tidewater Planters on the Eve of Revolution*. Princeton: Princeton University Press.

Briscoe, John. 1694. *Discourse on the Late Funds of the Million-act* [...]. London: s.n.

Bryan, Dick, and Michael Rafferty. 2006. "Money in Capitalism or Capitalist Money?" *Historical Materialism* 14, no. 1: 75 – 95; https://doi.org/10.1163/156920606776690893.

Buchanan, Neil H. 2013. "If You're Explaining, Everyone's Losing (Platinum Coin Edition)." Accessed March 16, 2023. http://www.dorfonlaw.org/2013/01/if-youre-explaining-everyones-losing.html.

https://doi.org/10.1515/9783110760774-012

Buiter, Willem H. 2008. "Can Central Banks Go Broke?" Centre for Economic Policy Research Discussion Paper Series. Discussion Paper no. 6827.

Campbell, Martha. 1997. "Marx and Keynes on Money." *International Journal of Political Economy* 27, no. 3: 65–91; https://doi.org/10.1080/08911916.1997.11643952.

Campbell, Martha. 2017. "Marx's Transition to Money with No Intrinsic Value in *Capital*, Chapter 3." *Continental Thought & Theory* 1, no. 4: 207–230.

Carney, Mark. 2018. "The Future of Money." Bank of England. Paper presented to the inaugural Scottish Economics Conference, Edinburgh University. 2 March 2018. Accessed 26 January 2023 at https://www.bankofengland.co.uk/-/media/boe/files/speech/2018/the-future-of-money-speech-by-mark-carney.pdf.

Carruthers, Bruce G. 1996. *City of Capital: Politics and Markets in the English Financial Revolution.* Princeton: Princeton University Press.

Carson, Rebecca. 2018. "Money as Money: Suzanne de Brunhoff's Marxist Monetary Theory." *Consecutio Rerum* 3, no. 5: 407–427.

Carter, Zachary D. 2020. *The Price of Peace: Money, Democracy, and the Life of John Maynard Keynes.* New York: Random House.

Cencini, Alvaro. 1988. *Money, Income, and Time: A Quantum-Theoretical Approach.* London: Pinter.

Chambers, Samuel. n.d. "Marx's Unorthodox Account of Money." Unpublished manuscript (PDF), last modified November 2019.

Chambers, Samuel. 2014. *Bearing Society in Mind: Theories and Politics of the Social Formation.* London: Rowman and Littlefield International.

Chambers, Samuel. 2018. *There's No Such Thing as "The Economy."* Brooklyn: Punctum Books.

Chambers, Samuel. 2022. *Capitalist Economics.* London and New York: Oxford University Press.

Cheng, Jeffrey, and David Wesell. 28 January 2020. "What Is the Repo Market, and Why Does It Matter?" Up Front. *Brookings.* Accessed 3 February 2023 at https://www.brookings.edu/blog/up-front/2020/01/28/what-is-the-repo-market-and-why-does-it-matter/.

Choo, Kim-Kwang Raymond. 2015. "Cryptocurrency and Virtual Currency: Corruption and Money Laundering/Terrorism Financing Risks?" In *Handbook of Digital Currency: Bitcoin, Innovation, Financial Instruments, and Big Data.* Edited by David Lee Kuo Chuen. New York: Academic Press; 283–307.

Chuen, David Lee Kuo, ed. 2015. *Handbook of Digital Currency: Bitcoin, Innovation, Financial Instruments, and Big Data.* New York: Academic Press.

Clancy, Kevin. 1999. "The Recoinage and Exchange of 1816–17." PhD dissertation, University of Leeds.

Connolly, William. 1987. *Politics and Ambiguity.* Madison: University of Wisconsin Press.

Coy, Peter. 10 December 2021. "Can We Trust What's Happening to Money?" *New York Times.* Accessed 29 January 2023 at https://www.nytimes.com/2021/12/10/opinion/cash-crypto-trust-money.html.

Cronon, William. 1991. *Nature's Metropolis: Chicago and the Great West.* New York: W.W. Norton.

dacoinminster. 2012. "The Second Bitcoin Whitepaper." Vs. 0.5. Accessed 28 January 2023 at https://drive.google.com/file/d/18iRKDmZy44YDd3jyEtafouT1PA7dEi5e/view.

Dalton, George, ed. 1978. *Research in Economic Anthropology: An Annual Compilation of Research.* Vol. 1. Greenwich, Connecticut: JAI Press.

Davies, Glyn. 2002. *A History of Money: From Ancient Times to the Present Day.* Cardiff: University of Wales Press.

De Brunhoff, Suzanne. 1973. *Marx on Money*. Translated by Maurice J. Goldbloom. New York: Urizen Books.

De Vroey, Michel. 1984. "Inflation: A Non-Monetarist Monetary Interpretation." *Cambridge Journal of Economics* 8, no. 4: 381–399; https://www.jstor.org/stable/23596646.

Del Mar, Alexander. 1896. *The Science of Money*. Second edition. New York: Macmillan.

Desan, Christine. 2014. *Making Money: Coin, Currency, and the Coming of Capitalism*. Oxford: Oxford UP.

Despain, Hans G. 22 June 2020. "Book Review: The Deficit Myth: Modern Monetary Theory and the Birth of the People's Economy by Stephanie Kelton." *LSE Review of Books*. Accessed 29 January 2023 at https://blogs.lse.ac.uk/lsereviewofbooks/2020/06/22/book-review-the-deficit-myth-mod ern-monetary-theory-and-the-birth-of-the-peoples-economy-by-stephanie-kelton/.

Diehl, Stephen. 2021. "The Intellectual Incoherence of Cryptoassets." Accessed 29 January 2023 at https://www.stephendiehl.com/blog/crypto-absurd.html.

Douglas, Alexander X. 2016. *The Philosophy of Debt*. London: Routledge.

Drumetz, Françoise, and Christian Pfister. 2021. "The Meaning of MMT." Banque de France Working Paper no. 833.

Drumm, Colin. 2021. *The Difference That Money Makes: Sovereignty, Indecision, and the Politics of Liquidity*. eScholarship, University of California. https://escholarship.org/uc/item/57h0m1x1.

Drumm, Colin. 2022. "Bills of Exchange, Medieval and Modern." *Trial of the Pyx*, 10 August. https://tri alofthepyx.substack.com/p/bills-of-exchange-medieval-and-modern#footnote-anchor-2-68066428

Durand, Cédric. 2017. *Fictitious Capital: How Finance Is Appropriating Our Future*. Translated by David Broder. New York: Verso.

Dymski, Gary A. 2006. "Money and Credit in Heterodox Theory: Reflections on Lapavitsas." *Historical Materialism* 14, no. 1: 49–73; https://doi.org/10.1163/156920606776690929.

Dyson, Ben, Graham Hodgson, and Frank van Lerven. 2016. *Sovereign Money: An Introduction*. Positive Money. Accessed 29 January 2023 at http://positivemoney.org/wp-content/uploads/2016/12/SovereignMoney-AnIntroduction-20161214.pdf.

Earley, James S. 1994. "Joseph Schumpeter: A Frustrated 'Creditist.'" In *New Perspectives in Monetary Macroeconomics: Explorations in the Tradition of Hyman P. Minsky*. Edited by Gary Dymski and Robert Pollin. Ann Arbor: University of Michigan Press; 337–351.

Edgeworth, Francis. 1887. "Report on Monetary Standard." British Association for the Advancement of Science: 284–855.

Edgeworth, Francis. 1918. "*The Value of Money* by B.M. Anderson." *The Economic Journal* 28, no. 109: 66–69; https://www.jstor.org/stable/i312715.

Ehnts, Dirk, and Nicolas Barbaroux. 2017. "From Wicksell to Le Bourva to Modern Monetary Theory: A Wicksell Connection." Berlin School of Economics and Law Institute for International Political Economy Working Paper no. 92/2017.

Eich, Stefan. 2018. "Between Justice and Accumulation: Aristotle on Currency and Reciprocity." *Political Theory* 47, no. 3: 1–28; https://doi.org/10.1177/0090591718802634.

Eich, Stefan. 2019. "Old Utopias, New Tax Havens: The Politics of Bitcoin in Historical Perspective." In *Regulating Blockchain: Techno-Social and Legal Challenges*. Edited by Philipp Hacker, Ioannis Lianos, Georgios Dimitropoulos, and Stefan Eich. Oxford: Oxford University Press; 85–98.

Eich, Stefan. 2022. *The Currency of Politics: The Political Theory of Money from Aristotle to Keynes*. Princeton: Princeton University Press.

Elliott, Douglas J., and Larissa de Lima. 2018. *Crypto-Assets: Their Future and Regulation*. Oliver Wyman, a Marsh & McLennan Company. Accessed 25 January 2023 at https://www.oliverwy

man.com/content/dam/oliver-wyman/v2/publications/2018/october/Oliver_Wyman_Crypto-as
sets_Their%20Future%20and%20Regulation.pdf.

Ellis, Howard S. 1934. *German Monetary Theory, 1905 – 1933*. Cambridge, Massachusetts: Harvard
University Press.

European Central Bank. 2019. "Stablecoins – No Coins, But Are They Stable?" November 2019. *In
Focus* no. 3.

Faure, David. 2006. *China and Capitalism: A History of Business Enterprise in Modern China*. Hong
Kong: Hong Kong University Press.

Federal Deposit Insurance Corporation. 1984. *The First Fifty Years: A History of the FDIC, 1933 – 1983*.
Accessed 27 January 2023 at https://www.fdic.gov/bank/historical/firstfifty/.

Federal Deposit Insurance Corporation. 2017. *Crisis and Response: An FDIC History, 2008 – 2013*.
Accessed 27 January 2023 at https://www.fdic.gov/bank/historical/crisis/.

Federal Deposit Insurance Corporation. 2022. "Capital." In *Risk Management Manual of Examination
Policies*, Section 2.1. Accessed 27 January 2023 at https://www.fdic.gov/regulations/safety/
manual/section2 – 1.pdf.

Federal Reserve System. 2016. *The Federal Reserve System: Purposes & Functions*. Tenth edition.
Federal Reserve System Publication; https://doi.org/10.17016/0199 – 9729.10

Feinig, Jakob. 2022. *Moral Economies of Money: Politics and the Monetary Constitution of Society*.
Stanford, California: Stanford University Press.

Ferguson, Frances. 2019. "Bitcoin: A Reader's Guide (The Beauty of the Very Idea)." *Critical Inquiry*
46, no. 1: 140 – 166; https://doi.org/10.1086/705302.

Fichte, Johann Gottlieb. 2012. *The Closed Commercial State*. Translated by Anthony Curtis Adler.
Albany: SUNY Press.

Fields, David, and Matías Vernengo. 2013. "Hegemonic Currencies During the Crisis: The Dollar
Versus the Euro in a Cartalist Perspective. *Review of International Political Economy* 20,
no. 4: 740 – 759; https://doi.org/10.1080/09692290.2012.698997.

Fine, Ben, and Costas Lapavitsas. 2000. "Markets and Money in Social Theory: What Role for
Economics?" *Economy and Society* 29, no. 3: 357 – 382; https://doi.org/10.1080/
03085140050084561.

Fisher, Irving. 1911. *The Purchasing Power of Money: Its Determination and Relation to Credit, Interest,
and Crises*. New York: Macmillan. Accessed 27 January 2023 at https://oll.libertyfund.org/title/
brown-the-purchasing-power-of-money.

Fisher, Irving. 2010. *The Money Illusion*. Milton Keynes, UK: Lightning Source.

Foley, Duncan K. 1983. "On Marx's Theory of Money." *Social Concept* 1, no. 1: 5 – 19.

Foley, Duncan K. 2013. "Rethinking Financial Capitalism and the 'Information' Economy." *Review of
Radical Political Economics* 45, no. 3: 257 – 268; https://doi.org/10.1177/0486613413487154.

Foucault, Michel. 1978. *History of Sexuality: The Will to Knowledge*. Volume 1. Translated by Robert
Hurley. New York: Vintage Books.

Friedman, Jeffrey, and Wladimir Kraus. 2011. *Engineering the Financial Crisis: Systemic Risk and the
Failure of Regulation*. Philadelphia: University of Pennsylvania Press.

Friedman, Milton. 1991. "The Island of Stone Money." The Hoover Institution at Stanford University
Working Papers in Economics no. E-91 – 3.

Fullwiler, Scott, Stephanie Kelton, and L. Randall Wray. 2012. "Modern Money Theory: A Response to
Critics." http://dx.doi.org/10.2139/ssrn.2008542.

Funke, Jayson J. 2017. "Demystifying Money: Fictions of Capital and Credit." *Human Geography* 10,
no. 1: 20 – 35; https://doi.org/10.1177/194277861701000103.

Galbraith, James K. 2008. "The Collapse of Monetarism and the Irrelevance of the New Monetary Consensus." Paper presented at the 25th Annual Milton Friedman Distinguished Lecture at Marietta College, Marietta, Ohio. Accessed 27 January 2023 at https://artsonline.uwaterloo.ca/rneedham/sites/ca.rneedham/files/needhdata/documents/CollapseofMonetarismdelivered.pdf.

Galbraith, James K. 2018. "The Past and Future of Political Economy." Review Essay. *American Affairs* 2, no. 4: 79–86.

Galbraith, James K. 2019. "Sparse, Inconsistent and Unreliable: Tax Records and the *World Inequality Report 2018.*" *Development and Change* 50, no. 2: 329–346; https://doi.org/10.1111/dech.12475.

Ganßmann, Heiner. 2011. *Doing Money: Elementary Monetary Theory from a Sociological Standpoint.* London: Routledge.

Gardiner, Geoffrey. 1993. *Towards True Monetarism.* London: Dulwich.

Gerson, Kelcie, Matthew Hornbach, and Guneet Dhingra. 2019. "Back to a Bigger Balance Sheet." U.S. Interest Rate Strategy, North America, Morgan Stanley Research.

Gerson, Kelcie, Matthew Hornbach, Guneet Dhingra, Betsy L. Graseck, Jay Bacow, Zuri Zhao, Philip Salandra. 18 September 2019. "TOMOs, POMOs, and Bills, Oh My! FAQ on the Repo Surge." US Interest Rate Strategy, North America, Morgan Stanley Research.

Goldberg, Dror. 2015. "Money, Credit, and Banking in Virginia, 1585–1645." Draft manuscript. Accessed 26 January 2023 at https://economics.yale.edu/sites/default/files/goldberg-paper.pdf.

Goldstein, Jacob. 2020. *Money: The True Story of a Made-Up Thing.* New York: Hachette.

Gorton, Gary B., and Andrew Metrick. 2009. "Securitized Banking and the Run on Repo." NBER Working Paper no. 15223. Accessed 28 January 2023 at http://www.nber.org/papers/w15223.

Gould, J. D. 1964. "The Price Revolution Reconsidered." *The Economic History Review* 17, no. 2: 249–66; https://doi.org/10.2307/2593005.

Graeber, David. 2011. *Debt: The First 5,000 Years.* Brooklyn, New York: Melville House.

Graseck, Betsy L., Manan Gosalia, Jeffrey Adelson, Ryan Kenny, Brad Fitter, and Emmanuel Nimarko. 23 September 2019. *What Large Cap Bank Investors Are Asking: What Happened in the Repo Market This Past Week?* Morgan Stanley Research.

Greenspan, Alan. 1966. "Gold and Economic Freedom." Accessed 22 December 2017 at http://www.321gold.com/fed/greenspan/1966.html.

Grey, Rohan. Forthcoming. "Administering Money: Coinage, Debt Crises, and the Future of Fiscal Policy." https://ssrn.com/abstract=3536440.

Grierson, Philip. 1978. "The Origins of Money." In *Research in Economic Anthropology: An Annual Compilation of Research.* Vol. 1. Edited by George Dalton. Greenwich, Connecticut: JAI Press; 1–35.

Hamilton, Alexander. 9 January 1790. *First Report on the Public Credit. Secretary of the Treasury.* Report communicated to the House of Representatives, 14 January 1790. Accessed 28 January 2023 at https://founders.archives.gov/documents/Hamilton/01-06-02-0076-0002-0001.

Hawtrey, R. G. 1919. *Currency and Credit.* London: Longmans, Green, and Co.

Hayek, F. A. 1990. "Denationalisation of Money: The Argument Refined; An Analysis of the Theory and Practice of Concurrent Currencies." Third edition. London: The Institute of Economic Affairs.

Hayes, M. G. 2018. "The Liquidity of Money." *Cambridge Journal of Economics* 42, no. 5: 1205–1218; https://doi.org/10.1093/cje/bey018.

Hazell, A. P. 1898. "Two Typical Theories of Money: The Quantity Theory of Money from the Marxist Stand-Point." *Journal of Political Economy* 7, no. 1: 78–85; http://www.jstor.org/stable/1825461.

Hazlett, Peter K., and William J. Luther. 2020. "Is Bitcoin Money? And What That Means." *Quarterly Review of Economics and Finance* no. 77: 144–149.

Heidegger, Martin. 1962. *Being and Time*. Translated by John Macquarrie and Edward Robinson. New York: Harper & Row.

Heidegger, Martin. 1972. *On Time and Being*. Translated by Joan Stambaugh. New York: Harper and Row.

Heidegger, Martin. 2000. *Introduction to Metaphysics*. Translated by Gregory Fried and Richard Polt. New Haven and London: Yale University Press.

Heinrich, Michael. 2009. "Reconstruction or Deconstruction? Methodological Controversies about Value and Capital, and New Insights from the Critical Edition." In *Re-reading Marx: New Perspectives after the Critical Edition*. Edited by Riccardo Bellofiore and Roberto Fineschi. London: Palgrave Macmillan; 71–98.

Heinrich, Michael. 2012. *An Introduction to the Three Volumes of Karl Marx's* Capital. Translated by Alexander Locascio. New York: Monthly Review.

Herian, Robert. 2019. *Regulating Blockchain: Critical Perspectives in Law and Technology*. London: Routledge.

Hicks, J. R. 1962. "Liquidity." *The Economic Journal* 72, no. 288: 787–802; https://www.jstor.org/stable/i338976.

Hobart, Byrne. 14 November 2022. "Money, Credit, Trust, and FTX." *The Diff* (blog). Accessed 29 January 2023 at https://www.thediff.co/p/money-credit-trust-ftx.

Howell, Alison, and Melanie Richter-Montpetit. 2020. "Is Securitization Theory Racist? Civilizationism, Methodological Whiteness, and Antiblack Thought in the Copenhagen School." *Security Dialogue* 51, no. 1: 3–22; https://doi.org/10.1177/0967010619862921.

Huber, Joseph. 2013. "Modern Money and Sovereign Currency." *Real-World Economics Review* no.66: 38–57.

Hull, John C. 2009. *Options, Futures, and Other Derivatives*. Seventh edition. London: Pearson Prentice Hall.

Ingham, Geoffrey. 1996. "Money Is a Social Relation." *Review of Social Economy* 54, no. 4: 507–529; https://www.jstor.org/stable/29769872.

Ingham, Geoffrey. 1998. "On the Underdevelopment of the 'Sociology of Money.'" *Acta Sociologica*, 41, no. 1: 3–18; https://doi.org/10.1177/000169939804100101.

Ingham, Geoffrey. 2000. "'Babylonian Madness': On the Historical and Sociological Origins of Money." In *What Is Money?* Edited by John Smithin. London: Routledge; 16–41.

Ingham, Geoffrey. 2001. "Fundamentals of a Theory of Money: Untangling Fine, Lapavitsas and Zelizer." *Economy and Society* 30, no. 3: 304–323; https://doi.org/10.1080/03085140120071215.

Ingham, Geoffrey. 2004a. *The Nature of Money*. Cambridge, UK: Polity.

Ingham, Geoffrey. 2004b. "The Emergence of Capitalist Credit Money." In *Credit and State Theories of Money: The Contributions of A. Mitchell Innes*. Edited by L. Randall Wray. Cheltenham, UK: Edward Elgar; 173–221.

Ingham, Geoffrey. 2004c. "The Nature of Money." *Economic Sociology: European Electronic Newsletter* 5, no. 2: 18–28; http://hdl.handle.net/10419/155831.

Ingham, Geoffrey. 2006. "Further Reflections on the Ontology of Money: Responses to Lapavitsas and Dodd." *Economy and Society* 35, no. 2: 259–278; https://doi.org/10.1080/03085140600635730.

Ingham, Geoffrey. 2012. "Revisiting the Credit Theory of Money and Trust." In *New Perspectives on Emotions in Finance: The Sociology of Confidence, Fear, and Betrayal*. Edited by Jocelyn Pixley. London: Routledge; 121–139.

Ingham, Geoffrey. 2015. "'The Great Divergence': Max Weber and China's 'Missing Links.'" *Max Weber Studies* 15, no. 2: 160–191; https://www.jstor.org/stable/24579905.

Ingham, Geoffrey. 2016. "The Nature of Money: A Response to Stefano Sgambati." *European Journal of Sociology* 57, no. 1: 199–206; https://doi.org/10.1017/S0003975616000060.

Ingham, Geoffrey. 2018. "A Critique of Lawson's 'Social Positioning and the Nature of Money.'" *Cambridge Journal of Economics* 42, no. 3: 837–850; https://doi.org/10.1093/cje/bex070.

Ingham, Geoffrey. 2019. "Money, Credit, and Finance in Capitalism." In *The Oxford Handbook of Max Weber*. Edited by Edith Hanke, Lawrence Scaff, and Sam Whimster. Oxford Handbooks. Oxford: Oxford University Press; 69–87; https://doi.org/10.1093/oxfordhb/9780190679545.013.4.

Ingham, Geoffrey. 2020. *Money: Ideology, History, Politics*. Cambridge UK: Polity.

Ingham, Geoffrey. 2021. "In Defence of the Nominalist Ontology of Money." *Journal of Post Keynesian Economics* 44, no. 3: 492–507; https://doi.org/10.1080/01603477.2021.1913755.

Ingham, Geoffrey. 2022. Email message to author, 4 November 2022.

Ingham, Geoffrey. Forthcoming. "Modern Money Theory: Sociology and Economics." Cheltenham, UK: Edward Elgar.

Ingves, Stefan. 2018. "The e-Krona and the Payments of the Future." Paper presented at Di Framtidens betalningar, June 2018. Accessed 25 January 2023 at https://www.bis.org/review/r181115c.pdf.

Innes, A. Mitchell. 1913. "What Is Money?" *Banking Law Journal* 30: 377–408.

Innes, A. Mitchell. 1914. "The Credit Theory of Money." *Banking Law Journal* no. 31: 151–168.

International Monetary Fund. 2022. "Special Drawing Rights: 7 Things You Need to Know about SDR Allocations." Accessed 29 January 2023 at https://www.imf.org/en/Topics/special-drawing-right/seven-things-you-need-to-know-about-sdr-allocations.

Itoh, Makoto. 2006. "Political Economy of Money, Credit and Finance in Contemporary Capitalism: Remarks on Lapavitsas and Dymski." *Historical Materialism* 14, no. 1: 97–112; https://doi.org/10.1163/156920606776690974.

Jaag, Christian, and Christian Bach. 2015. "The Effect of Payment Reversibility on E-commerce and Postal Quality." In *Handbook of Digital Currency: Bitcoin, Innovation, Financial Instruments, and Big Data*. Edited by David Lee Kuo Chuen. New York: Academic Press; 139–151.

Jessop, Bob. 2015. "Hard Cash, Easy Credit, Fictitious Capital: Critical Reflections on Money as a Fetishised Social Relation." *Finance and Society* 1, no. 1: 20–37; https://doi.org/10.2218/finsoc.v1i1.1369.

Jevons, William Stanley. 2011. *Money and the Mechanism of Exchange*. New York: D. Appleton and Company. Accessed online 28 January 2023 at https://oll.libertyfund.org/title/jevons-money-and-the-mechanism-of-exchange.

Kahn, Charles M., Francisco Rivadeneyra, and Tsz-Nga Wong. 2018. "Should the Central Bank Issue e-Money?" Federal Reserve Bank of St. Louis Working Paper no. 2019–003 A. https://doi.org/10.20955/wp.2019.003.

Kalecki, Michał. 1937. "A Theory of the Business Cycle." *Review of Economic Studies* 4, no. 2: 77–97; https://doi.org/10.2307/2967606.

Kelton, Stephanie. 2020. *The Deficit Myth: Modern Monetary Theory and the Birth of the People's Economy*. New York: Public Affairs.

Kemmerer, Edwin Walter. 1935. *Money: The Principles of Money and Their Exemplification in Outstanding Chapters of Monetary History.* New York: Macmillan.

Keynes, John Maynard. 1914. "What Is Money? By A. Mitchell Innes." Review essay. *The Economic Journal* 24, no. 5: 419–421.

Keynes, John Maynard. 1930. *A Treatise on Money.* Two volumes. Cambridge, UK: Cambridge University Press.

Keynes, John Maynard. 1936. *The General Theory of Employment, Interest, and Money.* London: Palgrave Macmillan.

Keynes, John Maynard. 1978. *The Collected Writings of John Maynard Keynes: Volume 5, A Treatise on Money.* Edited by Elizabeth Johnson and Donald Moggridge. London: Royal Economic Society.

Killeen Alyse. 2015. "The Confluence of Bitcoin and the Global Sharing Economy." In *Handbook of Digital Currency: Bitcoin, Innovation, Financial Instruments, and Big Data.* Edited by David Lee Kuo Chuen. New York: Academic Press; 485–503.

Kim, Jongchul. 2011. "How Modern Banking Originated: The London Goldsmith-Bankers' Institutionalisation of Trust." *Business History* 53, no. 6: 939–959; https://doi.org/10.1080/00076791.2011.578132.

Kincaid, Jim. 2006. "Finance, Trust and the Power of Capital: A Symposium on the Contribution of Costas Lapavitsas; Editorial Introduction." *Historical Materialism* 14, no. 1: 31–48; https://doi.org/10.1163/156920606776690992.

Knapp, Georg Friedrich. 1924. *The State Theory of Money.* London: Macmillan.

Koddenbrock, Kai. 2017. "What Money Does: An Inquiry into the Backbone of Capitalist Political Economy." Max Planck Institute for the Study of Societies Discussion Paper no. 17/9. Accessed 28 January 2023 at https://www.econstor.eu/bitstream/10419/162118/1/889808678.pdf.

Kofman, Sarah. 1993. *Nietzsche and Metaphor.* Translated by Duncan Large. Stanford: Stanford University Press.

Konings, Martijn. 2018. *Capital and Time: For a New Critique of Neoliberal Reason.* Stanford, California: Stanford University Press.

Kregel, Jan. 2019. "Democratizing Money." Levy Economics Institute of Bard College Working Paper no. 928. Accessed 28 January 2023 at https://www.levyinstitute.org/publications/democratizing-money.

Kristof, Andras. 2015. "National Cryptocurrencies." In *Handbook of Digital Currency: Bitcoin, Innovation, Financial Instruments, and Big Data.* Edited by David Lee Kuo Chuen. New York: Academic Press; 67–80.

Krugman, Paul. 27 March 2012. "Minsky and Methodology (Wonkish)." The Conscience of a Liberal. *New York Times.* Accessed 3 February 2023 at https://archive.nytimes.com/krugman.blogs.nytimes.com/2012/03/27/minksy-and-methodology-wonkish/.

LabCFTC. 17 October 2017. "A CFTC Primer on Digital Currencies." Commodity Futures Trading Commission. Accessed 30 January 2023 at https://www.cftc.gov/sites/default/files/idc/groups/public/documents/file/labcftc_primercurrencies100417.pdf.

Lanchester, John. 2016. "When Bitcoin Grows Up." *London Review of Books* 38, no. 8. Accessed 16 January 2018 at https://www.lrb.co.uk/the-paper/v38/n08/john-lanchester/when-bitcoin-grows-up.

Lange, Elena Louisa. 2019. "Money versus Value? Reconsidering the 'Monetary Approach' of the 'Post'-Uno School, Benetti/Cartelier, and the Neue Marx-Lektüre." *Historical Materialism* 28, no. 1: 51–84; https://doi.org/10.1163/1569206X-00001851.

Lapavitsas, Costas. 2000. "Money and the Analysis of Capitalism: The Significance of Commodity Money." *Review of Radical Political Economics* 32, no. 4: 631–656; https://doi.org/10.1016/S0486-6134(00)90004-4.

Lapavitsas, Costas. 2003. "Money as 'Universal Equivalent' and Its Origin in Commodity Exchange." Working Paper. Accessed 25 January 2023 at https://www.soas.ac.uk/sites/default/files/2022-10/economics-wp130.pdf.

Lapavitsas, Costas. 2005. "The Social Relations of Money as Universal Equivalent: A Response to Ingham." *Economy and Society* 34, no. 3: 389–403; https://doi.org/10.1080/03085140500112137.

Lapavitsas, Costas. 2006. "Relations of Power and Trust in Contemporary Finance." *Historical Materialism* 14, no. 1: 129–154; https://doi.org/10.1163/156920606776690956.

Lau, Jeffrey. 2006. "The Capitalist Development of China: A Monetary and Financial Analysis." Unpublished manuscript.

Lavoie, Marc. 2003. "A Primer on Endogenous Credit-money." In *Modern Theories of Money: The Nature and Role of Money in Capitalist Economies.* Edited by Louis-Philippe Rochon and Sergio Rossi. Cheltenham, UK: Edward Elgar; 506–543.

Lavoie, Marc. 2013. "The Monetary and Fiscal Nexus of Neo-Chartalism: A Friendly Critique." *Journal of Economic Issues* 47, no. 1: 1–32; https://doi.org/10.2753/JEI0021–3624470101.

Lavoie, Marc. 2019. "Modern Monetary Theory and Post-Keynesian Economics." *real-world economics review* no. 89.

Law, John. 1705. *Money and Trade Considered: With a Proposal for Supplying the Nation with Money.* Glasgow: R. & A. Foulis.

Lawson, Tony. 2016. "Social Positioning and the Nature of Money." *Cambridge Journal of Economics* 40, no. 4: 961–996; https://doi.org/10.1093/cje/bew006.

Lawson, Tony. 2018a. "Debt as Money." *Cambridge Journal of Economics* 42, no. 4: 1165–1181; https://doi.org/10.1093/cje/bey006.

Lawson, Tony. 2018b. "The Constitution and Nature of Money." *Cambridge Journal of Economics* 42, no. 3: 851–873; https://doi.org/10.1093/cje/bey005.

Lawson, Tony. 2019. *The Nature of Social Reality: Issues in Social Ontology.* London: Routledge.

Lawson, Tony. 2022. "Two Conceptions of the Nature of Money: Clarifying Differences between MMT and Money Theories Sponsored by Social Positioning Theory." *real-world economics review* no. 101.

Lee, Benjamin, and Randy Martin, eds. 2016. *Derivatives and the Wealth of Societies.* Chicago: University of Chicago Press.

Lerner, Abba P. 1947. "Money as a Creature of the State." *American Economic Review* 37, no. 2: 312–17.

Levin, Richard B., Aaron A. O'Brien, and Madiha M. Zuberi. 2015. "Real Regulation of Virtual Currencies." In *Handbook of Digital Currency: Bitcoin, Innovation, Financial Instruments, and Big Data.* Edited by David Lee Kuo Chuen. New York: Academic Press; 327–360.

Levine, Matt. 14 July 2015. "Banks Forgot Who Was Supposed to Own Dell Shares." Money Stuff. *Bloomberg.* Accessed 26 January 2023 at https://www.bloomberg.com/opinion/articles/2015-07-14/banks-forgot-who-was-supposed-to-own-dell-shares.

Levine, Matt. 14 February 2022. "Shareholders Like Any Old Merger." Money Stuff. *Bloomberg.* Accessed 26 January 2023 at https://www.bloomberg.com/opinion/articles/2022-02-14/share holders-like-any-old-merger.

Levine, Matt. 30 November 2022. "The Nickel Market Almost Broke." Money Stuff. *Bloomberg.* Accessed 26 January 2023 at https://www.bloomberg.com/opinion/articles/2022-11-30/matt-lev ine-s-money-stuff-nickel-market-almost-broke.

Levine, Matt. 2022. "The Crypto Story." *Bloomberg Businessweek,* 31 October 2022 edition. Accessed 17 December 2022 at https://www.bloomberg.com/features/2022-the-crypto-story/.

Levrero, E. S. 2018. "Sraffa on Taxable Income and Its Implications for Fiscal Policy. *Cambridge Journal of Economics* 42, no. 4: 1087–1106; https://doi.org/10.1093/cje/bex050.

Lewis, Michael. 2010. *The Big Short: Inside the Doomsday Machine.* New York: W.W. Norton.

Lim, Jonathan W. 2015. "A Facilitative Model for Cryptocurrency Regulation in Singapore." In *Handbook of Digital Currency: Bitcoin, Innovation, Financial Instruments, and Big Data.* Edited by David Lee Kuo Chuen. New York: Academic Press; 361–381.

Macfarlane, Laurie, Josh Ryan-Collins, Ole Bjerg, Rasmus Hougaard Nielsen, and Duncan McCann. 2017. *Making Money from Making Money: Seigniorage in the Modern Economy.* London: The New Economics Foundation. Accessed 28 January 2023 at https://research.cbs.dk/en/publications/mak ing-money-from-making-money-seigniorage-in-the-modern-economy.

MacKenzie, Donald. 2006. *An Engine, Not a Camera: How Financial Models Shape Markets.* Cambridge, Massachusetts: MIT Press.

Macleod, Henry Dunning. 1889. *The Theory of Credit.* Volume 1. London: Longmans, Green, and Co.

Mankiw, N. Gregory. 2010. *Macroeconomics.* Seventh edition. New York: Worth Publishers.

Mariz, Paul. 2023. "Blockchain for Everyone." Accessed 31 January 2023 at https://inquisitivists.s3.us-west-2.amazonaws.com/Blockchain_For_Everyone.pdf.

Markell, Patchen. 2006. "Ontology, Recognition, and Politics: A Reply." *Polity* 38, no. 1: 28–39; https://www.jstor.org/stable/3877088.

Marx, Karl. 1858. "Money as Means of Payment." *Second Draft of Critique of Political Economy.* In *MECW.* Volume 29: 430–507.

Marx, Karl. 1973. *Grundrisse.* Translated by Martin Nicolaus. New York: Penguin.

Marx, Karl. 1977. *A Contribution to the Critique of Political Economy.* Translated by S.W. Ryazanskaya. Moscow: Progress Publishers.

Marx, Karl. 1978. *Capital: A Critique of Political Economy.* Volume 2. Translated by David Fernbach. Edited by Frederick Engels. New York: Penguin.

Marx, Karl. 1981. *Capital: A Critique of Political Economy.* Volume 3. Translated by David Fernbach. Edited by Frederick Engels. New York: Penguin.

Marx, Karl. 1990. *Capital: A Critique of Political Economy.* Volume 1. Translated by Ben Fowkes. New York: Penguin.

Marx, Karl. 1996. *Later Political Writings.* Edited by Terrell Carver. Cambridge, UK: Cambridge University Press.

Marx, Karl. 2015. *Marx's Economic Manuscript of 1864–1865.* Translated by Ben Fowkes. Edited by Fred Moseley. Leiden: Brill.

Massa, Annie, and Caleb Melby. 21 May 2020. "In Fink We Trust: BlackRock Is Now 'Fourth Branch of Government.'" *Bloomberg Businessweek.* Accessed 28 January 2023 at https://www.bloomberg.com/news/articles/2020-05-21/how-larry-fink-s-blackrock-is-helping-the-fed-with-bond-buying.

Mattick, Paul, Jr. 1997. "Editor's Introduction." *International Journal of Political Economy* 27, no. 3: 3–5; https://doi.org/10.1080/08911916.1997.11643949.

Mazzucato, Mariana. 2018. *The Value of Everything: Making and Taking in the Global Economy.* New York: Public Affairs.

McKinney, Ralph E., Jr., Lawrence P. Shao, Duane C. Rosenlieb, Jr., and Dale H. Shao. 2015. "Counterfeiting in Cryptocurrency: An Emerging Problem." In *Handbook of Digital Currency: Bitcoin, Innovation, Financial Instruments, and Big Data*. Edited by David Lee Kuo Chuen. New York: Academic Press; 173–187.

McLeay, Michael, Amar Radia, and Ryland Thomas. 2014a. "Money Creation in the Modern Economy." Bank of England. *Quarterly Bulletin* 54, no. 1: 14–27.

McLeay, Michael, Amar Radia, and Ryland Thomas. 2014b. "Money in the Modern Economy: An Introduction." Bank of England. *Quarterly Bulletin* 54, no. 1: 4–13.

Mehrling, Perry. 2000. "Modern Money: Fiat or Credit?" *Journal of Post Keynesian Economics* 22, no. 3: 397–406; http://www.jstor.org/stable/4538686.

Mehrling, Perry. 2011. *The New Lombard Street: How the Fed Became the Dealer of Last Resort*. Princeton: Princeton University Press.

Mehrling, Perry. 2012. "The Inherent Hierarchy of Money." Paper prepared for Duncan Foley festschrift volume and conference, 20–21 April 2012. Accessed 28 January 2023 at https://ieor. columbia.edu/files/seasdepts/industrial-engineering-operations-research/pdf-files/Mehrling_P_ FESeminar_Sp12-02.pdf.

Mehrling, Perry. 2014. "Why Central Banking Should Be Re-Imagined." *Re-Thinking the Lender of Last Resort*. BIS Papers no. 79: 108–118. Accessed 28 January 2023 at https://www.bis.org/publ/ bppdf/bispap79i.pdf.

Mehrling, Perry. 2015. "Economics of Money and Banking." Online course, Columbia University. Accessed 15 January 2023 at https://www.coursera.org/learn/money-banking.

Mehrling, Perry. 2016. "The Economics of Money and Banking." Handout for ECON V3265, Barnard College, Columbia University. Fall 2016.

Mehrling, Perry. 2017. "Financialization and Its Discontents." *Finance and Society* 3, no. 1: 1–10; https://doi.org/10.2218/finsoc.v3i1.1935.

Mehrling, Perry. 2020. "Payment vs. Funding: The Law of Reflux for Today." Institute for New Economic Thinking Working Paper no. 113. https://doi.org/10.36687/inetwp113.

Meister, Robert. 2016. "Liquidity." In *Derivatives and the Wealth of Societies*. Edited by Benjamin Lee and Randy Martin. Chicago: University of Chicago Press; 143–173.

Meister, Robert. 2017. "Reinventing Marx for an Age of Finance." *Postmodern Culture* 27, no. 2. Accessed 28 January 2023 at https://www.pomoculture.org/2020/09/24/reinventing-marx-for-an-age-of-finance/.

Menger, Carl. 2009. *On the Origins of Money*. Translated by C.A. Foley. Auburn, Alabama: Ludwig von Mises Institute.

Michaelides, Panayotis, and John Milios. 2004. "Hilferding's Influence on Schumpeter: A First Discussion." Paper presented at the European Association for Evolutionary Political Economy Sixteenth Annual Conference on Economics, History, and Development. Crete, Greece. 28–31 October 2004.

Michell, H. 1951. "The Gold Standard in the Nineteenth Century." *The Canadian Journal of Economics and Political Science* 17, no. 3: 369–376; https://www.jstor.org/stable/137693.

Milios, John. 2001. "Marx's *Critique of* (Ricardian) *Political Economy*, the Quantity Theory of Money and Credit Money." 2001. Paper presented at the Year 2001 Mini-Conference on Value Theory and the World Economy. Crowne Plaza Hotel, Manhattan. 23–25 February 2001.

Milios, John. 2002. "Theory of Value and Money: In Defence of the Endogeneity of Money." Paper presented at the Sixth International Conference in Economics, Economic Research Center. METU, Ankara. 11–14 September 2002.

Milios, John. 2003. "Marx's Value Theory Revisited: A 'Value-form' Approach." *Proceedings of the Seventh International Conference in Economics.* Ankara: METU. Accessed 28 January 2023 at http://users.ntua.gr/jmilios/F2_3.pdf.

Milios, John. 2006. "*Capital* after Louis Althusser: Focusing on Value-Form Analysis." Paper presented at the Conference Rileggere *Il Capitale:* La lezione di Louis Althusser. Department of Historical Studies of the University Ca' Foscari. Venice, Italy. 9 – 11 November 2006.

Milios, John. 2009. "Rethinking Marx's Value-Form Analysis from an Althusserian Perspective." *Rethinking Marxism* 21, no. 2: 260 – 274; https://doi.org/10.1080/08935690902743518.

Milios, John. 2015. "Marx's Monetary Theory of Value, Fictitious Capital and Finance." Paper presented at the Second International Seminar on the 150th Anniversary of *The Capital* (1867 – 2017). Bogota, Columbia: 3 – 6 November 2015.

Minsky, Hyman. 1960. "The Pure Theory of Banking." University of California Department of Economics, Fall Semester.

Minsky, Hyman. 2008. *Stabilizing an Unstable Economy.* New York: McGraw Hill.

Mirowski, Philip. 1988. *Against Mechanism: Protecting Economics from Science.* Lanham, Maryland: Rowman and Littlefield.

Mirowski, Philip. 1989. *More Heat than Light: Economics as Social Physics; Physics as Nature's Economics.* Cambridge, UK: Cambridge University Press.

Miyazawa, Kazutoshi. 2006. "The Anarchic Nature of the Market and the Emergence of Money." *Historical Materialism* 14, no. 1: 113 – 128; https://doi.org/10.1163/156920606776690875.

Moseley, Fred, ed. 2005. *Marx's Theory of Money: Modern Appraisals.* London: Palgrave Macmillan.

Moseley, Fred. 2016. *Money and Totality: A Macro-Monetary Interpretation of Marx's Logic in* Capital *and the End of the 'Transformation Problem.'* Leiden: Brill.

Mosler, Warren B. 1994. "Soft Currency Economics." Accessed 28 January 2023 at https://mosler economics.com/wp-content/uploads/2018/04/Soft-Curency-Economics-paper.pdf.

Mueller, Reinhold C. 2019. *The Venetian Money Market: Banks, Panics, and the Public Debt, 1200 – 1500.* Baltimore, Maryland: Johns Hopkins University Press.

Munro, John H. n.d. "The Bill of Exchange, Draft, or Acceptance Bill." Accessed 18 July 2018 at https://www.economics.utoronto.ca/munro5/THE%20BILL%20OF%20EXCHANGE.pdf

Murray, Patrick. 1993. "The Necessity of Money: How Hegel Helped Marx Surpass Ricardo's Theory of Value." In *Marx's Method in* Capital: *A Reexamination.*" Edited by Fred Moseley. New Jersey: Humanities; 37 – 61.

Nakamoto, Satoshi. 2009. "Bitcoin: A Peer-to-Peer Electronic Cash System." Accessed 3 February 2023 at https://bitcoin.org/bitcoin.pdf.

Nesiba, Reynold F. 2013. "Was Money Created to Overcome Barter?" *New Economic Perspectives.* Accessed 14 April 2020 at https://neweconomicperspectives.org/2013/09/money-created-over come-barter.html.

Newcomb, Simon. 1885. *Principles of Political Economy.* New York: Harper.

Nian, Lam Pak, and David Lee Kuo Chuen. 2015. "Introduction to Bitcoin." In *Handbook of Digital Currency: Bitcoin, Innovation, Financial Instruments, and Big Data.* Edited by David Lee Kuo Chuen. New York: Academic Press; 5 – 30.

Nietzsche, Friedrich. 1967. *On the Genealogy of Morals.* Translated by Walter Kaufmann and R.J. Hollingdale. New York: Vintage Books.

Nietzsche, Friedrich. 1979. *Philosophy and Truth: Selections from Nietzsche's Notebooks of the Early 1870s.* Edited and translated by Daniel Breazeale. New Jersey: Humanities Press International.

Noizat, Pierre. 2015. "Blockchain Electronic Vote." In *Handbook of Digital Currency: Bitcoin, Innovation, Financial Instruments, and Big Data.* Edited by David Lee Kuo Chuen. New York: Academic Press; 453–461.

OCC (Office of the Comptroller of the Currency), Administrator of National Banks. 2003. *National Banks and the Dual Banking System.* Accessed 28 January 2023 at https://www.occ.treas.gov/pub lications-and-resources/publications/banker-education/files/pub-national-banks-and-the-dual-banking-system.pdf.

O'Hara, Phillip Anthony. 2000. "Money and Credit in Marx's Political Economy and Contemporary Capitalism." *History of Economics Review* 32 no. 1: 83–95; https://doi.org/10.1080/10370196.2000. 11733343.

Ong, Bobby, Teik Ming Lee, Guo Li, and David Lee Kuo Chuen. 2015. "Evaluating the Potential of Alternative Cryptocurrencies." In *Handbook of Digital Currency: Bitcoin, Innovation, Financial Instruments, and Big Data.* Edited by David Lee Kuo Chuen. New York: Academic Press; 81–135.

Orrell, David. n.d. "Quantum Economics." Accessed 28 January 2023 at http://etdiscussion.worldeco nomicsassociation.org/wp-content/uploads/2017/10/Orrell-july-18.pdf.

Palermo, Giulio. 2017. "Competition: A Marxist View." *Cambridge Journal of Economics* 41, no. 6: 1559–1585; https://doi.org/10.1093/cje/bex006.

Palley, Thomas, & Matías Vernengo. 2018. "Milton Friedman's Presidential Address at 50." *Review of Keynesian Economics* 6, no. 4: 419–420.

Palley, Thomas. 2019. "What's Wrong with Modern Money Theory (MMT): A Critical Primer." Hans-Böckler-Stiftung Macroeconomic Policy Institute Forum for Macroeconomics and Macroeconomic Policies Working Paper no. 44.

Peacock, Mark. 2013. *Introducing Money.* London: Routledge.

Pieters, Gina C. 2018. "How Global Is the Cryptocurrency Market?" Accessed 25 January 2023 at https://www.atlantafed.org/-/media/documents/news/conferences/2018/1018-financial-stability-im plications-of-new-technology/papers/pieters_bitcoin_international.pdf.

Pozsar, Zoltan. 29 January 2018. "Repatriation, the Echo-Tapper, and the €/$ Basis." Credit Suisse Global Strategy. Global Money Notes no. 11.

Pozsar, Zoltan. 21 August 2019. "Sagittarius A*." Credit Suisse Economics. Global Money Notes no. 24.

Pozsar, Zoltan. 31 March 2022. "Money, Commodities, and Bretton Woods III." Credit Suisse Economics.

Public Address. 2021. "Love is a Rose." Accessed 31 January 2023 at https://thispublicaddress.com/ 2019/11/21/love-is-a-rose/.

Quarles, Randal K. 2021. "Parachute Pants and Central Bank Money." Paper presented at the 113th Annual Utah Bankers Association Convention, Sun Valley, Idaho, June 2021.

Rancière, Jacques. 1989. "The Concept of 'Critique' and the 'Critique of Political Economy.'" In *Ideology, Method, and Marx: Essays from Economy and Society.* Edited by Ali Rattansi. London: Routledge; 74–180.

Rebrovick, Tripp. 2015. "Routine Maintenance: Forming, Reforming, and Transforming Social Formations." PhD dissertation, Johns Hopkins University; https://jscholarship.library.jhu.edu/bit stream/handle/1774.2/40285/REBROVICK-DISSERTATION-2016.pdf?sequence=1.

Ricardo, David. 2001. *Principles of Political Economy and Taxation.* Kitchener, Ontario: Batoche Books.

Robinson, Joan. 1953. "The Production Function and the Theory of Capital." *The Review of Economic Studies* 21, no. 2: 81–106; https://doi.org/10.2307/2296002.

Robles-Báez, Mario L. 1997. "On Marx's Dialectic of the Genesis of the Money Form." *International Journal of Political Economy* 27, no. 3: 35–64; https://doi.org/10.1080/08911916.1997.11643951.

Rubin, Isaak Illich. 1924. "Fundamental Features of Marx's Theory of Value and How It Differs from Ricardo's Theory." In *Responses to Marx's Capital: From Rudolf Hilferding to Isaak Illich Rubin.* Edited by Richard B. Day and Daniel F. Gaido. Leiden: Brill; 536–582.

Saito, Tetsuya. 2015. "A Microeconomic Analysis of Bitcoin and Illegal Activities." In *Handbook of Digital Currency: Bitcoin, Innovation, Financial Instruments, and Big Data.* Edited by David Lee Kuo Chuen. New York: Academic Press; 231–248.

Samid, Gideon. 2015. "How Digital Currencies Will Cascade up to a Global Stable Currency: The Fundamental Framework for the Money of the Future." In *Handbook of Digital Currency: Bitcoin, Innovation, Financial Instruments, and Big Data.* Edited by David Lee Kuo Chuen. New York: Academic Press; 403–415.

Sapovadia, Vrajlal. 2015. "Legal Issues in Cryptocurrency." In *Handbook of Digital Currency: Bitcoin, Innovation, Financial Instruments, and Big Data.* Edited by David Lee Kuo Chuen. New York: Academic Press; 253–266.

Scharf, J. Thomas. 1879. *History of Maryland from the Earliest Period to the Present Day.* 3 vols. Baltimore: John B. Piet.

Schumpeter, Joseph A. 1956. "Money and the Social Product." Translated by A. W. Marget. *International Economic Papers* no. 6: 148–211.

Schumpeter, Joseph A. 1954. *History of Economic Analysis.* Edited by Elizabeth Boody Schumpeter. New York: Routledge.

Seaford, Richard. 2004. *Money and the Early Greek Mind: Homer, Philosophy, Tragedy.* Cambridge, UK: Cambridge University Press.

Semenova, Alla. 2011. "The Origins of Money: Evaluating Chartalist and Metallist Theories in the Context of Ancient Greece and Mesopotamia." PhD dissertation, University of Missouri-Kansas City; https://doi.org/10.1111/j.1536-7150.2011.00779.x.

Sgambati, Stefano. 2015. "The Significance of Money: Beyond Ingham's Sociology of Money." *European Journal of Sociology* 56, no. 2: 307–339; https://doi.org/10.1017/S0003975615000144.

Sgambati, Stefano. 2020. "Historicizing the Money of Account: A Critique of the Nominalist Ontology of Money." *Journal of Post Keynesian Economics* 43, no. 3: 417–444; https://doi.org/10.1080/01603477.2020.1788396.

Sharpe, William F. 2019. *Retirement Income Analysis with Scenario Matrices.* Accessed 29 January 2023 at https://web.stanford.edu/~wfsharpe/RISMAT/.

Siegel, Rachel. 1 September 2020. "A Penny Pinch: How America Fell into a Coin Shortage." *Washington Post.* Accessed 26 January 2023 at https://www.washingtonpost.com/business/2020/09/01/coin-shortage-pandemic/.

Sieroń, Arkadiusz. 2019. *Money, Inflation and Business Cycles: The Cantillon Effect and the Economy.* Translated by Martin Turnau. London: Routledge.

Simmel, Georg. 2004. *The Philosophy of Money.* Third edition. Edited by David Frisby. Translated by Tom Bottomore, David Frisby, and Kaethe Mengelberg. London: Routledge.

Skingsley, Cecilia. 2016. "Should the Riksbank Issue e-Krona?" Paper presented at FinTech Stockholm 2016, Stockholm, November 2016. Accessed 25 January 2023 at https://www.bis.org/review/r161128a.pdf.

Smith, Adam. 1869. *The Wealth of Nations.* Books 1–3. London: Penguin Books.

Smithin, John, ed. 2000. *What Is Money?* London: Routledge.

Sraffa, Piero. 1951. "Introduction." In *The Works and Correspondence of David Ricardo.* Vol. 1. Edited by Piero Sraffa and Maurice H. Dobb. Cambridge: Cambridge University Press; xiii–lxii.

Steuart, James. 1767. *An Inquiry into the Principles of Political Economy.* Vol. 1. London: Millar & Cadell.

Stiglitz, Joseph, and John Driffill. 2000. *Economics.* New York: W. W. Norton.

Streeter, S. F. 1 February 1858. "Sketch of the Early Currency in Maryland and Virginia." *Historical Magazine:* 42–45.

Tarasiewicz, Matthias, and Andrew Newman. 2015. "Cryptocurrencies as Distributed Community Experiments." In *Handbook of Digital Currency: Bitcoin, Innovation, Financial Instruments, and Big Data.* Edited by David Lee Kuo Chuen. New York: Academic Press; 201–222.

Taylor, Charles. 1985. *Philosophy and the Human Sciences.* Vol. 2 of *Philosophical Papers.* Cambridge, UK: Cambridge University Press.

Teo, Ernie G. S. 2015. "Emergence, Growth, and Sustainability of Bitcoin: The Network Economics Perspective." In *Handbook of Digital Currency: Bitcoin, Innovation, Financial Instruments, and Big Data.* Edited by David Lee Kuo Chuen. New York: Academic Press; 191–200.

Tether. 2014. *Tether: Fiat Currencies on the Bitcoin Blockchain.* Accessed 29 January 2023 at https://as sets.ctfassets.net/vyse88cgwfbl/5UWgHMvz071 t2Cq5yTw5vi/ c9798ea8db99311bf90ebe0810938b01/TetherWhitePaper.pdf.

Thornton, Henry. 1802. *An Enquiry into the Nature and Effects of the Paper Credit of Great Britain.* London: n.s.

Tooze, Adam. 2018. *Crashed: How a Decade of Financial Crises Changed the World.* New York: Penguin.

Tooze, Adam. 2021. *Shutdown: How Covid Shook the World's Economy.* New York: Viking.

Tooze, Adam. 27 February 2022. "Sanctions and MAD: Will a financial panic in Moscow accelerate the "logic" of escalation?" *Chartbook #88.* https://adamtooze.substack.com/p/chartbook-88-sanc tions-and-mad-will

Treynor, Jack L. 1987. "The Economics of the Dealer Function." *Financial Analysts Journal* 43, no. 6: 27–34; https://www.jstor.org/stable/4479073.

Tribe, Laurence H., and Jeremy Lewin. 15 April 2022. "$100 Billion: Russia's Treasure in the U.S. Should Be Turned against Putin." *New York Times.* Accessed 29 January 2023 at https://www.ny times.com/2022/04/15/opinion/russia-war-currency-reserves.html.

Trivellato, Francesca. 2019. *The Promise and Peril of Credit: What a Forgotten Legend about Jews and Finance Tells Us about the Making of European Commercial Society.* Princeton: Princeton University Press.

Ugolini, Stefano. 2017. *The Evolution of Central Banking: Theory and History.* London: Palgrave Macmillan.

Vernengo, Matías. 2022. "The Inflationary Puzzle." *Catalyst* 5, no. 4: 90–113.

Vinketa, Darko. 2022. "From Labor as Bondage to Labor as Tragedy: Scenes of Production in Hegel and Nietzsche." Chapter, PhD dissertation, in progress at Johns Hopkins University.

Walker, Francis A. 1878. *Money.* New York: Henry Holt.

Walker, Francis A. 1879. *Money in Its Relations to Trade and Industry.* New York: Henry Holt.

Walton, Jo Lindsay. 2022. "Bitcoin and Stone Money: Anglophone Use of Yapese Economic Cultures, 1910–2020." *Finance and Society* 8, no. 1: 42–66; https://doi.org/10.2218/finsoc.7126.

Weber, Beat. 2016. "Bitcoin and the Legitimacy Crisis of Money." *Cambridge Journal of Economics* 40, no. 1: 17–41; https://doi.org/10.1093/cje/beu067.

Weber, Max. 1978. *Economy and Society: An Outline of Interpretive Sociology.* Edited by Guenther Roth and Claus Wittich. Translated by Ephraim Fischoff, Hans Gerth, A.M. Henderson, Ferdinand

Kolegar, C. Wright Mills, Talcott Parsons, Max Rheinstein, Guenther Roth, Edward Shils, and Claus Wittich. Berkeley: University of California Press.

Werner, Richard A. 2014. "Can Banks Individually Create Money out of Nothing? The Theories and the Empirical Evidence." *International Review of Financial Analysis* 36: 1–19; https://doi.org/10.1016/j.irfa.2014.07.015.

White, Molly. 17 July 2022. "Cryptocurrency 'Market Caps' and Notional Value." *Molly White* (blog). Accessed 29 January 2023 at https://blog.mollywhite.net/cryptocurrency-market-caps-and-notional-value/.

Wicksell, Knut. 1962. *Interest and Prices: A Study of the Causes Regulating the Value of Money.* Translated by R.F. Kahn. New York: Sentry.

Wikipedia, s.v. "Judy Shelton." Last modified 28 March 2022, 19:28. Accessed 3 February 2023 at https://en.wikipedia.org/wiki/Judy_Shelton.

Wilkins, Inigo, and Bogdan Dragos. 2022. "Money as a Computational Machine." *Finance and Society* 8, no. 2: 110–28; Accessed 30 January 2023 at http://financeandsociety.ed.ac.uk/article/view/7762/9683.

Williams, Michael. 2000. "Why Marx Neither Has Nor Needs a Commodity Theory of Money." *Review of Political Economy* 12, no. 4: 435–451; https://doi.org/10.1080/09538250050175127.

Wood, Ellen Meiksins. 2002. *The Origin of Capitalism: A Longer View.* New York: Verso.

Wood, Gavin, and Aeron Buchanan. 2015. "Advancing Egalitarianism." In *Handbook of Digital Currency: Bitcoin, Innovation, Financial Instruments, and Big Data.* Edited by David Lee Kuo Chuen. New York: Academic Press; 385–402.

Wray, L. Randall. 1998. *Understanding Modern Money: The Key to Full Employment and Price Stability.* Cheltenham, UK: Edward Elgar.

Wray, L. Randall. 2000. "Modern Money." In *What Is Money?* Edited by John Smithin. London: Routledge; 42–66.

Wray, L. Randall. 2004. "Conclusion: The Credit Money and State Money Approaches." In *Credit and State Theories of Money: The Contributions of A. Mitchell Innes.* Edited by L. Randall Wray. Cheltenham, UK: Edward Elgar; 223–262.

Wray, L. Randall. 2012. "Introduction to an Alternative History of Money." Levy Economics Institute of Bard College Working Paper no. 717.

Wray, L. Randall. 2014. "From the State Theory of Money to Modern Money Theory: An Alternative to Economic Orthodoxy." Levy Economics Institute of Bard College Working Paper no. 792.

Wray, L. Randall. 2015. "Minsky on Banking: Early Work on Endogenous Money and the Prudent Banker." Levy Economics Institute of Bard College Working Paper no. 827.

Wray, L. Randall, and Stephanie Bell. 2004. "Introduction." In *Credit and State Theories of Money: The Contributions of A. Mitchell Innes.* Edited by L. Randall Wray. Cheltenham, UK: Edward Elgar; 1–13.

Yermack, David. 2015. "Is Bitcoin a Real Currency? An Economic Appraisal." In *Handbook of Digital Currency: Bitcoin, Innovation, Financial Instruments, and Big Data.* Edited by David Lee Kuo Chuen. New York: Academic Press; 31–43.

Zelizer, Viviana. 2000. "Fine Tuning the Zelizer View." *Economy and Society* 29, no. 3: 383–389; https://doi.org/10.1080/03085140050084570.

Zuboff, Shoshana. 2019. *The Age of Surveillance Capitalism: The Fight for a Human Future at the New Frontier of Power.* New York: Public Affairs.